BODY
THIEVES

BODY *THIEVES*

Help Girls Reclaim Their Natural Bodies and Become Physically Active

by
Sandra Susan Friedman
BA, BSW, MA

SALAL BOOKS
Vancouver
British Columbia
Canada

National Library of Canada Cataloguing in Publication Data
Friedman, Sandra Susan, 1942-
  Body thieves

  ISBN 0-9698883-3-3

  1. Teenage girls–Psychology. 2. Teenage girls–Counseling of. 3. Eating disorders in adolescence. 4. Body image in adolescence. 5. Self-perception in adolescence. I. Title.
HQ798.F735 2002   649'.125   C2002-910498-X

Cover design by Leon Phillips   <www.leonphillips.ca>

Text editing & DTP production by Dan Fivehouse for:
    SALAL BOOKS
    #309, 101-1184 Denman Street
    Vancouver, British Columbia, Canada   V6G 2M9
    ☎ + FAX 604-689-8399   <www.salal.com>

Printing: FRIESENS Corporation
         One Printers Way
         Altona, Manitoba, Canada   R0G 0B0
         ☎ 204-324-6401   FAX 204-324-1333   <www.friesens.com>

First printing: June 2002

In Memoriam

This book is dedicated to...

Lori Michelle Irving
(1962 – 2001)

She fought the body thieves with courage,
integrity and passion and tried to make
the world a better place.

We miss you!

Acknowledgements

This book would not have been possible without the help, support and encouragement of many other people who are committed to fighting the body thieves in their lives and in their work.

Jacki Abbott showered me with resources the first time we met in Portland, Oregon and has been a source of support ever since. I thank her for reading the manuscript and for all the feedback that she gave me. Jacqui Gingras lent me her entire set of *Healthy Weight Journals* and continuously emailed me articles on obesity and nutrition. Michael Levine invited me onto his list serve and kept me informed of whatever interesting information he came across.

Lindsay Hall of Gürze Books provided the impetus for this book and gave me valuable feedback on the first draft. Akka Janssen of HaperCollins (Canada) continues to provide me with ongoing support. Sharon Young, as usual, provided me with the link to and perspective of public health.

I owe the chapters on physical activity and sport to the generosity and mentoring of Bryna Kopelow (past chair) and Jennifer Fenton (my co-chair) of Promotion Plus who know more about girls and gender equity and physical activity and sport than anyone else in Canada. They shared their gender stories, their resources (including Jennifer's Master's thesis), their expertise and their passion and were always there for endless discussions. Their feedback on these chapters was invaluable. Dawna Moon was patient and helpful the many times I phoned or visited Bryna and Jen at the PSAP office. I would like to acknowledge all my fellow Promotion Plus board members: Holly Rogers, Colleen Reid, Lynda Cannell, Patti Hunter, Indy Baath, Dena Coward, Diane Murphy, Simone Longpre and Janet Ready.

Sydney Millar shared her experiences and knowledge around getting girls active and the barriers that they face. Sydney also read the manuscript with an eagle eye.

Lynn Sackville brought her experience as a professional editor and mother of twelve year old Clea to her reading of the manuscript. Her words are quoted on the back cover and her suggestions are integrated throughout the text.

Ken Bro and Brenda Glenn provided technical support and introduced me to artist Leon Phillips (a West End neighbor—which in Vancouver is a great thing to be!!) who did such a fabulous job designing the covers.

I would like to thank Niva Piran whose commitment to feminism and work in prevention continue to provide me with inspiration, and Lorna Medd who started all this in 1992 when she invited me to develop the prevention program which evolved into *Just for Girls*. Thanks to my friends Carol Herbert, Marion Crook, Louise Doyle and Raine McKay for their ongoing support.

Finally, I would like to express my appreciation and love for Dan Fivehouse. As my husband and friend he has constantly encouraged me to pursue my dreams and to be the very best. As my partner in Salal Communications he has applied his considerable talents to editing, producing, publishing and marketing my work.

Table of Contents

Introduction

The teenage girl comes bounding up the stairs, makes a bee-line to my office and plunks herself down on the couch. Her smile and her energy fill the room. A year ago she lay in the hospital for the third time, anxiety soaring and weight plummeting as anorexia nervosa played havoc with her body and mind. Today she is a normal, feisty sixteen year old who is making sense of her world and taking charge of her life.

Several hours later, a second girl trudges up the walkway. With her shoulders slumped she looks like she is carrying the weight of the world. And in a way she is. At eleven she is already dealing with society's negative attitudes towards people who are fat. In our counseling sessions together we work on how she can fight back against the teasing she encounters daily, on how she can be fat with dignity, and how she can make her body strong.

These two girls represent the opposite ends of the weight spectrum. There are thousands of others in between who, in varying degrees, struggle for ownership of their bodies and a sense of themselves. What they have in common is that they have all fallen victim to *body thieves* who hold them hostage to the bathroom scale, destroy their sense of self, and block them from getting on with their lives.

The Body Thieves are:

Society's emphasis on thinness as the predominant measure of worth—which robs girls of their ability to accept their natural bodies.

The silencing of girls' voices. When girls come to distrust their own experiences and knowledge, they lose their voices, and their bodies become surrogate selves that speak in their absence—too often telling tales of self-loathing.

Society's attitudes and prejudices towards fat which girls internalize at an early age and which become entrenched as they mature.

Antifat crusaders who reinforce society's negative attitudes towards fat by spreading myths about obesity and encouraging us all to diet.

Dieting which robs girls of their natural bodies and puts them at risk for eating disorders, obesity and the medical consequences of constant weight cycling.

Mothers, teachers and other mentors who themselves diet and transfer their attitudes toward fat and weight loss practices onto girls.

We are now in the midst of a societal crisis. At one end of the spectrum of weight-related concerns the number of girls with eating disorders is rising dramatically and the age of onset is becoming lower and lower. At the other end of the spectrum childhood obesity is increasing at an alarming rate. Societal hatred towards people who are fat is becoming more intense at the same time that opportunities for girls to use their bodies are diminishing as neighborhoods are judged unsafe for girls to play outside, families are stressed out and physical education is disappearing from school curriculums or not serving the needs of girls.

As an educator, therapist and social activist whose entire career has been spent trying to empower girls and women, I am afraid of what is happening to them. I am also downright angry. I wrote this book because I want to stop the body thieves and I want to enlist your help. Whether you are a parent, teacher, concerned adult or older adolescent, *Body Thieves* will provide you with the skills to fight the body thieves and in doing so help girls reclaim their natural bodies, become physically active and get on with their lives. I invite you to join with me in becoming Size Acceptance Warriors who are fighting to raise girls who are healthy and strong.

This book will provide you with a societal context for girls' development and the issues that concern them. It will enable you to challenge your own beliefs, attitudes and assumptions about body size so that you will get off your diet and/or help girls get off theirs.

How This Book Came About

This book incorporates my personal and professional interests and experiences developed over the past thirty years. I taught elementary and high school for a dozen years and then went back to university for an MA in psychology. Equipped with a better understanding of my issues around food and weight, and vowing never again to diet, I went into private practice as a therapist in 1980. Ten years later I shifted my focus to prevention and developed the *Just for Girls* group program that is in use throughout Canada and the United States.

When I began to get inquiries from mothers and professionals who wanted more specific information about girls and puberty, I wrote *When Girls Feel Fat: Helping Girls Through Adolescence*. To my great delight this book also became a hit with teenaged girls who wanted to learn more about themselves.

In 1998 I became involved with designing and facilitating workshops on eating disorder prevention and intervention for parents, professionals and lay people as part of Eating Disorders Project North in British Columbia. *Nurturing girlpower: Integrating Eating Disorder Prevention/Intervention Skills into Your Practice* evolved out of these workshops.

A workshop participant asked one day if next time I would talk about girls who are fat. That opened the door to my interest in childhood obesity and the war against fat. It also exposed my blind spot. Years of dieting, quitting smoking and a ruptured disk had moved me from someone who had once only felt fat to someone who was fat. Looking at the myths around fat allowed me to deal with the remaining issues that I had around my weight, with my need to reclaim my natural body and to renew my commitment to helping girls reclaim theirs.

In 1997 I joined the Board of Directors of Promotion Plus: Girls and Women in Physical Activity and Sport. Marrying physical activity and sport to building healthy self-expression became the logical link to fighting the body thieves and helping girls take charge of their lives.

How to Use This Book

Think of *Body Thieves* as a kind of partnership. I provide you with stories and information, skills to use and suggestions to try—all of which I hope will be helpful. You bring your own life and professional experiences and your relationships with girls. If you are a teacher or someone who works with girls this book will help you enhance the skills you already bring to your work. If you are a parent, keep in mind that you are the best authority on your daughter—no matter how much information I hope to give you. You don't have to become perfect yourself or make major changes in your life to fight the body thieves You just have to be open, willing to try new things and have a sense of humor!

Body Thieves is made up of fifteen chapters which cover different issues in girls' lives. The first two chapters address female development and what happens to girls in the process of growing up that diverts them away from developing their self-worth toward defining themselves by numbers on the bathroom scale. While some of this information might seem familiar to those of you who have read my other books, it is important to reiterate because it provides the framework upon which the rest of the book is built. I also talk briefly about boys so that you can understand the differences in their development and culture.

The chapter 'Building Relationships with Girls' will help you develop or enhance your connection with the girls in your life. It teaches 'schmoozing'—a communication ritual that allows you to get real with girls instead of talking at them. 'The War on Fat' confronts the myths around obesity and indicates how we can fight fat prejudice. The 'Deadly Quest to be Thin' provides us with a context for eating disorders and helps us support girls who we consider to be at risk. 'When Girls *are* Fat' looks at why girls are fat, and how we can confront our own fat prejudice and help girls be fat with dignity.

The rest of the book provides skills to fight the body thieves and help girls reclaim their natural bodies and become physically active. The end of each chapter describes featured resources that you can use in parenting, teaching and working with girls. 'Fighting the Body Thieves' addresses the basic elements of prevention. 'Translating Fat Talk' teaches about the *grungies*–a term coined to describe the negative voice that girls develop (such as 'feeling fat'). It provides us with the skills to help girls become aware of their grungies and to tell the stories that lie underneath. It teaches us how to help girls express their feelings in a constructive way, and how to talk to the other person in such a way that he or she will be receptive.

'Celebrating Girls' Bodies' looks at body image and provides us with body awareness skills as well as ways to diffuse the power of appearance. 'Getting Girls Off Diets' also provides us with the skills to get off our own. 'Food, Glorious Food' looks at how girls can normalize their relationship to food. 'Becoming Physically Active' and 'Sports' look at how we can help girls take charge of their bodies by using them. 'Media' provides tools for media literacy and to fight against propaganda. 'With Determination and Courage' looks at where we go from here.

As you read this book you might find parts where you agree with me and others where you don't. I hope this opens the door for good discussions with your friends and colleagues. Some of this information may be new to you and in some cases you may find that your experience and knowledge are greater than mine. You are the best judge of what is valuable to you.

Use the parts you agree with and feel most connected to. Pick and choose and adapt these suggestions to what works best for you. Remember we all come from different orientations, experiences and points of view. You may find areas of the book repetitive. This is because I have tried to provide you with a context for each chapter that is set in girls' development and the realities of their lives.

I hope you enjoy this book and I hope you begin to fight the body thieves in whatever way is comfortable for you and makes sense to you so that you, too, can help girls reclaim their natural bodies, become physically active and get on with their lives.

Please come visit me at <www.salal.com> and if you have comments or concerns, contact me through salal@salal.com

1

∞

Gender and Development

With their wedding party scattered 3000 miles, the bride and groom did much of their planning by e-mail. As a first anniversary gift one of their bridesmaids compiled all the wedding correspondence into a handmade book. Messages between the groom and his friends made up 10 per cent of the book and consisted mainly of wedding jokes and reminders of tuxedo fittings. These messages were briefer than those between the bride and her friends, more utilitarian and more functional.

About 90 per cent of the book consisted of messages sent between the bride and her bridesmaids. The women held forth not just on wedding minutiae like high heels and earring styles but also on stories about their days, support over little frustrations, congratulations on their triumphs. 'A message is a bright spot in the day,' commented the bride. 'It's like a kaffeklatch of girlfriends getting together to talk. My husband thinks that the e-mailing that I do with my friends is odd. That's not surprising since he's a guy.'

Excerpt from the *New York Times*[1]

Consider the e-mail habits of the bride and groom with their friends as a good introduction to this chapter on gender and development because it illustrates differences in behavior between women and men that are familiar to us. From the moment we are born girls and boys grow up in two different cultures with different ways of interpreting and responding to the world.

There was a time in the 1980s when many people believed the differences between us were mainly because of gender—the social and cultural aspects attached to one's biological sex—and were the results of socialization. They believed that because what is learned can also be unlearned, girls and boys raised exactly the same way would grow up to behave the same.

Despite continued attempts to make children androgynous, little girls continue to arrange their cars and trucks into families and little boys point their Barbie dolls at one another and shout 'bang, bang.'

The notion that we can narrow or eliminate the 'gender gap' between girls and boys by teaching girls competitive sports and encouraging boys to be more sensitive by giving them dolls doesn't begin to address the fundamental differences in the ways in which girls and boys experience and respond to the world. This is because differences in behavior are the result of both biology and gender. Biology and culture form a circle in which one influence feeds the other, making it difficult to pinpoint if something is exclusively biological or cultural or the result of the interplay between them.[2]

Understanding biological and gender differences and the separate worlds that girls and boys inhabit helps us understand how the genders develop their unique identities, the ways in which they perceive and measure self-esteem, their communication patterns, their friendships, how they engage in play and in physical activity and how they learn. It provides us with a framework so that we can parent girls and boys and teach and work in ways that are appropriate for each of them.

As you read on, you might find that some girls and boys you know (or women and men) don't quite fit into the female and male gender cultures that I am describing. For example, the girls may be aggressive and the boys quite nurturing. This doesn't mean you or the girls and boys in your life 'failed gender' or that the information is incorrect.

Please keep in mind that in considering generalities I am not writing about single individuals but about groups of women and men who have certain things in common and share similar characteristics. A good way to look at generalities would be in looking at height: If we put 500 randomly chosen women and men in a room, we would find that most of the men would be taller than most women even though a few women might be taller than certain men. While as individuals we occupy a unique place on the continuum of human behavior, we also share characteristics that are common to our specific gender.

How Differences Develop

From conception, girls and boys are programmed to march to different drummers. When the sperm fertilizes the egg the genetic blueprint embedded in the fetus is determined by twenty-three paired sets of chromosomes. One set comes from the egg cell and the other comes from the sperm cell. The chromosomes determine specific traits from each parent (and their ancestors) such as hair and eye and skin color, body type, intelligence, abilities, talents and vulnerabilities to diseases and disorders. The twenty-third set of chromosomes determines the biological sex of the fetus: the egg cell from the mother contributes one X chromosome while the sperm cell from the father contributes either an X or a Y. An XX combination will result in a fetus that is female while an XY combination will produce a fetus that is genetically male.[3]

For the first six or seven weeks after conception all fetuses develop along female lines and appear the same. They are female by default or in the words of anthropologist Helen Fisher 'Women are the first sex.'[4] Then chemical messengers in the form of sex hormones (steroids) called androgens and estrogens ensure that the designated genetic programs are carried out. A fetus destined to be female (XX), develops cells that produce and bath it in estrogen.[5] By the thirteenth week of gestation gonads appear in the form of ovaries. These produce tiny amounts of testosterone that influence the development of the female brain.[6]

Cells producing androgens (the main one being testosterone) develop in a fetus that is genetically male (XY). The androgens instruct the body not to develop female gonads but instead to stimulate the development of embryonic male genitalia. At a certain point in gestation, testosterone interacts with the nerve cells (neurons) that make up the brain and stimulates dramatic changes that alter the brain from one that is female into one that is distinctly male.[7] The levels of testosterone that the fetus receives at this point are four times the level experienced throughout infancy and boyhood.

Differences in behavior between girls and boys are evident shortly after birth. Girl babies show a tendency to be interested in people and communication. Infant girls reach out to touch their mothers more than infant boys do.[8] Studies of babies who are two to four days old show that girls pay attention longer when adults are speaking and spend almost twice as long maintaining eye contact. They are more tuned in to facial expressions and emotional nuances and will lose interest once the connection is broken. At four months most girls can distinguish between photographs of people they know and those of strangers.[9] The female brain responds more intensely to emotion. Feelings (especially sadness) activate neurons in an area eight times larger in the female brain than in the male. Even before they can understand language, girls seem to be better at identifying the emotional content of speech.[10] As girls grow older they can detect the emotions of others more accurately than boys can. Girls learn to speak before boys and develop better language skills. They can follow more than one train of thought and do more than one thing at a time.

For boys the interpersonal connection is less important than activity. Boys tend to be interested in dynamic activity and in objects. Male babies will continue to jabber away at toys long after the adult has ended the contact. Boys are more active and wakeful than girls. They are more sensitive to bright light and focus more on depth perception and perspective than on the wider picture. Boys tend to take in less sensory information than girls. They smell less, taste less, and get less input and soothing feedback from tactile information. They hear less well, and hear better through one ear than through the other.[11] Boys receive more testosterone and less serotonin (the neurotransmitter that inhibits aggression). As a result boys are more aggressive and impulsive than girls are.[12] Because the male brain is a problem-solving one, it can often take boys up to seven hours longer to process emotional data.

Girls and boys have different perceptions, priorities, behaviors and skills because of differences in their brains and in the ways that they process information. The female brain is 10 to 15% smaller than the male brain but the regions dedicated to higher cognitive functions such as language are more densely packed with neurons. It is more diffuse than the male brain. The functional division between the left and right sides of the brain is less clearly defined so that both sides are used in verbal and visual activities. This means that girls learn to speak earlier than boys do and develop more skill at verbal memory, which helps them master grammar and the intricacies of language at an earlier age.

Male brains are more compartmentalized and therefore more specialized than female ones. The left side is almost exclusively set aside for the control of verbal abilities including speaking, writing, reading and language. The right side controls visual abilities including spatial relations and abstract thoughts. The focused structure of the male brain means that boys can concentrate more intensely than girls can on one thing at a time. They are task-oriented because their brain turns on and off between tasks. Their attention span and motor activity are shorter than those of girls but are made up of more intensely active periods. Boys have better hand-eye coordination and greater ability to manipulate objects in space. They have better spatial relations. As they mature they will be better at interpreting maps, solving mazes, and doing the kinds of mathematics that involve abstract concepts of space, relationships and theory.[13]

It is important to know that neither brain structure is superior to the other. Nor are girls and boys restricted in what they do. Girls and boys acquire certain skills at different times and the ways that they learn to perform these skills are often different.[14] As well, different parts of the brain become susceptible to sex hormones at different times. Because levels of hormones fluctuate continuously, one region of the brain can be affected by powerful sex hormones that make it more masculine while other regions are untouched and are therefore feminine.

Each of us is a complex mix of feminine and masculine traits that lies on a continuum that ranges from the hypermasculine on one end to the hyperfeminine on the other. The amount of male hormone we receive and when we receive it contributes to behaviors that include aggressively competitive girls and boys who are preoccupied with clothes and dolls. It determines which girls are better than others in math, and which boys are less aggressive and more cooperative in nature than other boys.'[15]

Societal culture builds and expands upon what we bring into the world. As a result, the theories that describe the psychological development of girls and boys evolve out of and are influenced by the biological proclivities of each gender and the cultural beliefs of a particular time.

Girls' Development

Relational theory of female development demonstrates the divergent paths that girls and boys follow. Girls grow up with a perception of the world that is more contextual and less individualistic than that of boys. Because they are not encouraged to separate emotionally from their mothers at an early age, girls develop a core structure of self-in-relation[16] which evolves out of this close relationship. Female identity is based on girls' experience of themselves in relationships–first with their mother and then with significant people in their lives. Healthy relationships involve mutual understanding, emotional support and the commitment of both individuals to the development of each person and to the relationship itself.

Because of the emphasis on relationships, girls grow up to be interdependent. They learn to evaluate situations not only in terms of their individual responses, but also within the context of whatever 'others' may be involved.[17] They are concerned not only with their own individual well being, but also with the well-being of all those systems in which they participate.

Understanding Female Gender Culture

The relational and contextual perspective girls develop forms the basis of their female gender culture. It influences how they learn, the stories they tell (and the ways in which they tell them), what they think is important, and how they get things done.

Girls play in small groups that are based on communication and connection. They like to talk and listen because that is what their brains are better designed to do.[18] Their conversations focus on home, friendship and emotions. The games that girls play teach them empathy and sensitivity and have fewer rules than those of boys. Girls will change the rules to accommodate situations that arise. While competition can be a part of their games, girls tend to place more emphasis on inclusion and on taking turns. In games such as skipping and hopscotch the competition is indirect. The emphasis is not on being the best, but on being included—something that is really important to girls.

Girls handle conflict by trying to compromise and negotiate with one another. If there is no resolution, they learn to use relational rather than physical aggression towards each other. The use of exclusion such as "everyone is coming to my birthday party but you can't come," is generally more hurtful and more effective than using physical force.[19]

Relationships play a major part in the sense of well-being of most girls and, later on, are also their greatest source of angst. Girls have a best friend. They tell each other secrets. Their friendships are based on intimacy, connection and sharing.[20] When girls reach puberty they begin to participate in ongoing, committed relationships that demand more of them than just doing things for each other. They are possessive of each other—because it takes considerable time and effort to make a close friend. In order to feel secure, girls continuously check each other out to see how close or how distant they feel from the other person and how vulnerable they can be with her. Underlying their interactions are the questions: "Do you love me?" "Do you want to be with me?" and "What do I need to do to maintain the connection with you?"

Girls use language and communication as a way of drawing people closer to them. They engage with one another on many levels and provide clues as to how they feel through their body language and through empathic sounds they make. The exchange of similar experiences ensures that girls are equal in vulnerability and therefore in power. For example: attempting to offer advice before establishing equality places the person giving the advice on top and impairs the balance of the relationship.[21]

Because girls are interdependent they travel in pairs. Whenever they need to solve problems and make decisions they talk to a friend. If the problem or decision is a big one, they talk to two friends (or more). Sharing reassures girls they are not alone in how they feel and that they have the right to feel the way they do. Talking allows them to try out different solutions and to ask for and receive feedback before they make up their mind.

When girls enter new situations they assess how close or how distant they are from the other person. Their sense of security depends on feeling connected. When girls experience distance, they become anxious and often blame themselves for the failure to connect. Girls work best together through a process that involves verbally sharing things about themselves to establish intimacy and connection, then working to discover a commonality in order to develop equality, then finally addressing the task at hand.

Boys' Development

The traditional psychological theories that describe boys and men are based upon performance and accomplishment rather than on relationship. These theories tend to see development as taking place in progressive or hierarchical stages. Once you complete one stage, you rise to the next one. Each stage reinforces the qualities and abilities you mastered before and teaches you new ones that are considered to be increasingly more appropriate and mature.[22]

Traditional theories make the assumption that in order for boys to develop a male identity, they need to separate from their mothers at an early stage. This assumption is presently being challenged by some psychologists and viewed as creating a psychological impasse that harms boys at an early age.[23]

According to traditional theories of development, boys must master the stages of separation and individuation in order to become distinct individuals who can stand on their own two feet. They develop a sense of self-in-separation[24] that is based on accomplishment—how well they perform out in the world. Intimacy, and the ability to form relationships, does not enter into the male development scheme until boys reach adolescence. For many boys, it tends to be intertwined with (and sometimes inseparable from) sexuality.

Understanding Male Gender Culture

The activities boys are involved in and the ways that they carry them out serve to reinforce their goal-oriented sense of self and form the basis for their self-esteem. Boys grow up with tremendous energy and exuberance, a willingness to venture into the unknown, to take action, and a need to test their limits.[25] They want to explore areas, spaces and things because their brain bias predisposes them to these aspects of the environment.[26]

In pre-school and kindergarten boys tend to be interested in building structures of toppling heights out of blocks and playing with any kind of vehicle, especially transformers. They are more physical than girls are and their games are more rough-and-tumble. Boys tend to gather in larger, competitive groups where they can exercise their need for physical activity and for controlling more territory. Even in pre-school, boys play games with winners and losers and bluster through their games boasting about their skills. Later on, team sports reinforce the importance of rules, of winning and losing, and of being the best— being on top—as competition offers boys a way in which to feel worthy.[27]

Boys are better able to tolerate and depersonalize conflict than girls. They tend to argue more than girls over objects, fight with one another and pursue their own individual goals. They are also more physical with one another and try to get their own way by dominating one another.[28] Conflict is often a part of play. It provides boys with a way to relate to each other, check each other out and take a first step towards friendship.

Loyalty and fairness play a big part in the friendships that boys develop. Standing up for and being there for friends is very important. Boys support each other by diffusing emotional intensity and cheering each other up. They feel most comfortable with interpersonal communication when it takes place in the context of an activity or when boys are side-by-side, rather than face-to-face.[29] For example, when I taught a course in basic counseling skills at the local college, the men in the class found that sitting directly across from and maintaining eye contact with another man made them feel threatened. They felt that the other person was invading their space. When they repositioned their chairs so they didn't have direct eye contact, the tension decreased.

Despite the importance of friendships many boys tend to solve problems on their own rather than make themselves vulnerable by talking to someone else. They protect themselves from being misjudged, labeled, and seen as weak and losing face.

Boys assess each situation in terms of how adequately they perform in relation to one another. Their comfort level comes from knowing where they fit in and what they must do to improve or maintain their status in order to gain respect. Possession of information allows boys to gain power over someone else. Male language, which is based upon logical reasoning, serves as a way for boys to capture and hold onto another person's attention and to put forth their opinions and views in such a way that they 'win' the discussion (or at least hold their own).[30]

Experiencing Gender Differences in Our Lives

This initial chapter provides a context for all of the concepts and topics addressed throughout this book. Before we can put our knowledge of gender and development to use in parenting and in our work with girls (and boys) it helps to first understand how we experience these differences in our own lives. Our adult relationships with the opposite sex illustrate gender most vividly, so I have used them in the following examples:

In a *Sally Forth* cartoon the interaction between Sally Forth and her husband Ned illustrate how men and women give and interpret directions differently:

Sally: "Hillary wants me to take her shopping at the Jeans Jungle. Do you know how to get there?"

Ned: "Get on 152 and head…"

Sally (interrupting): "Does 152 have a name? Names are easier."

Ned: "Dunham Road. Turn north on Dunham and go..."

Sally (interrupting again): "Give me a direction."

Ned (growing impatient): "North is a direction."

Sally: "North is a compass point. Right is a direction."

Ned: "Okay, turn right on Dunham, go about three miles. Then turn west, I mean left at Stonehenge Circle."

Sally: "Give me a landmark."

Ned: "You make giving directions very difficult."

Sally: "No I don't. All I am asking for is something like 'Right on Dunham, go three miles, left at the blue house with the ugly curtains.' What's so difficult about that?"

The conversation between Sally and Ned is happening because women tend to have 'location memory.' They navigate by means of stationary objects spread across a landscape. When they give directions, they specify twice as many concrete landmarks as men do.[31] Men usually navigate by distances and cardinal directions. When they give directions, they give twice as many quantitative and cardinal references as women do.[32]

A common and familiar gender difference is around the subject of feelings. In my practice as a therapist I often hear the following complaint:

She: "Whenever I ask him how he feels he looks annoyed. He never shares his feelings. He just doesn't love me."

He: "She is constantly asking me how I feel. I love her but every time she asks me I just feel pressured and go blank."

Women can express their emotions in words easier than men can. The emotional side of the female brain is more integrated with the verbal side so what women feel is transmitted more effectively to the verbal side of their brain. Men keep their emotions on the right side of their brain, while the power to express their feelings in speech lies on the left. It is more difficult for them to express their emotions because the information is flowing less easily to the verbal (left) side of their brain.[33] The difference in brain structure is what causes women to believe that men don't want to share their feelings and men to feel pressured to do something they cannot do at that specific time.

Imagine you are having coffee with a small group of women. You are talking about your kids, spouses or mates. One of the men in your office comes in and joins you. What happens to the conversation? Most likely there is an awkward pause as either you change the subject to accommodate him, or he changes the direction in which the conversation is going.

In women-only groups we practice the communication style of our female gender culture, which is informal and personal and includes details of our lives. When a man joins our group we tend to adapt ourselves to his cultural pattern of communication instead of continuing with or asking him to adapt to ours–because we have been socialized to fit into the dominant culture.

Imagine you are having a discussion with a small group of your friends. You are talking about a book or article that you have read or a movie you have seen. Everyone is passionate about the subject. The room is alive with your energy. Now imagine you have to make a presentation to a large group of people about this very same subject. How you present to a group of women might be very different from how you present to a group of men. The informal personal way in which you expressed yourself now seems inadequate. You begin to translate your ideas into male language and style of communication. In the process you lose your context. This causes you to doubt yourself and your ability. You ask yourself 'what do I know?' You are afraid of getting this wrong and begin to doubt yourself even more.

As girls we grow up and play in small groups. Contrast our intimate style of communication with that of boys who play in large groups and use language to win arguments and gain power over others. When we make presentations or speak to large groups we adopt the male style of communication which requires us to 'translate' from one gender culture to another. Asking us to speak in larger, more formal groups is similar to asking someone whose first language is English to do a presentation in French. No wonder it is difficult!

Endnotes

1. Cohen, Joyce. "He-Mails, She-Mails: Where Sender Meets Gender." *New York Times.* May 19, 2001

2. Blum, D. (1997) *Sex on the Brain: The Biological Differences Between Men and Women.* New York: Viking, p. 77

   3. Moir, A. & D. Jessel. (1991) *Brain Sex: The Real Difference Between Men and Women.* New York: Bantam Doubleday Dell, pp. 23-30

4. Fisher, H. (1999) *The First Sex: The Natural Talents of Women and How They are Changing the World.* New York: Random House, p. xviii

5. Blum, D. (July 1999) "What's the Difference Between Boys and Girls?" *Life Magazine.* p. 46

6. Gorski, R. (1991) "Sexual differentiation of the brain," in Krieger, D.T. and J.C. Hughes. (Eds.) *Neuroendocrinology.* Sunderland, MA: Sinauer Associates, pp. 215-222

7. Moir and Jessel. pp. 23-24

8. Hall, J. (1984) *Nonverbal Sex Differences: Communication Accuracy and Expressive Style.* Baltimore: Johns Hopkins University Press

9. Moir and Jessel. p. 56

10. Ibid. p. 55

11. Ibid. p. 58

12. Ibid. pp. 53-65

13. Ibid, p. 15

14. Berger-Sweeny, J. (February 9, 1996) "The Developing brain: Genes, Environment and Behavior," AAS Symposium

15. Reinish, J.M. (1974) "Fetal hormones, the brain and human sex differences: A heuristic Integrative review of the recent literature" *Archives of Sexual Behavior.* 3:51-90

16. Surrey, J. L. "The self-in-relation: A theory of women's development" in J. Jordan, A. G. Kaplan, J.B. Miller, I.P. Stiver and J. L. Surrey. (Eds.) (1991) *Women's Growth in Connection: Writings From the Stone Center.* New York: Guilford Press, pp. 51-64

17. Ibid

18. Moir and Jessel, p. 59

19. Sheldon, Amy. "Pickle fights: Gendered talk in preschool disputes." In Deborah Tannen. (Ed.). (1993) *Gender and Conversational Interaction.* New York: Oxford University Press, pp. 83-109

20. Tannen, D. (1990) *You Just Don't Understand: Women and Men in Conversation.* New York: Ballantine Books

21. Ibid

22. Erikson, E. (1968) *Identity, Youth and Crisis.* New York: W.W. Norton

23. Pollack, W. (1998) *Real Boys: Rescuing Our Sons from the Myths of Boyhood.* New York: Random House

24. Surrey, pp. 51-64

25. Gurian, M. (1996) *The Wonder of Boys: What Parents, Mentors and Educators Can Do To Make Boys Into Exceptional Men.* New York: Tarcher/Putnam, p. 37-38

26. Moir and Jessel, p. 58

27. Gurian
28. Sheldon, pp. 83-109
29. Pollack
30. Tannen
31. Silverman, E. and M. Eals. "Sex differences in spatial abilities: Evolutional theory and data," in J. Barkow, L. Cosmides and J. Tooby. (Eds.) (1992) *The Adapted Mind: Evolutionary Psychology and the Generation of Culture.* New York: Oxford University Press, pp. 533-539
32. Miller, L. K. and V. Santini. (1986) "Sex differences in spatial abilities: Strategic and experiential correlates," *Acta Psychologica.* 62: 225-235
33. Moir and Jessel. p. 48

2

Socialization

Two newborn infants lie side by side in the nursery. "Look at how cute and delicate Jennifer is," her parents boast to the other onlookers. "She's so quiet. We've never seen such a good baby."

"That's our Michael beside her," respond the other parents. "Listen to the lungs on him. He sure lets us know what he wants," they exclaim. "He's so strong and sturdy. He's going to be a real handful."[1]

If Jennifer and Michael's parents had looked at the hospital charts, they would have found that Jennifer was bigger than Michael and weighed more. Most likely her lungs were more powerful than his because boys' lungs are often underdeveloped at birth. That probably wouldn't have made a difference in how they perceived their babies, however, because from the moment they knew the sex of their child, the process of gender socialization ensured that gender stereotyping was already in place.

It is the process of gender socialization that reinforces, amplifies, and maintains those behaviors that are associated with being female or male. Although we are born predisposed to certain behaviors because of our biological makeup and are further influenced by our environment or culture, gender socialization teaches us how to be girls and boys (and then women and men) according to the rules of our society. Factors such as family, culture, education, socio-economic status, religion, ethnicity, peer group and the media also play important roles.

Socialization is also responsible for the creation of stereotypes or characterizations of people that are used to differentiate the treatment of girls and boys. Often they are based upon narrow and frequently incorrect assumptions. The stereotype illustrated on the previous page assumes that because Jennifer is female she must be delicate and because Michael is male he must be strong. While we have traits and behaviors that are common to our gender, stereotypes exaggerate and lock us into behaviors, characteristics and traits associated with being female and male whether they apply to us personally or not.

The Impact of Gender Socialization on Female Development

Before girls reach adolescence, they tend to thrive in their female gender culture. They mature faster than boys. Their female brain structure equips them to learn math and reading skills earlier. Because they develop better control of their small motor skills they are better able to write before boys can.[2] In the period between preschool and puberty girls are physically active. They are as tall as boys and weigh the same and can run as fast, jump as high and hit a ball just as far.

Before puberty girls speak their minds and voice their opinions—just try arguing with an eight or nine year old, especially about something she thinks is unfair. They break up with their best friends and come back together. They get angry and express strong feelings.[3] They quarrel and they fight because they have confidence in their ability to make up.

Before adolescence girls' behavior and sense of self is relatively unrestricted from societal pressure. However, in the period between childhood and budding adulthood, between elementary/middle school and high school, girls' bodies begin to change and so do their lives. They begin to suffer from depression, anxiety, stress and other signs of psychological distress. They begin to worry a lot about their own safety and the safety of others, about the unknown and especially about how they look and what they eat.[4]

Changes in Girls' Bodies

Puberty refers to all of the physical changes that happen inside and outside of a child's body as it transforms into an adult body with the capacity to reproduce. It marks the beginning of adolescence, the stage between childhood and adulthood. At a biologically determined time, the pituitary gland sends a message to the sex glands and puberty begins. The changes that occur in girls' bodies happen slowly and gradually over an extended period of time. This can begin to happen as early as seven or eight or as late as sixteen and continues for many years.

The changes in girls' bodies are gradual until they reach puberty and so girls are easily able to accommodate themselves to them. When they enter puberty girls go through so many changes so rapidly that their bodies feel new and strange and out of control. Remember what it was like to go to bed at night wondering if your jeans were going to fit the next day and not knowing when all these changes would end. Girls ride the roller coaster of hormones and Premenstrual Mood Swings (PMS). One grade seven girl in a group that I facilitated said, "I feel like my head is in a bubble and the pressure inside builds and builds until I want to scream and scream." Because we don't give girls enough relevant information, they think their bodies are not normal and something is wrong with them. At a community talk that I gave, a ten-year-old girl wanted to know if she had cancer because her breasts hurt. A twelve-year-old girl talked about being afraid because she didn't get her period each and every month.

Because girls begin puberty at different times, they can feel out of step with their peers. Some must deal with teasing and with being sexualized because they mature early. Many of these girls have a tendency to diet because they see themselves as different from their friends and therefore as 'fat'. When boys and men make comments about their bodies, girls come to feel that their bodies are not their own. Some girls must deal with the angst of being a late bloomer—the only one who doesn't yet have breasts.

When girls get their periods we don't celebrate their rite of passage in the same way we make a fuss over facial hair on boys. Instead, we teach them to keep this information hidden. Whenever I ask girls what would happen if they came into class and announced "I got my period, I got my period," I am met with uncomfortable giggles and horror that I would suggest such a thing. "Leave your purse out of it!" a television commercial for Tampax exclaims. "The Tampax compact applicator is so small you can hide it in your hand." If we do talk about our periods, the word blood never crosses our lips. Nor is it ever mentioned or shown in the commercials for sanitary napkins and tampons which use blue liquid instead.

During puberty girls are especially vulnerable to becoming preoccupied with body weight and shape. The adolescent growth spurt, the normal tendency to gain weight and the significant increase in body fat necessary to female development are in direct contradiction to society's message to girls that they must look like pencils—but with breasts and muscle tone. Society's emphasis on thinness as a measure of value and worth robs girls of their ability to accept their natural bodies and replaces childhood joy with adolescent shame. At a time when they need the most nourishment, girls begin to restrict their food intake because of their fear of getting fat. In community after community girls ask me, "Can't I go through puberty without gaining weight or getting fat?"

Girls measure themselves against each other and reinforce the societal message that they must constantly try to change their natural bodies in order to fit in. Many girls deal with the changes to their bodies by disengaging from their inner and/or kinesthetic experience and focusing largely on their external appearance. In doing so, they disconnect and dissociate from their bodies and thus from themselves.

Changes in Girls' Lives

According to psychologists Carol Gilligan and Lynn Mikel Brown, girls continue to develop the capacity for authentic relationships up to the time of adolescence. Because girls develop their identity in the context of their relationships, they flourish when their relationships are open, honest and mutually supportive. However, when girls reach adolescence the way in which they practice and negotiate their relationships begins to change. Girls lose their ability to know what is relationally true or real and therefore lose the ability to trust their own instincts and feelings.[5]

From the time girls are young, society (people such as us) tells them that it is better to be 'kind and nice' and not hurt anyone's feelings than to be honest and say what they really think and feel. These messages are intensified when girls reach adolescence. Society holds up to girls the model of the 'perfect girl' who is calm, controlled, independent and confident. She is thoughtful of others but able to assert her rights and fight for the rights of others—all the while not offending anyone or drawing too much attention to herself. She is also, inevitably, thin.[6]

Girls fall victim to the 'tyranny of kind and nice'[7] which places them in a terrible dilemma. If they are honest with their feelings and opinions they will be shunned by other girls and will jeopardize their relationships. If they are perfect (and therefore 'kind and nice') they will lose touch with who they are, how they feel and what is important to them. They will also lose their real connections with others. Because the fear of hurting someone is very powerful, girls struggle with wanting to be honest and with feeling that they should be nice. I am often asked "How do you say no to someone without hurting her feelings?" and "How can you express your feelings without hurting someone?" As adult women we continue to ask the same questions ourselves.

Girls learn to silence themselves in their relationships rather than hurt someone else or risk open conflict that might lead to rejection and isolation and perhaps even violence against them. Nice girls make more friends. People like them. Girls learn that the way to stay close and be perfect is to hide parts of themselves. They begin to hold back their feelings and opinions in order to fit into their peer group and conform to the expectations of society. Many girls repress their desires and dismiss or reframe their feelings and thoughts into happy ones. As they focus on the other person's experience and point of view they lose their own.

Girls often ask, "What should I do with my anger if I don't like someone?" Being kind and nice and perfect leaves girls with no way to deal directly with anger and conflict so girls do so indirectly. Their friendships take on a dark side and the intimacy that once nourished them goes bad. Girls develop secrets that they use against one another. They form cliques. They learn that alliances are elusive and that it is not safe to be direct. Pretending to be a perfect girl in a world of in-groups can assure you of inclusion, attention and love.

Because girls learn to put the needs of others ahead of their own, they have a difficult time with boundaries. They are afraid that if they say 'no' they will be rejected and that if they say 'yes' or appear to want to take care of their own needs, they will be seen as selfish. Girls who become interested in boys may have sex when they don't really want to, or have unsafe sex because they don't want to hurt the boy's feelings by asking him to use a condom, or get into cars with guys who are drunk. For many girls it is far less scary to become pregnant or develop a sexually transmitted disease or even risk death than have the boy not like you or not ask you out again—even if he is somebody that you don't particularly care for.

The profound changes that girls experience in their relationships create an impasse in their psychological development. Because these relationships are based on a desire to please the other person, girls have difficulties in speaking their truths and this leaves them feeling unheard or not listened to. They are left to deal with the absence of mutual empathic responses and with the feeling of not being able to convey or to believe in their own experiences.[8] Girls begin to distrust their experiences and knowledge and to disconnect from their selves. This silencing of girls' voices is a *body thief* because as the girls' voices are repressed, their bodies become the 'selves' that speak—too often telling them that they are fat.[9]

How Girls Deal with Societal Pressures

The pressures to be kind and nice, to please others and to hold back their feelings and opinions cause girls to split into two selves: the false outward pleasing persona and the real person inside.[10] Girls move back and forth across this chasm fulfilling what is expected of them as opposed to what they think and feel and hide inside. The more practiced their pleasing persona becomes, the more girls lose their inner voice—that awareness of their own needs and their ability to trust their own perceptions.

This causes them to look outward for definition instead of being the center of their own experiences. Girls no longer interact with the world in terms of 'I.' Instead, they relate to it in terms of 'you.' Instead of asking themselves 'what do I want' and 'how comfortable am I with you' they ask 'what do you want?' and 'what do you think of me?'

Society socializes girls to internalize distress and boys to externalize it. Girls learn to draw their pain into themselves and to blame themselves and feel angry with themselves while boys hit out and blame others. A good illustration is the story of the couple that wanted to go for a ride in their car. When the car door didn't open, the man exclaimed, "What's wrong with the car? The door won't open." The woman asked, "What's wrong with me? I can't open the door?"

When girls cannot express their feelings and opinions directly, they do so indirectly. Girls learn to speak about themselves in a negative voice. They tell themselves they feel ugly and stupid. They tell themselves they are such losers that nobody will like them. Many girls deflect feelings they cannot express onto their bodies. Because fat is labeled bad in our society, girls begin to feel fat.

Girls learn to encode their feelings in a *language of fat* and to speak 'fat'. They feel fat when they are angry, sad, lonely and insecure and when they have no language for their emotions or feel unsafe in expressing themselves. Speaking fat causes girls to shift their focus from their inner experiences to their external self. It reinforces the disconnection that girls experience from their bodies and from their selves.

Girls try to alleviate emotional pain or stress in their lives by trying to change their physical bodies or by focusing on the outside instead of addressing what's real on the inside. Many girls deal with the discomfort and disconnection of feeling fat by dieting. Feeling fat is the first clear indicator of a risk factor that might lead to disordered eating (and subsequently to eating disorders) as well as to yo-yo dieting which alters girls' metabolism and increases their body weight. In Chapter 8 we will look at how to translate fat talk and help girls express the real feelings that are hidden underneath.

Putting it into Practice

Take some time to sit quietly and think back over the
time when you were growing up.

- What was puberty like for you?

- How did you feel about your body?

- Were you a late bloomer or an early bloomer?

- What were your greatest fears?

- What would you have liked to have known then that you
  know now?

- What changes happened in your life once you became an
  adolescent?

- Are you still affected by those changes?

  Go back over the past week or two. Think of a situation
  where you wanted to say no to someone:

- Were you able to do it?

- What did it feel like afterwards?

- Did you ask anyone for support?

- If you were not able to do it, what happened to the feelings
  that you had?

- Do you feel like moving towards that person or moving
  away? Why?

- How does being 'kind and nice' affect your life today?

- How does it affect your relationship with the girl(s) in your
  life?

- How do you reinforce it to the girl(s) in your life?

Endnotes

1. Adapted from Rubin, J.Z., and E. Provenzano and Z. Luria. (1974) "The eye of the beholder: Parents' Views on the sex of their newborns," *American Journal of Orthopsychiatry*, No. 44. pp. 512-519
2. Shakeshaft, C. (March 1986) "A gender at risk," *Phi Delta Kappan.* Vol. 67, No. 7. pp. 500-503
3. Gilligan, C. & L. M. Brown. (1992) *Meeting at the Crossroads: Women's Psychology and Girl's Development.* Cambridge: Harvard University Press, p. 59
4. Steinberg, L. and J. Belsky. (1991) *Infancy, Childhood and Adolescence: Development in Context.* New York: McGraw Hill, p. 344
5. Brown and Gilligan, p. 54
6. Thanks to Lynn Sackville
7. Brown and Gilligan, p. 53
8. Ibid, p. 55
9. Steiner-Adair, C and A. P. Vorenberg. (1999) "Resisting weightism: Media literacy for elementary-school children," in Piran, N., and M.P. Levine and C. Steiner-Adair (Eds.) *Preventing Eating Disorders: A Handbook of Interventions and Special Challenges.* Philadelphia: Brunner/Mazel, p. 106
10. Pipher, M. (1994) *Reviving Ophelia: Saving the Selves of Adolescent Girls.* New York: Ballantine Books, pp. 19-23

3

∞

Building Relationships with Girls

"The thing that I like best about working with girls is the experience of learning about their lives from the girls themselves." Community Health Nurse

"One way I found of getting my kids to open up is to talk with their friends when they are over. Their friends tend to be chatty with you and your daughter opens up. I find this works well when we're all sitting around the table after school having a snack."
Lynn, mother of 12 year old Clea

Until girls reach puberty it's very easy and gratifying to have a relationship with them. They want to hang out with us, do things with us and include us in their lives. Once girls reach adolescence it's like someone pulled a switch. The relationship suddenly changes. The same girl who wanted to spend time with you just a short while ago now looks at you blankly and says 'whatever.' We've all had versions of the following conversation:

You: "So, Jessica, how was your day?"

Jessica: "Fine"

You: "What went on?"

Jessica: "Nothing."

As the previous chapter illustrated, when girls reach adolescence they split into two selves: the pleasing one that they show to society and the real one inside. Before girls will share their true feelings and opinions and reveal their vulnerability they carefully assess every relationship to see how 'safe' the other person is. The bottom line for most adolescent girls is—especially with adults—'I'll show you mine, but only if you show me yours!'

In order to build relationships with girls that facilitate growth we need to be active participants in our interactions with them instead of the passive observers that most of us have been taught to be. As women the essential ingredients that we bring to our relationships are the common characteristics of our gender that we share with girls, our own experiences of growing up female and our willingness to model healthy female relationships by engaging honestly with them by letting them know what we actually think and feel and by sharing our own experiences of the world—instead of just trying to tell them what to do. While the gender dynamics are somewhat different for men, they can still be open and honest with girls and interested in learning about what it is important to them.

Schmoozing—the Art of Sharing Ourselves

Girls are more willing to communicate with adults when we share ourselves with them. However, we need to remember that we are the adults and they are not, so we don't tell them about our messy divorce or use them as a sounding board for issues that we are still in the process of working out. We don't depend on them to take care of our feelings nor do we appropriate their experiences. It means that we selectively share similar experiences of ours as a way of validating and normalizing theirs. It means giving them permission to raise certain topics, and giving them language to help them when they have trouble describing what they feel. By sharing our experiences with girls we validate theirs and form a connection that facilitates their growth. By sharing our opinions we provide girls with a sounding board that they can use in the process of formulating their own opinions.

One of the most powerful ways for us to share ourselves with girls is to schmooze with them. Schmoozing is a Yiddish word that has made its way into the English language. It means talking informally or 'chewing the fat.' When we phone a friend to catch up on the details of her life and to get the dirt we schmooze. I like to use the term schmoozing to describe the communication ritual that women use with each other, especially when we share our problems.

It goes like this: when I have a problem I telephone a friend and say "Oh, I can't believe what just happened! I really need to talk!" When I put the problem into words it makes it real. This is important because many of us tend to minimize our experiences.

My friend responds to the description of my problem with comments such as "Ooh, that's terrible, that's really difficult, I can't believe it, you must be so upset!" Her empathic response validates my feelings and lets me know that I have a right to the way I feel. This step is important because we tend to minimize our feelings and focus on other people instead of ourselves.

My friend might say "Oh, the same thing happened to me!" If she doesn't have a similar problem, she shares someone else's. Knowing that other people have similar experiences reassures me that I am normal and helps me feel less isolated. After we have schmoozed for a while she might give me feedback or brainstorm strategies with me. When I hang up the phone, the problem might still be there, but the schmoozing (expressing the feeling and taking it seriously and having it validated and normalized) makes me feel better about myself and makes the problem easier to resolve.

SCHMOOZING

Talking about our problem makes it real...
...because we tend to discount our experiences.

Empathy from others lets us know that we have a right to the way we feel...
...because we tend to negate our feelings or focus on how the other person felt instead of on ourselves.

The sharing of a similar problem lets us know that we are not alone in how we feel...
...because we think we are abnormal and the only one that feels the way we do.

When Men Schmooze

Women enter into conversation to create intimacy and to bring people closer to them. They do this by sharing the details of their lives. Schmoozing with all its interruptions—the sharing and validation—conforms to this means of communication. Schmoozing can be difficult for men because the patterns of communication that they learn as they grow up are different from those of girls and women.

Men enter conversation to solve problems. They wait to hear the whole story so that they can figure out the logic of the problem and then try to help by telling the other person what to do to fix it. Because of these differences in communication styles some men tend to become frustrated when girls don't get to the point. How can they fix the problem if they don't know what it is? Schmoozing can be difficult for men who are not socialized (and therefore not practiced) in sharing the details of their lives.

When men give girls advice before they have schmoozed (or dealt with the emotional content), girls feel unheard and resentful. Even though men might have difficulties in schmoozing that doesn't mean that they cannot form connections with girls. It just means that men will do it differently. Sometimes it helps to acknowledge to the girl that what you really want to do is fix things but you know that she is not ready for that. This will remove the onus to perform, lessen your tension and allow you to listen. Providing empathic responses (such as 'that sounds terrible') gives you something to do and at the same time allows the girl to feel heard. With time and patience and practice you can adapt the schmoozing ritual so that it works for you and for the girls and women in your lives.

Talking at Girls

As adult women, we schmooze mainly with other adults. We rarely schmooze with girls. Instead we try to make things better for them and we tell them what to do. Yet just as we don't want or expect the men in our lives to fix things for us, our girls don't want us to fix things for them. Sometimes it is difficult for us to not do this.

As parents, it's hard not to get nervous when we look at girls and see their bodies begin to change. We look at the world they are about to enter and at the pressures on them to be perfect and thin. We worry about their safety and the all of the risks to which they are vulnerable. On our worst days we imagine our daughter having unsafe sex with a drunk driver while smoking a cigarette as a way of coping with her eating disorder and sexually transmitted disease and then, after all of that, being abducted by the person next door.

Because we want to keep girls safe we feel compelled to tell them what to do: We say 'don't have sex,' 'don't hang out with those people,' 'don't drink,' 'don't speak to strangers or come home too late.' We ourselves have been conditioned to believe that if we just give girls a logical rationale for not doing something; they will listen to us and change their behavior. But when we talk at girls instead of engaging with them, they distance themselves from us and just tune us out.

Sharing tales of our own adolescence can be painful for some of us because it brings up memories we consider best left forgotten. Often we don't share our experiences with girls because we are afraid to 'burden' them. We think that if we don't talk to girls about the guys (or women) who dumped us or we don't share our own moments of insecurity and doubt or talk about issues that we are presently grappling with we will spare them that pain. By not talking with girls about our experiences, we rob them of a context for their own. Instead of giving them support, we set them adrift.

I'm the Authority, You're the Girl

Developing relationships with girls requires that we adults bring our personal selves into our professional lives. Sharing ourselves with girls can be difficult for those of us who have been trained to view our professionalism as based on hierarchy, on maintaining a distance from the other person and on viewing girls' issues and concerns as their individual problems.

Sometimes we become afraid that if we say something personal about ourselves we will lose our authority because girls will use the information that we give them against us. We also worry that they will try to take care of us instead of our being able to help them. When our relationships with girls are based on honest connection, these fears rarely materialize. If we want to parent, teach or work with girls in a healthy way then we must find ways of connecting to them and this means learning to share ourselves. Because this is a new skill we need to give ourselves the time and patience to practice it and to use it in a way that feels comfortable to us.

The Issues that Girls Raise

As women and men who parent and teach and work with girls we must constantly try to understand what life looks like for girls–to continuously ask them about their feelings and what their experiences mean to them in the context of their lives. We need to be careful as we do this that the conversation isn't one-sided and we don't grill girls or else they will turn off and tune us out. It is through understanding, articulating and sharing their knowledge of their own truths and their own personal experiences that girls are able to begin the process of change.

Once girls begin to share their feelings and talk about their concerns we find the issues they are dealing with are the same (or very similar) to the ones that we constantly deal with as grown women. Girls talk about relationships and their difficulties in being true to themselves while not hurting anyone else. They talk about the pain of rejection and how hard it is to be regarded as different. They talk about sexuality and harassment and their ambivalent feelings about their changing bodies. They talk about taking care of others and not getting their own needs met. And while we want to validate their experiences by sharing our own, it's not easy when the issues that girls raise are the ones that are so emotionally charged for us, or when their value systems or means of coping are very different from ours.

We need to monitor ourselves for commonalities when we relate to the girls (and especially when we don't relate to their experiences). We still need to find a way to validate them without judging them or minimizing their feelings or feeling the need to 'fix' their lives.

Working with girls makes us take stock of our *shoulds*–we should always be right, know the answer, agree with other people, be patient, share when we don't want to, never get angry, never say no. When we turn off our heads and open our hearts we know when we feel connected to someone else and when we feel safe, heard, understood and accepted–regardless of whether they agree with us or not. When that connection is broken, we feel abandoned, judged, wronged and criticized.

Girls respond when they feel an emotional bond with women and men who are honest about their feelings and opinions. We don't always have to know the answer, or be patient, or agree with their behavior or points of view as long as we are honest in our interactions with them. We need to listen, listen, listen and not jump to conclusions. We lose girls the moment that we cease to be ourselves. When we assume our formal and authoritative adult voices, we become part of the dominant culture. Girls close down, show us their pleasing persona and stonewall us. Many feel unsafe because of the dissonance between what we are telling them and what they experience.

Supporting the Girls We Work With

When we teach girls the skills that help them develop a healthy sense of self, we introduce them to an image of women and girls that it is different from those prevailing in our society. We offer them dynamic choices and encourage self expression in place of the mantle of passivity and self-repression that they are expected to assume as they grow up.

In encouraging girls to be assertive and in steering them back to their own culture, we may put them at risk of disapproval and adverse reaction from their parents, their teachers and their friends. The father of one girl in a group that I facilitated complained that until his daughter did the group she 'knew her place.' Now she was beginning to question him and to tell him how she felt and he didn't like it.

If we are going to teach girls new behaviors and encourage them to practice a different way of being in the world, then we must also be there to give them support. This means we must be willing to be advocates for them when they need it and model the same behavior we are teaching them. It is up to us as women and men who parent, teach and work with girls to care for them and provide them with a solid foundation for their roots so they can feel safe in expressing their feelings and opinions and in being true to themselves.

Giving Girls Feedback

Because we want the best for our girls, we try to help them in what they do, encourage them, correct their mistakes and teach them skills. Sometimes, despite our best intentions girls feel criticized instead of helped. This is because when we give girls feedback we tend to concentrate only on what they did wrong and how it could be fixed. We point out their spelling mistakes, make suggestions about how they could improve the composition or how they could throw the ball or hit the puck with more accuracy.

Girls need praise and acknowledgement about what they have done right before they can hear about what they did wrong or need to improve. The women in one workshop that I facilitated described this as 'giving roses and onions.' When we don't give girls 'a rose' first and acknowledge how hard they tried, how interesting their characters are or how much they have improved it makes them feel that their efforts go unacknowledged and unseen. No matter how much we want to help girls, they won't take in our suggestions when they feel criticized.

When we give girls feedback we need to do so from within the context of our relationship with them. Girls need to know that the connection will still be intact despite whatever criticism we are going to give them. Validating them and their efforts before giving feedback assures them that the relationship is on sure ground despite whatever is coming next.

Girls can take in our feedback and respond to us when we are able to say, "I noticed that you have been working hard on your spelling. Would you like me to point out the few places that you missed?" and "I really liked the characters in your composition. Can I make a suggestion about how you can make your work stronger?" and "You are really passing the puck well.

You might want to try to straighten the blade of your hockey stick the next time you shoot from the point." When we get to the chapter on sport you will see that it is especially this dynamic that makes coaching girls different from coaching boys.

Trusting Ourselves

As you read the rest of this book it is important that you remember three things: there is no one specific way to help girls reclaim their natural bodies; we all negotiate relationships differently; and (most important) that as long as we are willing to be real, we cannot fail parenting/working with girls.

We all bring with us certain skills and talents. We all have some ability to relate to others. We enter into the learning process at our own particular level of experience and interest. We need to respect who we are. When we get caught up in performance anxiety, we lose our curiosity—the main ingredient that we need in order to connect with girls and learn new things ourselves.

It is important that we trust ourselves instead of entering into our relationships with girls with the fear of doing something wrong. If you keep asking yourself what you are learning and need to learn from the girls and what you are learning about yourself it will be easier for you to give up your need to do everything perfectly the first time. As you become more comfortable interacting with girls you will gradually develop your own style and make the strategies your own.

Putting it into Practice

Take a few moments to think or write about the following:

- What three special personal qualities do you bring to your work/relationships with girls?
- What two skills do you bring to your work/relationships with girls?
- What are you most curious about in working with girls?
- What do you find most difficult in working with girls?
- What would you need to feel more confident?
- Where can you get that support?

4

∞

The War on Fat

When her GP looked at Katie, he saw rolls of flesh, he saw
mammae hanging like two heavy flour sacks from her shoulders, he saw a stomach that drooped to cover her pubis and
skin that was cratered with cellulite. She was carrying so
much weight on her frame that she would live for a year on
her own tissues without eating, and if the doctor was to be
believed, the fat was moving in on her vital organs. If she
didn't do something to curb herself at the table, he declared
each time she saw him, she was going to be a gonner.

'Heart failure or stroke, Kathleen,' he told her with a shake
of his head. 'Choose your poison. Your condition calls for
immediate action and that action is not intended to include
ingesting anything that can turn into adipose tissue. Do you
understand?' But the truth of the matter was that her GP
was the only person in Katie's life who had difficulty accepting her as the fat girl she'd been from childhood.[1]

from *A Traitor to Memory* by Elizabeth George

We live in a society that has declared war on fat. We are constantly bombarded with urgent warnings that obesity is on the
rise, that we are in the midst of a health crisis where obesity will
make us sick and even kill us, that we all need to lose weight
and that all of our health dollars are being drained by irrespon-
sible people who are fat. "Obesity Greater Health Risk than
Smoking," one newspaper headline screams. "Obese People
Have Twice the Chronic Health Troubles than People of
Normal Weight."[2] This is 'no time to be thin-skinned,' blames a
newspaper editorial. "The medical evidence overwhelmingly
concludes that overweight and obesity are linked to premature
illness and an early grave—which a lot of people are digging
with their own knives and forks."[3]

Our society has created a powerful and influential *Antifat
Crusade* that is waging a war against a paper tiger—the myth that

fat is necessarily bad. The weapons of choice are weight loss, guilt and humiliation. Between 40 to 70% of Americans are trying to lose weight.[4] Each year they spend roughly forty billion dollars ($40,000,000,000.00) on diet products and programs.[5] The numbers are comparable in Canada. If diets by themselves don't work, there is a thriving pharmaceutical industry (with physicians on its Boards) to help fat people lose weight even if the pills kill them[6] or make them sick,[7] nutritionists to help them keep their diets on track, a fitness industry to help them continuously recycle their fat and a fashion industry to reinforce whatever feelings of insecurity they have about their bodies. Concerned health care professionals help them deal with their low self-esteem, their seemingly out-of-control appetites and reinforce the message they are responsible for getting themselves into the mess that they are in.

Studies show that 95 to 97% of people who lose weight by dieting regain that weight *plus more* within 4 to 5 years.[8] Set point theory suggests that we all have a genetically determined weight range that our body attempts to maintain.[9] When we diet, physiologically determined set point mechanisms counteract our efforts to change our weight by slowing down our metabolism and burning fewer and fewer calories in order to protect our body from starvation. When we go off the diet, the body adjusts to this modern form of famine by storing more and more fat and raising the set point.[10] Even though we now weigh more and it's harder to lose weight, the pressure continues and the dream remains alive. While diet center franchises flourish from guaranteed repeat business, we feel worse about ourselves. Because we don't learn about how our set point mechanisms work, we blame our difficulty on losing weight on ourselves and reinforce our sense of failure.

The Antifat Crusaders have created and continue to reinforce their own worst nightmare to the detriment of us all. Because diets don't take the set point mechanism into consideration, the harder people try to rid themselves of fat, the fatter they become. The average person is fatter now than at any time in history. Between 1960 and 1980 one quarter of the population (24%) were considered either overweight or above average weight. By 1991 these numbers increased to one third (33%).[11] From 1991 to 1999 the prevalence of adult obesity increased by 57%.[12] Children in the United States, Canada, Europe and Australia are becoming progressively fatter. From 1981 to 1996 the prevalence of overweight increased by 92% in boys and 57% in girls.[13] The rate of obesity among boys aged seven to thirteen has nearly tripled from 5% to 13.5% over this same period of time while the prevalence of obesity among girls of the same age more than doubled to 11.8%.[14]

The 'Size Acceptance Warriors' Fight Back

The work and efforts of the Antifat Crusaders have not gone unchallenged. Since the 1970's many people have questioned if diets really work, if they are at all healthy and if, in fact, they are the only way to go. They include many counselors, physicians, nutritionists, fitness instructors and others who have worked with the devastating effects of dieting, and fat people who are tired of being marginalized and discriminated against. The warriors of the Size Acceptance movement are challenging societal beliefs around fat, the benefits and claimed success of dieting, and the research attempting to show a relationship between weight and various health risks.

The Size Acceptance Warriors have found that as of 1995 there has not been one study that has truly evaluated the effects of weight alone upon health. Not one study has shown weight as an independent cause of health problems or an independent risk factor for premature mortality.[15] According to Thomas Moore, author of *Lifespan: Who Lives Longer and Why*, most leading obesity researchers are either consultants to pharmaceutical companies or the diet industry, or conduct research for these companies, or present their results at conferences sponsored by these companies—or all three. These researchers often review proposals that receive government funding, and provide peer reviews for weight-related articles in scientific journals. Because of their economic interests and bias, research not supporting weight loss is very rarely funded or published.[16]

While no one questions hypertension, high cholesterol and diabetes exist or that they place people at risk, what is being questioned is whether these conditions develop as a result of obesity and fatness or are the consequences of futile attempts of yo-yo dieting and lack of physical activity. Is it the disease or the cure we have to address? Is it the cure that in fact generates the disease? Let's look at how fat got its bad name and at some of the myths around obesity.

Obesity

Obesity is the medical term for the degree of fatness at the far end of the continuum of weight or at the 95th percentile. It is generally regarded as a body weight of 20% or more above what is considered to be 'normal' or 'ideal'.[17] The word 'obese' comes from the Latin *obesus* or grown fat by eating. Obesity is usually measured by using either body weight, percentage of body fat or—most commonly and popularly—the Body Mass Index (BMI) that is based upon a simple ratio of height to weight. To determine your own BMI multiply your weight by 700 and divide it by your height in inches squared. Most charts today put the recommended BMI range between 20 and 26. Some charts are even lower.

The BMI is not a scientific device but rather an artificial practice. What we consider an 'ideal' result at any time depends upon the degree of fat phobia in our society, our medical beliefs and the zeal with which the war on fat is being carried out. The question we need to ask is just how fat is 'dangerously' fat? Are there other ways of evaluating people to determine how healthy they are rather than how much fat they have on their bodies; and how did the BMI get the power it has?

The Body Mass Index

According to Glenn Gaesser, author of *Big Fat Lies: The Truth about Your Weight and Your Health*, the Body Mass Index was developed by the life insurance companies at the turn of the century as a cheap way to screen applicants for policies to maximize their profits. The first height/weight tables published between 1897 and 1912 were based on the average of policyholders who ranged in age from 15 to 70. The tables took into account that as people aged they tended to gain weight. They believed mortality did not increase until a person was at least 20% above the average weight. The weight loss industry was born when the companies advocated the use of the tables as a way of measuring health and recommended weight loss as a way of promoting health.

In 1943, the Metropolitan Life Insurance Company published new tables. As the basis for the ideal weights they used the lowest mortality rates of 20 to 29 year old Caucasians who were of northern European descent and lived on the east coast of the United States. These weights varied by the size of one's frame. The weight people gained with age was now ascribed to overeating. Once again, weight loss was the cure.

In 1959 the Metropolitan Life Insurance Company released another table of 'desirable' (rather than 'ideal') weights that were lower than before. In the early 1980's it reversed itself and promoted weights that were even heavier than those recommended in 1952. Rather than applaud the fact that these tables were more humane and closer to reality, the new standards came under attack by many leaders in the fields of health care and nutrition who would not believe the data. Today we are being told that we should weigh at least 10 to 15% below the ideal weight for our age. All of a sudden—according to the statistics—75% of adults have become too fat and obesity has become an epidemic.[18]

Tearing Down the Paper Tiger: Confronting the Myths of Obesity

In 1951, the primary cause for cardiovascular and kidney disease and cancer and diabetes—the leading causes of death—were attributed to obesity. Dieting was prescribed as the major form of treatment. In 1985, obesity was promoted from being the cause of disease to being a disease itself. In 2001 the National Heart Lung and Blood Institute's *Expert Panel on the Identification, Evaluation and Treatment of Overweight and Obesity in Adults* concluded that obesity is a complex, multifactorial chronic disease[19] with a relapsing nature and need for lifelong therapy[20]— in the form of weight loss and drugs.

Yet the cure seems to be more dangerous than the disease. The continuous cycle of weight-loss and regain makes people fatter and puts them at risk. The diet drugs that are supposed to help people lose weight have also been linked to irreversible heart valve and lung damage. The recent offering, Merida (sibutramine), has already been recalled in the U.S. and is being investigated by Health Canada for side effects such as increased/irregular heart rate, increased blood pressure, chest pain, eye pain and eye hemorrhage. So who benefits—besides the pharmaceutical companies?

The myths around obesity and fat are pervasive and powerful. They enter into the very fabric of our lives including the fiction that we read—as evidenced by the excerpt at the beginning of this chapter. When we hear the same messages again and again it's hard not to get scared and give in to the pressure to diet or to hold them up as truths even when they are not. In order to tear down the paper tiger, we need to begin by confronting and destroying its myths.

Myth #1 Obesity is a risk for premature death

Studies show that being fat is not a risk for premature death. For example, a German study followed 6,053 obese patients for an average of 14 years. Although a BMI of 20 to 26 is considered 'normal' there was no significant increase in mortality rates up to a BMI of 32 and only moderate risk up to 36. In the heaviest group with a BMI of 40 or more, the risk was double for women and triple for men.[21]

Myth #2 Obesity causes cardiovascular disease

Because obese people have more fat on their bodies, it is assumed they must also have more fat in their arteries— the chief underlying cause of cardiovascular disease. This is not so. Studies show there is no connection between fat-clogged arteries and obesity. Fat in the arteries and fat on the body are different and unrelated.[22] However, there is an increased risk of cardiovascular disease in women who have dieted their way through repeated cycles of weight gain. These women tend to have lower levels of the 'good' high-density lipoprotein cholesterol (HDL).[23]

Myth #3 Obesity worsens the outcome of heart failure

In heart failure the heart does not pump blood around the body as efficiently as it should. While it is treatable with drugs, there is no cure. People with heart failure who are above average weight or are obese are advised to lose weight because of the assumption that if you are thin, your heart will have less to do.

However, researchers in California surveyed 1200 people with heart failure and found above average weight and obesity do not worsen the outcome of heart failure. In fact, carrying excess weight may be even helpful. One and two years after the start of the study people who were obese or above average in weight had a higher survival rate. At five years, there was no significant difference in survival based on body weight.[24]

Myth #4 Obesity causes hypertension

Hypertension or high blood pressure—the silent killer— is two to three times more common in people who are obese. However, this may be because of the cycles of weight-loss/regain they undergo, rather than a direct influence of fat tissue.[25] A study of rats showed that the net impact of genetic obesity is protective. However, blood pressure rises markedly if they are fed a high salt diet or when the loss of weight on a low-calorie diet is alternated with overeating. The rats that lost and regained weight showed increases in systolic blood pressure well as cholesterol, triglycerides and plasma glucose.[26]

Myth #5 Thinness equals health

Because we equate fat with sickness we believe people must be healthy if they are thin. This may be true...up to a certain point. Extreme thinness that comes from weight-loss strategies such as fasting, purging and over-exercising can be life-threatening. The risks of being very thin are not just limited to eating disorders. One epi-demiological study following 1.8 million Norwegians for 10 years found those in the lowest weight category were at highest risk for premature death. Women who were considered morbidly obese or very very fat and who weighed twice the recommended weight standard had a higher chance of survival than thin women in the lowest category.[27] As well, thin women are more vulnerable to hip fractures than heavy women. The Osteoporosis Society in the United Kingdom reported more women die of complications from hip fractures due to osteoporosis than from cancers of the cervix, uterus and breast com-bined.[28]

Myth #6 Obesity causes diabetes

The condition most strongly linked to obesity is Type 2 diabetes. While being fat is a sign that a person may be at risk, correlation is not the same as causation. Not all fat people develop diabetes. Diabetes has a lot to do with genetics. Studies have shown that if one identical twin over the age of 50 has Type 2 diabetes, there is a 91% chance the second twin will also develop it even if the twins have been raised in separate environments.[29]

Myth #7 People cause their own weight problems by un-controlled eating

While the image of fat people who cannot push them-selves away from the table is a popular one, it is a stereo-type that is simply not true. Twelve of thirteen studies found obese people ate the same or lesser amounts of food than non-obese people.[30] Studies that have exam-ined more specific eating habits have found no major dif-ferences in food choice, the amount of calories, carbo-hydrates, protein or fat consumed or other food related behaviors.[31] Many fat people eat less than people who are thin. Years of dieting have altered their metabolisms so it takes them a much longer time to burn off the calo-ries they take in.

Myth #8 You can't be fat and fit

One of the most pervasive myths in our society is that thinness is equated with fitness. According to our prevailing belief system, if you are thin you are not only healthy but also fit by default.

Not true! According to Steven Blair, director of research at the Cooper Institute for Aerobics Research in Dallas, obese people who exercise have half the death rate of those who are trim but don't exercise. It is of little or no consequence health-wise if you are 50 pounds or more over weight—if you are physically fit.[32] Once people are fat, exercise does not necessarily make them thin. But it does make them healthy.

Pat Lyons, co-author of *Great Shape: The First Fitness Guide for Large Women*[33] developed a fitness program for fat women. Of the one hundred and four non-dieting fat women who completed the eight weekly sessions of the Great Shape Program, forty-one percent had started to exercise more than three times a week as a result of being in the program. Fifty nine percent reported improvements in health such as lowered blood pressure, lowered blood sugar, fewer aches and pains, increased energy, less depression and more optimism about their selves and their lives.[34]

Fat is Not the Problem

When we dispel the myths around obesity we find that fat is not the core problem but rather our society's obsession with getting rid of it. While some fat people are unhealthy there are many who are fat and healthy. Weight by itself is not a health risk. While my doctor friend argues that losing just a few pounds would make a difference in many medical situations, I remind her that for women who have spent their lives on diets, losing just a few pounds is similar to being just a little bit pregnant. Once you start trying to lose even just a few pounds it is very difficult to not get caught up in the yo-yo dieting or weight cycling that puts people at risk.

Each of us has a natural weight where our body feels comfortable and healthy. And this varies over the course of time. Some of us are meant to be thinner than our culturally and medically imposed standards while some of us are better off being fat.[35] Once we are fat we will likely remain so.[36] If we are to continue using measurements such as the Body Mass Index they need to be recalculated and redefined. We would be much better off evaluating the health of people by taking into account their body type, age, genetic inheritance, level of fitness and ethnicity.

The repeated attempts of the Antifat Crusaders to measure fat and cure obesity only create a barrage of problems that put us at medical risk from dieting itself and at psychological risk from the fat prejudice which the Antifat Crusaders reinforce. As long as we spend our time trying to be thin, we never look at how we can be fat and healthy. Worst of all we also pass our attitudes and behaviors onto the girls in our lives thereby perpetuating yet another generation of women who are defined by and can't get off the bathroom scale.

Becoming a 'Size Acceptance Warrior'

You can be a Size Acceptance Warrior to fight fat prejudice and help girls reclaim their natural bodies:

• If your doctor focuses on weight tables or tries to make you or your daughter lose weight, discuss what you have learned about fat facts.[37] Insist on not being weighed and on not dieting.

• Ask your doctor to write a "Green Prescription" describing a particular regime of physical activity instead of encouraging people to diet. Doctors in New Zealand write "Green Prescriptions" with the same ease and frequency as they write prescriptions for drugs. And when things are written down, people tend to take them more seriously.[38]

• Write letters to newspapers, media outlets and advertisers protesting misinformation and fat prejudice. Chapter 14 will teach you how to do this.

• Visit Body Acceptance websites. There is strength in numbers (see Resources).

• Make lists of the following and share them with parent organizations and teachers and coaches and with girls.[39]

  ▪ Television shows that depict fat characters either positively or negatively.

  ▪ Advertising which insults or enhances fat people's self-image.

  ▪ Articles or ads that make especially blatant weight loss claims or which promote especially dangerous diets.

• Refuse to engage in conversations about diets, weight loss or fat. I have two seasonal responses that I use. In the summer I counter comments about weight loss or dieting with "How about those Toronto Blue Jays?" In the winter I use "So what do you think about the Vancouver Canucks?" People might look at me strangely but they stop talking about fat.

• Don't let people make comments about your body. Adapt the Jays and Canucks response to fit your own sports interests and geography or chose your own way of changing the subject.

• Don't compliment people who lose weight. That just reinforces our fat prejudice.

• Stop bashing yourself. Every time you criticize your body or use phrases such as "I shouldn't eat this but…" or place those tacky anti-fat magnets on your fridge you reinforce fat prejudice and make the Antifat Crusaders stronger.

• Hardest of all, perhaps – get off your own diet!!!

Endnotes

1. George, E. (2001) *A Traitor to Memory*. New York: Bantam Books
2. Los Angeles, *Associated Press*, June 7, 2001, pp. 1-2
3. *Vancouver Sun*, June 2001
4. Centers for Disease Control and Prevention. (1991) "Body weight perceptions and selected weight management goals and practices of high school students," *JAMA* :2811-2812
5. Council on Size and Weight Discrimination, Inc. 2000
6. AP, Los Angeles, *Bismark Tribune*, August, 1997, "Death reveals liposuction risks," in Healthy Weight Journal 1997: 11:6, 106
7. Gaesser, Glenn A. (1996) *Big Fat Lies: The Truth About Your Weight and Your Body.* New York: Fawcett Columbine, p. 23
8. Garner, D. M. & D. Wooley. (1991) "Confronting the failure of behavioural and dietary treatments for obesity," *Clin Psychol Rev:* 729-780
9. Nisbett, R.E. (1972) "Hunger, obesity and the ventromedical hypothalamus," *Psychological Review,*79:433-533
10. Brownell, K.D., Greenwood, M.R.C., Stellar, E. & E.E. Shrager, (1986) "The effects of repeated cycles of weight loss and regain in rats." *Physiology and Behavior*, 38:459-464
11. Gaesser, p. 26
12. Mokdad, A.H., Sedrula, M.K., Dietz, W.H., Bowman, B.A., Marks, J.S. & J.P. Koplan (2000) "The continuing epidemic of obesity in the United States, " *JAMA* 284: 1650 - 1
13. Anderson, R. E. (2000) "The spread of the childhood obesity epidemic," *Canadian Medical Association Journal*, 163(11): 1461-1462
14. Tremblay, M. S. and D. Willms (2000) "Secular trends in the body mass index of Canadian children," *Canadian Medical Association Journal*, 163(11): 1429-1433
15. Gaesser, p. 86
16. Moore, T. (1993) *Lifespan: New Lives Longer and Why*. New York, Touchstone
17. US Department of Health, Education and Welfare, 1979
18. Gaesser, pp. 32-58
19. *Obesity Research*, 1998, quoted in a letter by Dr. Michael Jensen, president of the North American Association for the Study of Obesity (NAASO) to the Centers of Medicare and Medicaid Services, http://www.hcfa.gov/coverage
20. In Dr. Jensen's letter
21. Spraul, M., et al. (1997) "Mortality in obesity," *International Journal of Obesity*, 21 (Suppl 2):S24
22. Barrett-Conner, E. "Obesity, Atherosclerosis and Coronary Heart Disease," paper presented at the conference on Health Implications of Obesity in Bethesda, MD
23. "Weight cycling appears to lower levels of HDL-C in women." Westport, CT, Reuters Health 11/1/00: *J Am Coll Cardiol* 2000, 26: 1565-1571
24. Aldridge, S. (September, 2001) "Obesity and heart failure," *Journal of the American College of Cardiology*
25. Gaesser, p. 8

26. Ernsberger, P. & R. J. Koletsky , "Rational for a wellness approach to obesity," in *Healthy Weight Journal*, Vol. 14 No. 1, January/February 2000, pp 8-15

27. Waaler, H.T. (1984) "Height, weight and mortality: The Norwegian experience," *Acta Med Scan Suppl*: 1-56

28. Gaesser, p.106

29. Ernsberger and Koletsky, p. 2

30. Garrow, J. (1974) *Energy Balance and Obesity in Man.* New York: American Elsevier

31. Gaesser, p. 34

32. Lee, C.D., Jackson, A.S. and S.D. Blair (1998) "US weight guidelines: Is it also important to consider cardiorespiratory fitness?" *Int J Obes Relat Metabl Disord*, August: 22, Suppl 2:S2-7

33. Lyons, P. A. & D. Burgard (1988, 2000) *Great Shape: The First Fitness Guide for Large Women,* Lincoln, NB: iUnivers.com.Inc

34. Lyons, P. (1996) "Fat and fit: An idea whose time has come," *Melpomene*, Fall, Vol. 15, No. 3

35. Gaesser, p. 86

36. Garner and Wooley

37. Maine, M. (2000) *Body Wars: Making Peace with Women's Bodies.* Carlsbad, CA: Gurze Books, p.39

38. Thanks to Jennifer Fenton who learned about this in New Zealand

5

∞

The Deadly Quest to be Thin

"Girls can be really brutal to each other. People can not like you because you're not what they think is perfect. All the models in the TV ads and magazines have body types where they are all so skinny and tall. Everybody measures themselves by these messages and if you're not close to perfect they tease you."

Katie, a 15 year old girl

"Girls become anorexic so that they can be models and be liked. We cringe at how skinny these girls are but underneath we long to be like that too."

Jessica, a 14 year old girl

It's almost impossible to grow up female without being preoccupied with food and weight and body shape. As the previous chapters have shown, we live in a society that has a tremendous aversion to fat and a definition of health that 'accepts' a range of body sizes—just so long as they are not one pound over what is considered to be 'average'. We also grow up under tremendous pressure to define ourselves by how we look.

From the time girls are born we teach them they have to be attractive to be valued and being attractive means being thin. We perpetuate the myth everyone can achieve the look that society espouses. If they can't, it is not that there is something wrong with that degree of thinness but rather with girls who cannot achieve it. We've taken our reverence for thinness to such great heights and have endowed it with so many unrealistic and magical characteristics it wouldn't be surprising to see people choose a surgeon according to the size of her thighs!

Our strong morality around food and body size, the loss of voice that girls experience during adolescence and society's hatred and fear of fat are all *body thieves* that have caused a large number of girls and women to experiment with disordered eating amid their never-ending quest for thinness. In North

America, 1 to 2 % of female adolescents develop anorexia nervosa, a slightly higher percentage develops bulimia nervosa, and the prevalence of eating disorders among preteen and young adolescents is still on the rise.[1]

According to the Mayo Clinic, anorexia nervosa has been increasing by 36% every five years since the 1950s.[2] Three out of every one hundred girls will develop anorexia nervosa or bulimia—often in the wake of puberty.[3] Thirteen percent of teenage girls (although not yet diagnosed with full-blown eating disorders) engage in anorectic and bulimic behaviors such as self-induced vomiting, skipping meals, abuse of laxatives and diet pills, and cycles of binge eating and dieting.[4]

For a large numbers of girls who may never actually develop eating disorders, these disordered eating practices and the preoccupation with body shape and weight have a profoundly negative impact on their lives, on their relationships with others and on their self-esteem. The problem is so insidious as to be considered a 'normal' fact of teenage life, not a medical issue that is carried too far by a few.

Imagine the girls in your local school:

• Some girls will start to feel fat in grade three, sometimes earlier. A large number of girls will feel fat by grade seven.

• Many of these girls will become preoccupied with food, weight and body shape. They will think a lot about what they eat and feel fat quite often. A number of elementary school girls will begin to diet.

• When girls enter junior high school, a fair number will experiment with dieting, bingeing, purging and exercising to excess.

• Some girls will get caught up in these dynamics and will develop eating disorders.

• A small number of girls will develop medical complications from these behaviors.

• A small number will end up in the hospital at medical risk.

• Some of these girls will die.[5]

When I began working as a psychotherapist in 1980, we thought that anyone who binged and purged had an eating disorder. Today, bingeing and purging have become part of the teenage culture. Anorexia and bulimia are at the end of a continuum of disordered eating that includes body dissatisfaction, weight preoccupation, chronic 'normalized' dieting, compulsive over-eating, dysfunctional eating and eating disorder practices. Girls with eating disorders are only one or two steps down the continuum from the rest of us.

Not every girl who is preoccupied with food and weight develops an eating disorder. Many girls who compulsively over-eat and/or continually diet will become fatter. Many girls will become women who spend their entire lives chronically dieting and restricting their food. The preoccupation with food and weight and the weight-loss practices around them exact a tremendous toll from girls and from women in terms of their self-esteem, their relationships with others and their performance at school and at work.

Eating Disorders

An eating disorder develops when the preoccupation with food and weight and associated behaviors escalate to become such an obsession that everything girls do and all of their feelings are determined by what they have or have not eaten that day and by the numbers on the bathroom scale.

While eating disorders are expressions of food and weight issues, they are not merely problems with food or with weight and have very little to do with physiological hunger. In fact, most girls with eating disorders can't tell when they are hungry at all! Eating disorders are a complex expression of underlying issues with identity and sense of self. They are disorders of human relationships that have been displaced onto the arena of food, appetite and hunger.[6]

As the chapter on gender indicated, girls develop their identity in the context of their relationships. During adolescence the societal devaluation of girls and the silencing of their voices may contribute to the development of psychological disempowerment, making it difficult for them to sort out their values and develop a strong sense of relationship and therefore a strong sense of themselves. Without these assets, girls look outward for definition and become overly pleasing. Unable to acknowledge or express their feelings directly, they redirect them onto their bodies and encode them in a language of fat. They then engage with the fear of fat instead of what is really going on underneath.

Eating Disorder Behaviors are Coping Mechanisms

Eating disorders are coping mechanisms whose behaviors can make us sick. We all have coping mechanisms. From the moment we are born we have to learn to deal with the world around us, with our family dynamics, our feelings, our life experiences and the societal pressures and messages around our gender. Because we are not born with and often don't directly learn the skills to do this, we learn to do so indirectly.

Our coping mechanisms take various forms and vary in intensity depending upon the degree of distress that we experience. Some people use alcohol and drugs, some become workaholics, some develop psychosomatic diseases, some hold all the stress in their bodies and develop rigid skeletal structures, and some people just commit suicide.

A great number of people—predominately girls and women—use food and disordered eating behaviors to deal with feelings that are considered inappropriate or are too painful to express such as: loneliness, insecurity, anger, sexuality and need. They use them as a coping mechanism to deal with tension and anxiety, with emotional conflict and with difficulties they cannot resolve. Girls who compulsively over-eat use food to stuff down and anesthetize their feelings. Food provides the means for girls who are bulimic to symbolically purge their feelings. Not eating provides a sense of control for girls who are anorexic.

Eating disorders are also a response to the feelings of powerlessness that many girls and women feel in their lives. We all have a need to feel in control. For most of us the sense of control centers on choice—our ability to say yes or no. Imagine what it would be like if you had to go through an entire week never being able to say 'no', regardless of the request. Every time someone wanted something from you or you thought they did, you had to say yes.

When I ask women in professional training workshops what that would be like, they describe the sensation of hands pulling at them. They talk about feeling fear, revulsion and powerlessness and anger. When everything girls do is predicated on not hurting someone else, when taking control or saying yes/no means risking isolation and rejection and loneliness, girls create their own sense of control that seems less threatening to them. Controlling their body and their food intake becomes an external adaptation—a way of feeling in control of themselves and of their lives.

Disordered eating and eating disorder behaviors are a way of converting something scary on the inside to something that seems manageable on the outside. They externalize those parts of girls that are not acceptable to society.

To most girls the perfect girl is thin, confident, unemotional, in control and nice. In order to be like her, girls dissociate from those parts of themselves that do not fit this image. They dissociate from feelings such as insecurity, loneliness, sexuality, jealousy, competition, anger and need. They redirect what they see as the imperfect parts of themselves onto their fat, their bulimia and their anorexia. These become separate entities—almost like a suitcase that girls carry—that contain all of the feelings that are too scary to acknowledge and too difficult to express. Because coping mechanisms keep them safe, girls don't give them up easily—not until they are ready to do so and have something to replace them with.

A Multitude of Causes

There is no one single simple thing that causes a girl or woman to develop an eating disorder. It is usually a complex combination of factors. These include their biological predisposition to anxiety or to obsessive-compulsive disorder. Researchers believe that many genes work together with environmental factors to cause eating disorders.[7] Dr. Walter Kaye at the University of Pittsburgh found in an international study that

10% of patients with anorexia or bulimia had a relative who also had an eating disorder.[8]

Girls are more vulnerable to eating disorders at certain stages of development, especially during the onset of puberty and then through adolescence when they have to deal with separation and individuation and loss of voice and with the repercussions as their bodies and lives change in dramatic fashion.

Society plays its part in the development of eating disorders with its emphasis on body image and the preoccupation with thinness, the cultural prejudice towards fat, devaluation of the female gender culture and the adaptations girls have to make to be female in a male-defined world.

Families have a big influence on girls. Parents who don't have the capacity to tolerate the expression of feelings tend to encourage their girls to close down their feelings. Parents who are overly emotional tend to overwhelm their girls and drown out their feelings, causing them to repress their own needs and to become the caretaker of the parent instead of the other way around. In families where there is poor communication girls tend to redirect their distress onto themselves. Personality structure also is a factor. Girls who are obsessively perfectionists, who are overly concerned with doing things right and overly concerned either with not harming others or with doing things wrong are at increased risk.

GIRLS AT RISK OF DEVELOPING EATING DISORDERS MAY:

- Mature early
- Have low self-esteem
- Have a sense of ineffectiveness in their lives
- Lack intimate connections with others
- Have experienced changes or loss in their major relationships
- Have had problematic life experiences
- Have been sexually or physically abused
- Have parents who are chronically depressed
- Have parents who abuse alcohol or drugs
- Have families with rigid rules or with no boundaries

- May be teased about their weight
- Have mothers and friends who diet
- Read magazines that emphasize thinness and dieting

WARNING SIGNS THAT SOMEONE MAY BE AT RISK:

- Obsessed with her appearance
- Constantly 'feeling fat' and making comments about her weight
- Weighing herself at least once a day
- Avoiding eating with others
- Calculating the number of fat grams and calories in each bite she eats
- Categorizing her food into 'good' foods and 'bad' foods
- Putting herself down and being overly sensitive to others' opinions of her
- Frequently depressed, anxious or irritable
- Fasting, restricting, bingeing, purging or excessive exercising
- Needing to be perfect in everything she does
- Withdrawing from her friends or family
- Experiencing loss or disruption of friendships
- Experiencing disruption in her family

When Someone is Struggling with an Eating Disorder

It can be very scary when we think someone might be struggling with body image and weight concerns, and even more so when we think they might have an eating disorder. We're afraid anything we say is going to make it worse. We try to reason and say things such as "You know, Tara, that you can get sick doing this." We try to bargain with her with offers such as "If you eat you can go shopping/go away for the weekend/get your own phone" etc. We resort to guilt in the form of "If you really loved me, you would..." We try to take control by monitoring the purging and by preparing the food and supervising girls when they eat. When these things don't work, we get angry and very afraid because girls are not doing what we tell them to do.

If you are a mother it's hard not to blame yourself, even if you know intellectually that it's not your fault. If you're a father, you feel powerless. Your job is to take care of and protect your daughter and to fix things. This is one thing that you can't fix. If you are a teacher or if you work with girls you are afraid that anything you say or do will be wrong and that she will die right in front of you. If you are her friend, you want to be there for her even though you feel that you are in over your head.

What You Can Do[9]

• Pay attention to my Golden Rule of Counseling which also applies to parenting, teaching, and working with girls:

> You didn't break it. It's not your fault.
> You are not a plumber. You can't fix it.

• Eating disorders are coping mechanisms that develop over time. As long as you don't encourage weight loss or make the person feel guilty for not getting better, there is little you can say or do that will make it worse.

• Talk to her about your concerns. Describe specific things you see and the feelings you have had during those times. Use 'I' statements: "I see you are not eating breakfast or lunch. This makes me worried about you." "When I heard you throwing up yesterday, I got really scared."

• Try to avoid telling her what to do: "You have to eat something." "You have to stop throwing up." She'll just feel guilty and hide the behaviors.

• If she doesn't want to listen to you or becomes angry with you for calling attention to her behavior, just keep telling her you are concerned.

• Remember this is not about you. She won't change her behaviors because you tell her you love her or how hard it is on you.

• Take the focus off the food and off the fat and help her become curious about what is underneath the feeling fat and eating disorder behaviors. Chapter 8 will help you to do this.

• Remember that her disordered eating and body image issues did not develop overnight and won't go away overnight.

• Validate her feelings but remember that feeling fat is not a feeling. Reassure her there is no right or wrong feeling. Everyone is entitled to whatever she feels.

• Encourage her to seek help. Let her know that asking for help does not mean that she is weak. Reassure her that seeing a therapist does not mean that she has to give up the behaviors right away. Remember people don't give up their coping mechanisms until they are ready to do so and have something to replace them with.

• If you are a teacher or work with girls, talk to her parents.

• If you are a parent, seek professional help. Begin with her doctor to make sure that she is not at medical risk. Talk to your public health nurse or other helping people in your community. In the Resource section I have listed organizations that might be of help.

• If you are a friend and if the girl you are worried about is under 18, tell an adult that you trust. You can't help her by yourself. Have this person talk to her and/or tell her parents. Doing this may be difficult because it feels as if you are not being there for her and because she might become angry with you. But if she has become obsessed with eating or exercising or her body image, she probably needs professional help. It's important that you discuss your worries with someone early on before she has endured many of the damaging physical and emotional effects of eating disorders. Often as a friend you are the first person to know that something is wrong. Offer to help her find out where to go for help and then offer to go with her. Sometimes having a friend come with you makes it less scary.

Endnotes

1. Goldman, E. I. (1996) "Eating disorders on the rise in preteens, adolescents," *Psychiatry News*, 24 (2): 10
2. *Dying to Be Thin* video, Nova, December 12, 2000. Larking McPhee, director
3. Willard, S., De Paul Tulane Hospital in *Dying to be Thin*
4. Killen, J.D., Taylor, C.B., Telch, M.J., Saylor, K.E., Moaron, D.J. & Robinson, T.N. (1986) "Self-induced vomiting, laxative and diuretic use among teenagers: Precursors of the binge-purge syndrome," *Journal of the American Medical Association*, 255:1442-1449
5. Kaye, W. University of Pittsburg in *Dying to Be Thin* video
6. Kearney Cook, A. Eating Disorders Workshop. Washington State University, Vancouver Washington, February 23, 2001
7. BBC News, Thursday, January 21, 1999
8. Ibid
9. Adapted from National Eating Disorder Association pamphlet

6

∞

When Girls *are* Fat

A group of teenage girls was asked on a TV program if they would rather be a rich fat person with a fabulous career or be poor, thin and unemployed. They all said thin, of course, and looked at the interviewer with horror—that she would even suggest that there *was* such a choice!

WTN program *You, Me and the Kids*[1]

"When I'm at the mall trying on clothes and my friends wear little tank tops, sometimes I wish that I could be like everyone else."   Roberta, a 15 year old girl

It's difficult to be a fat girl in a thin world. Fat has been endowed with all kinds of negative characteristics and moral judgments. Being fat is seen as being inferior, out of control, weak, lazy and powerless. Fat remains one of the last socially sanctioned prejudices. It may no longer be acceptable to make comments about someone's sex, race, religion or sexual orientation but it is considered perfectly acceptable to make comments about their weight. Sound familiar? This is how society once described some minority groups before racism became politically incorrect.

Girls at one of my community talks shared their bad feelings about a well-meaning teacher who brought cookies for the class. Realizing too late that there were not enough to go around, the teacher said: "Only the thin kids will get cookies. The fat kids don't need them." Though this was her improvised response to an unintentional gaffe, the comments still stung the larger kids.

People often justify their prejudice by self-righteously expressing fear and concern about the health of people who are fat. Despite evidence to the contrary, many of us still believe we can change our size and body type if we try hard enough–that inside every fat person is a thin person struggling to get out.

Because it goes without saying, doesn't it, that everyone wants to be thin? We never consider the possibility that thin people are just size-challenged people waiting to become fully developed! Yet as Chapter 4 showed, it's not the fat that is the problem but the continuous cycling of weight loss and weight gain and the lack of physical activity that puts fat people at risk.

Society's prejudice towards fat is internalized by girls at an early age and becomes entrenched as they grow up. When preschool children are given the opportunity to play with dolls, all children (even those who could correctly identify that the fat dolls looked more like them) prefer to play with the thin dolls.[2] Nursery school children rate figure drawings of fat children more negatively than drawings of children with physical disabilities.[3] When shown silhouettes of fat and thin males and females, nine year old children rate the fat figures as having significantly fewer friends, being less liked by their parents, doing less well at school, being less content with their appearance and wanting to be thinner.[4]

Prejudice towards fat is a very powerful *body thief.* It robs fat girls of their self-esteem and makes it difficult for them to feel loved and accepted in a society that rejects them because it finds their size unacceptable. Their low self-esteem and hatred of their bodies is often caused not by being fat but by the shame that they are made to experience in a culture that only values people who are thin.

A Multitude of Reasons

Despite popular beliefs, being fat is not determined by a simple lack of will power or lack of self-control or just by unhealthy eating. People are fat for a multitude of reasons. Weight is a complex mix of biological, social, environmental and psychological issues as well as lifestyle practices. To understand why some people are fat we need to look at all of these factors as well as how they interact with each other.

Genetics

Body type and weight are genetically influenced. If Aunt Tessie, Uncle Al, your mother or father, grandmother or grandfather is fat, chances are that you, too, will tend to be fat if you tend to take after these people genetically. The risk of heavy newborns becoming fat adolescents is approximately 5 to 7 times higher when the mother is fat.[5] Studies of twins who were raised together and of twins who were given up for adoption have consistently found that fraternal and identical twins were similar in body weight regardless of whether they were reared together or apart.[6] Set-point theory also suggests that genetics affects weight, distribution of body fat, skeletal frame, metabolism and appetite.[7]

Faulty Hunger Mechanisms

All children are born with the ability to know when they are physiologically hungry and when they are full. This allows them to internally regulate how much they eat. When parents try to restrict their children's food they disrupt their children's hunger mechanism—too often at a very early age. A study followed a community sample of 216 newborns and their parents in the San Francisco Bay area from birth to 5 years. Mothers who dieted and wanted to be thin tended to restrict the amount their daughters ate. The daughters overate to compensate for not getting enough food.[8] They also ate when they were not hungry, chose the very foods being restricted and felt guilty when they ate.[9] In trying to stop their daughters from becoming fat, the mothers caused the very same condition they were trying to prevent.

Lack of Physical Activity

Girls lead increasingly sedentary lives. They have fewer opportunities for physical activity and burn off fewer calories in an average day. Many girls are driven to school and then on to the mall. They do fewer chores at home. Even small things such as using a remote control instead of getting up to change the TV channel and loading the dishwasher instead of washing dishes by hand rob them of the chance to use their bodies.

Protective parents would rather see their daughters safely inside watching television or working on the computer and surfing the internet than playing outside unsupervised. Sixty per cent of girls watch at least 2 hours of television a day.[10] The more they watch, the more likely it is that they will gain weight over time—for every hour they watch there is a 2% increase in adolescent fatness.[11]

Many schools have cut back on their physical education programs despite recommendations that children should participate in 30 minutes of physical activity a day.[12] When it's a toss up between spending school money on physical education and computers, the computers win all the time. Even when physical activity is available, it is not often geared towards a range of body types—causing fat girls to lose confidence in themselves and give up trying.

Emotional Eating

When girls gain weight rapidly (especially when they are young) it is often a sign that something is not right in their lives. Girls use food to deal with psychological distress by stuffing down and anaesthetizing feelings that are painful and difficult to express and for which they have no language. Many girls have to deal early on with changes in their family structure due to the birth of a new child, conflict, divorce, remarriage by a parent and/or chronic illness or death of a family member. Some girls must deal with sexual abuse and violence and/or the use of alcohol or drugs by their parents.

Moving from one neighborhood or city to another often means losing good friends and having to make new ones. Girls must contend with pressures at school and with being bullied and teased. During adolescence girls deal with many profound changes in their bodies and in their lives—including the silencing of their voices and disconnection from their selves. Weight gain is often the only visible sign that girls are not doing well and might need help.

Fast Food Junkies

Some girls are fat because of what they eat. A recent television commercial showed a mother coming home from a long day's work. As she makes her way across the lawn in her high heels and suit she trips over her son's toys and lands flat on her back, her briefcase flying through the air. Unable to face the thought of preparing dinner, she takes him to a fast food restaurant where he loads up with super-sized servings of high fat food. The mother in that commercial is not alone.

Where we once prepared food from scratch, we've come to rely on convenience foods to compensate for the lack of time in our lives. We teach children to pop pizza pockets into the microwave and feed them hot dogs and hamburgers when they are very young.

According to a national nutrition survey in the United States, fried potatoes made up almost one-third of the vegetable servings eaten by young people 2 to 19 years old. Less than one-fourth of children aged 6 to 11 met the recommended servings of fruit and vegetables. In the average American diet, over 40% of daily calories were taken from fat and added sugars.[13] It's not all that different in Canada.

Huge industries compete with each other to make their brand more enticing, more readily available and cheaper than that of competitors. Advertisers tempt children to eat sugary cereals and adolescents to eat high fat foods. Fast food restaurants offer 'super' sizes for just a few cents more. As a result of bombardment by television commercials, the consumption of soft drinks is on the rise. Each additional daily serving of sugar-sweetened drinks (including juice) raises the odds significantly for children becoming fat.[14]

Dieting and Binge Eating

Girls are beginning to diet at younger and younger ages. Dieting causes them to become obsessed with food and to engage in dysfunctional eating. A study that followed girls and boys between the ages of 9 to 14 for two years found that over one-quarter of 'normal weight' girls had dieted the previous year. Regardless of their intake of calories, fat, carbohydrates or their levels of physical activity or inactivity, 2.7% of the girls and 5.2% of the boys became overweight.

Normal weight girls who dieted were more likely to report binge eating at least monthly while 12.5% of frequent dieters binged.[15] While dieting is a prime risk factor for developing an eating disorder, yo-yo dieting (chronic dieting interspersed with overeating) makes you fat. Chapter 7 looks at how we can help prevent the rapid increase in childhood fatness.

Confronting Our Own Fat Prejudice

Girls come in all sizes and shapes. Those who are fat as children tend to be fat as adults, especially if they are fat during adolescence.[16] As they grow up they must deal with teasing and bullying, with stigmatization and discrimination and later with the medical consequences of yo-yo dieting in their attempts to lose weight. Worst of all they must deal with our good intentions. In our society's attempts to make girls 'healthy' we reinforce the negative attitudes and bad feelings that we instill in them and that they have about themselves.

As women and men who parent and work with girls we likewise are products of the culture in which girls mature and we are influenced by these same prejudices and biases. Despite our best intentions, we pass our attitudes along to the girls. When we encourage girls to diet, we are telling them that this person they are right now is somehow unacceptable. We set them on a dangerous road to yo-yo dieting, eating disorders and continuous weight-gain; we destroy their hunger mechanism and negate who they are right now.

While we may think we are being gracious when we compliment girls on their weight loss what are we going to tell them if they are already too thin—or when they gain the weight back? Ask yourself: in what other circumstance would you praise someone for their loss?

We invalidate girls' sense of self when we try to protect them from hurt by deliberately ignoring their fat—pretending something that is a major issue in their lives and a part of who they are doesn't exist. Our silence and avoidance tells them that they are somehow bad. When we tell girls who are fat that 'it's what's inside that counts' we're sending them a subtle message that you can't expect to be beautiful if you are fat. How often have your heard, "She has such a pretty face. It's a shame she's fat," as though the pretty face was wasted on a fat person.

As role models for girls we need to examine our own beliefs and attitudes about body size. We must be able to accept a range of body types and sizes, something that is often very difficult for parents who want their daughter to look like everyone else because they see her fat as a failure on their part. It is also difficult for those parents who may accept their daughter's body shape and size, but want to spare her from inevitable teasing and pain. Many professionals have difficulty getting past the belief that fat relates to bad lifestyle choices and focus on what they see as failure instead of relating to the girl. When we find the size of a particular girl disturbing, our reactions often are more about our own fear of fat than they are about her body.

As women and men who parent and work with girls, we must watch ourselves so we that we do not fall prey to the myth that equates being fat with being unhealthy or undisciplined, nor to the myth that everyone wants to be thin and can be if he or she tries hard enough. We need to be able to acknowledge our own weight prejudice and monitor our language and actions for signs of it. We need to be aware not only of overt fat prejudice but also of the subtle messages that seemingly promote size acceptance—as long as that size is not large. We need to value our bodies and girls' bodies as functional and beautiful no matter what size they are. We must also be able to value people for who they are and what they have to offer.

Because we are constantly bombarded by the same messages from the media as the girls themselves, we must consciously question and debate what those images of perfection are designed to advertise and what they mean.

Many women and men struggle to varying degrees with their natural bodies. When we are willing to talk about our own struggle and about the societal pressures that make us feel badly about our size we open the door for girls to talk about their own struggles with their body shape. If we see fat as bad, if we are presently dieting, if we have a strong belief that losing weight and eating only 'healthy' food or being physically fit will change our lives (or the lives of others) and/or if we regularly engage in fat talk, then whether we want to or not, we are doing the girls in our lives a disservice. It is difficult to help girls accept their natural bodies if, in our own hearts, we still believe that these bodies are wrong.

What You Can Do

We need to help girls who are fat feel good about themselves and their bodies. Many of the suggestions listed below are elaborated upon in further detail in different parts of this book, and most are applicable to all young people.

• Diffuse the value judgments around fat by using the word in the same way you use the words for other physical characteristics. The more we use the word fat, we more we defuse the negative charge we have constructed around it.

• Let your girl know she is beautiful. Imagine a world in which there was only one narrow definition of beauty. How boring the world would be if the only flowers in it were red tulips!

• Avoid telling her that it's 'what's inside that counts' and that she should develop her personality. This is true for children of all sizes and shapes, not just for those who are fat. It makes it sound like personality is some kind of consolation prize.

• Let her know that fat is a body type—not a character type.

• Listen to her feelings about being different without trying to fix things.

• Validate her feelings. It's hard to be fat in a thin world.

• Teach all children about genetics and metabolism. This lets them know that it is normal for them to come in all sizes and shapes and that there is no 'fault' attached to being fat.

• Look at pictures of your family together. Who does she most resemble? Talk about that person, tell his/her story.

• Bring in pictures of girls and women of a whole range of body sizes and talk about them in terms other than of how they look.

• Encourage her to use her body so she can be proud of her strength. Find physical activities that she can enjoy.

• Be physically active with her. Go for walks. Ride a bicycle. Snack on exercise several times a day. Walk to school with her and if the school is too far to do this, park the car a few blocks away and walk.

• Join with other parents and lobby your school to offer physical activities suited to all body types and abilities.

• Help her deal with teasing and bullying.

• Join with other parents to ensure that there is zero tolerance for bullying in your school.

• Help her find her passion. Move the focus away from how she looks to what stimulates her, makes her feel good about herself and provides her with a sense of satisfaction.

• Hug her often. Tell her how much you love to hug her body because it is so soft and comforting.

• Help her be fat with dignity. We all need to be proud of who we are right now. Many adults put their futures on hold—waiting until they lose weight for their 'life' to begin. Let's not do this to our girls!

Endnotes

1. WTN program *You, Me and the Kids* episode on body image. 1998
2. Rothblum, E.D. (1992) "The stigma of women's weight: Social and economic realities," *Feminism and Psychology*, 2: 61-73
3. Goodman, N., S.A. Richardson, S.M.Dornbush and A.H. Hastorf. (1963) "Variant reactions to physical disabilities," *American Sociological Review*, 28: 429-435
4. Hill & Silver.(1995) in M. I. Loewy, "Working with fat children in schools," *Radiance Magazine*, Fall Issue, 1998
5. Frisancho, A.R. (November, 2000) "Prenatal compared with parental origins of adolescent fatness," *American Journal of Clinical Nutrition*, 72(5): 1198-1190
6. Stunkard, A.J., Harris, J.R. Pederson, N.L et al. (1990) "The body mass index of twins who have been reared apart," *New England Journal of Medicine*, 1483-1487
7. Bennet, W. and J. Gurin. (1982) *The Dieter's Dilemma*. New York: Basic Books
8. Stice, E., W.A. Agras & L.D. Hammer (1990) "Risk factors for the emergence of childhood eating disturbances: A five year prospective study," *International Journal of Eating Disorders*, 26:375-387
9. Fisher, J.O. & L.L. Birch (July, 2000) "Parents' restrictive feeding practices are associated with young girls' negative self-evaluation of eating." J Am Diet Assoc. 100:1341-1346, taken from *Healthy Weight Updates*.
10. Anderson, R. E. (2000) "The spread of the childhood obesity epidemic," *Canadian Medical Association Journal*, 163(11): 1461-1462
11. Gortmaker, S.L., Dietz,W.H.,. Sobol, A.M. & C.A. Wehler. (1987) "Increasing pediatric obesity in the United States," *American Journal Dis Child*, 141:535-540
12. Canadian Association for Health, Physical Education, Recreation and Dance (CAHPERD), 1999
13. Continuing Survey of Food Intake by Individuals, 1994-1996
14. Ludwig, D.S., Peterson, K.E. & S.L.Gortmaker (2001) "Relations between consumption of sugar-sweetened drings and childhood obesity: a perspective, observational analysis," *The Lancet*. 357 (9255): 505-508
15. North American Association for the Study of Obesity, Annual Scientific Meeting. News release 11/1/00 from *Healthy Weight Updates*, July, 2000
16. Guo, S.S., Roche, A.F., Chumlea, W.C., Gardner, J.C. & R.M. Siervogel. (1994) "The predictive value of childhood body mass index values for overweight at age 35," American Journal of Clinical Nutrition, 59:810-819

7

⚛

Fighting the Body Thieves

"The *Just For Girls*[1] group was offered to us through our school. They said it was a group for grade seven girls to go talk and learn. As you can guess we thought it would be pretty boring. But we signed up anyway. I'm so glad we participated. It was the best group I've ever been to. Our facilitators were great. They always cared about how we were doing. We covered a lot of important issues such as puberty, families, friends and boyfriends and women in the media. We acted out our grungies and also learned that each one of us was great just the way we were. The group was a place where we could say anything and know that it would remain confidential."

Sarah, a grade 7 student

Prevention is the best and most effective weapon with which to fight the body thieves. This book addresses the prevention of a whole spectrum of weight issues and concerns that affect girls because these are all interrelated. Girls who diet—no matter what their natural weight may be—are at risk of getting caught in a cycle of weight-loss and regain and becoming progressively fatter and/or developing an eating disorder. This includes girls who gain a lot of weight in the aftermath of anorexia and get involved in a whole different experience of diet dynamics.

Genetics and physiology play a role in the development of eating disorders and of children being fat, but the dramatic increases we are seeing in the numbers of both result from environmental and social factors that can be addressed by prevention. Addressing the entire spectrum of weight issues all together, we can end the conflicting messages that girls receive about body image and their relationship with food. Focusing on one aspect of the problem, we might try to discourage girls from dieting and normalize their relationship with food and encourage them to accept their bodies at whatever size. Focusing on a different issue we instead encourage girls to diet and not stop until they are thin.[2] This just doesn't add up!

In writing this book I have struggled with the term 'obesity' which is medical terminology and has developed negative connotations because of society's attitudes toward fat. I have difficulty with the terminology of 'preventing childhood obesity' because this reinforces dieting behavior. By placing the emphasis on fat it reinforces the belief that fat—and fat people—are bad.

For the remainder of the book I will use the term *fat+plus* to describe those girls who are at the higher end of the weight spectrum. Instead of using the term 'childhood obesity' I will move the focus away from fat toward promoting and sustaining healthy development, encouraging girls to become and remain physically active as they grow up, and helping them establish a joyful relationship with food. It seems to me that if girls are healthy and use their bodies daily then it doesn't really matter what size they are.

Prevention Addresses the Changes in Girls' Bodies AND the Changes in Girls Lives'

Prevention equally addresses the changes that take place in girls' bodies and in their lives during adolescence. If we focus just on body image, the pressure to be thin, healthy eating, the hazards of dieting and on promoting physical activity then we run the risk of silencing girls in the same way the culture does, and inadvertently reinforce the very dynamics we say we are trying to change.

On the other hand, if we only address the silencing of girls' voices and their loss of self-esteem, then we leave them without the skills to normalize their eating and without the resources to fight back against societal pressure to disconnect from their bodies and define themselves solely in terms of how they look.

Prevention is about size acceptance and being active and healthy at whatever size we are. It integrates the *Health at Any Size* paradigm started by nutritionist and educator Frances Berg. *Health at Any Size* sees eating disorders, dysfunctional eating, being overweight and size prejudice as interrelated issues that are all influenced by today's unnatural obsession with thinness.[3]

MAJOR COMPONENTS OF PREVENTION*

BODY ISSUES:	LIFE/SELF ISSUES:
Puberty education	Dealing with the grungies
Metabolism/genetics	Understanding gender
Eating for health, energy and joy	Encouraging self-expression
Body awareness/ appreciation	Addressing bullying
Physical activity	Addressing fat prejudice
Media literacy	Media activism
Redirecting the emphasis on appearance	Building healthy relationships

* **Note:** The components of prevention that are starred herein are described in the following chapters of this book. Please see the Resource section to find out where you can obtain more information about the other components.

Body Issues

Puberty Education—teaches girls about the changes in their bodies. We need to provide them with a lot of information and with a safe place to ask the questions that are of real concern to them.

Metabolism and Genetics—lets girls understand why they have the body they do. Understanding why people have different body types and sizes helps normalize and break down the prejudices around fat.

Eating for Health, Energy and Joy*—teaches girls about balance, helps normalize food, helps resolve the uneasy relationship that girls develop around eating and gets girls off diets.

Redirecting the Emphasis on Appearance*—gives girls skills to fight back against the unrelenting pressure to be thin and helps them develop other ways of viewing and valuing themselves.

Body Awareness and Appreciation*—helps girls develop an internal and kinesthetic sense of their bodies so they can redirect their focus toward how they feel inside. It also teaches girls about the diversity of body shapes and types and encourages them to value their bodies regardless of their size.

Physical Activity*–encourages girls to use their bodies to develop physical strength, flexibility, body awareness and self-confidence, and to reconnect with them.

Media Literacy*–teaches girls how to critically evaluate and break down media images and how to challenge and change unrealistic standards.

Life/Self Issues

The Grungies*–this term was coined to describe your negative voice. Every time you tell yourself that you feel fat or ugly or stupid you have been 'hit by a grungie'. Underneath every grungie there is a real story waiting to be told (see Chapter 8).

Understanding Gender*–helps girls understand why their friendships are so important, why they travel in pairs, why it is sometimes so difficult to talk to boys and why they tend to behave the way that they do. This places their experiences in a social context so they don't view their preoccupation with weight and body shape as their individual problem.

Encouraging Self-Expression*–helps girls maintain their voice and confidence in their ideas and perceptions and feelings. It teaches girls how to recognize and express their feelings in a healthy way.

Building Healthy Relationships*–helps girls develop limits and boundaries, understand what draws them to people and what makes them move away. It teaches girls communication skills and conflict resolution skills.

Addressing Bullying–makes schools and other environments safer for girls. It teaches girls how to fight back.

Addressing Fat Prejudice*–helps parents, teachers, mentors and coaches recognize fat prejudice in themselves and work toward an acceptance of all sizes and shapes.

Media Activism*–encourages girls to protest or praise media products that have been analyzed and identified as conveying or challenging undesirable or unhealthy messages.

Prevention is about Nurturing Girlpower

Prevention is about promoting and sustaining healthy development, encouraging girls to use their bodies and teaching them to eat for strength and joy. Raising strong and healthy girls of all shapes and sizes means nurturing girlpower.[4]

GIRLS WITH _girlpower_

• Can express their feelings constructively

• Have a good sense of their boundaries

• Develop their self-esteem in areas other than looking good

• Have healthy connections with others

• Have a good sense of their bodies and are physically active

• Have a healthy relationship with food

Prevention Addresses Developmental Issues[5]

As much as we would like to find one, there is no one-size-fits-all approach to prevention, nor one miracle resource, nor one quick thing we can do to prevent eating disorders and fat+plus in children. While there are some skills we can use regularly to help girls meet life's challenges, we need a variety of programs and resources to address the different challenges that confront girls at each stage of development. We also need a variety of resources in order to address the different components of prevention.

Prevention begins in early childhood because feeding problems may lead to difficulties with food later on. Chapter 11 addresses how families who restrict their daughters' food or over-feed their girls destroy their hunger mechanism and their ability to know when they are hungry and when they are full. For girls under ten, the greatest risks are family dynamics, problematic life experiences and sexual and physical abuse. Once girls are preadolescent (around ten to twelve) they must also deal with the beginnings of the social, emotional and physical changes that occur during puberty.

Girls' bodies vary widely because of genetic and biological factors—yet they are all encouraged to look the same. A predisposition to perfectionism, as well as low self-esteem, and teasing and bullying about being fat all become risk factors. So do the changing dynamics of friendship. Girls must deal with the dark side of friendship including secrets and exclusionary practices. Shunning is a painful experience that peer groups reinforce. Often the one being shunned isn't even aware of the reason.

In early adolescence (around the ages of eleven to thirteen) girls continue to deal with the social, emotional and physical changes that occur during puberty. They also have to contend with the dismay of being an early bloomer or the disappointment of developing later than their friends. The transition to high school means giving up the security of a smaller school and entering unknown and overwhelming territory. It also means a rearrangement of friendships as old ones are lost and new ones are formed.

During early adolescence girls are faced with their sexuality and with problems with their parents as they attempt to gain more freedom. There is now greater pressure at school. At this time in their lives girls begin to experience the loss of their aerobic capacity as they stop using their bodies and start looking at them in mirrors instead.

During the period of middle adolescence (around the ages of fourteen to sixteen) girls must deal with increasing independence—with their need to experience themselves as separate from their parents. They must be encouraged to redefine their relationships with their parents to accommodate their growth instead of severing their connections or creating emotional distance. Girls worry about their worthiness as a friend and about their relationships with boys. They experience pressure not only to achieve but also to be perfect—which to them means being thin, nice and yet confident. Girls who are fat must deal with prejudice and stigmatization.

Do No Harm[6]

When we interact with girls, the terms _eating disorders_ or _disordered eating_ or _obesity_ should not cross our lips. Nor should we help or encourage fat girls to lose weight.

Be very careful about the approaches and activities you use

to broach this subject matter. Just about every girl in elementary school knows someone who has or has flirted with an eating disorder, so she knows what they are. Certain approaches can give girls–especially younger girls–negative information about how to control their weight by starvation, purging and excessive exercise. Talking about anorexia or bulimia to groups can be counter productive because it can inadvertently glamorize and normalize them.[7] Be wary of bringing in newspaper articles about young women who have eating disorders, or having discussions led by peers or older girls in recovery or enacting plays about girls with eating disorders. These activities don't deter girls because they don't address the underlying issues that make girls vulnerable to eating disorders.

Talking about the dangers of being fat makes fat girls feel guilty and self-conscious about their size. Encouraging them to diet causes emotional and psychological harm, endangers their health and increases their risk of developing an eating disorder. It also reinforces societal prejudice towards people who are fat.

Whenever teachers ask me to come into their classrooms to talk about the dangers of eating disorders and/or fat+plus I always reframe the subject so that I can talk about the underlying dynamics and teach skills instead.

When I visit elementary and middle school classes I talk about the diversity of body shapes and types. I engage the girls in discussions about the 'perfect' girl; about the pressures to be thin and kind and nice and the prejudice against being fat; about how girls can use their bodies to feel strong; about physical activity that is fun and about what makes girls feel good about themselves. Then (as I will explain in the next chapter) I teach them how to recognize their negative voice (the *grungies*) and tell the stories that lie underneath.

When I do presentations with high school girls I engage them in discussions about what goes on underneath the eating disorder behaviors without describing the behaviors themselves. We talk about what feeling fat means, how we deflect our feelings onto our bodies, the need to please other people, the dilemma around having a relationship with someone and still remaining true to yourself, the dynamics in their friendships that make girls feel insecure, what it means and looks like to feel out of control, and about fat prejudice and how to fight it.

We talk about the tremendous pressure on girls to diet and what really happens when they do this. The challenge with this age group is to make it safe enough for girls who are preoccupied with food and weight and engaging in eating disorder behaviors to come forward without giving a how-to lesson to the rest.

Do More Than Increase Knowledge

The traditional way of addressing prevention is to give girls information and to hope for the best. Many of us who are teachers or who work with girls have a lot of other demands on our curriculum time. Preventing eating disorders and fat+plus in children are important concerns, but we also want to do this quickly so that we can move on to the next risk that we will be asked to address.

Few parents today believe that just telling their girls what to do will keep them safe. But many professionals still seem to think that if we just give girls good information about healthy eating, body image, the importance of exercise, the dangers of eating disorders or being overweight, the girls will run right out and change those behaviors. After all, they now know better because we the authorities have so instructed them.

Increasing knowledge does not change or affect behavior. Think about all of the messages about smoking that you have seen on TV. Despite all of the icky lungs and other horrors presented to them, girls continue to smoke. Different studies show that attempts to improve body image and prevent eating disorders among adolescent girls by giving them information don't change their behavior in the least.[8][9][10] While the information increases the girls' knowledge, it does little to change their beliefs, attitudes and behaviors.[11] Nor does it teach them skills. A study that focused on preventing fat+plus in children produced the same results.[12]

It is important for girls to have information about the things that they need to know, not the behaviors that they have to change. For example, girls need to understand about genetics and metabolism so that they have a context for why girls are different sizes and why some girls gain weight faster than others. They need to know what happens when they diet and what different kinds of foods do to their bodies.

When we give girls information it is important that we have a dialogue with them instead of talking at them, that we give them time to think about the information and digest it, and that we provide them with the opportunity to come back to clarify what they don't understand.

Change Attitudes and Teach Skills

Prevention is about addressing the conditions that place girls at risk, teaching them skills with which to deal with the stressors in their lives, supporting them as they try out new behaviors, and creating an accepting environment for them. All of this is done in the context of girls' lives and experiences. For example, you can't talk about self-esteem without talking about why girls feel powerless and without providing them with skills to deal with bullying and teasing.

You can't expect girls to accept their bodies without acknowledging fat prejudice, teaching body awareness skills, helping girls to fight the power of appearance and encouraging girls to be physically active. And you can't encourage healthy self-expression without dealing with the tyranny of kind and nice and with how and why girls lose their voice. Girls will only use what makes sense to them—just as I hope you will with the information and exercises in this book.

Asking girls to change their behavior without providing an understanding of what created it and helping them become aware of their context (and its trigger) and providing them with skills, is setting them up to fail. That's like asking them to ride a bicycle with their hands tied behind their backs. This only adds to the sense of powerlessness that they already feel.

When to Include the Boys

There is an ongoing debate in the field of prevention as to whether programs (classes) should be separated by gender or if they should be addressed to girls and boys together. In making the decision about who to include in classes and groups we need to look at the stage of development that girls and boys are in and at the learning that we want to take place. If we want girls and boys to learn about each other or if we are giving information that both can benefit from and that is not about a vulnerable area in their lives, then we may keep them together.

If we want to prevent the silencing of girls' voices, encourage them to share their feelings, voice their opinions, validate each other and build and nurture their relationships and female culture and if we want to teach skills, then we need to keep the girls separate from the boys. This is especially important once girls reach adolescence because this is the time that they are most vulnerable and therefore at the greatest risk.

Adolescent girls are developmentally and socially more mature than boys their own age. They also want these potential boyfriends to like them. Having even one boy present changes the group dynamics as the girls stop sharing their real concerns and start focusing on the boy.

Where prevention strategies are implemented with boys, they should be adapted to and made appropriate for the male gender culture. They should also be implemented by men.

Providing On-Going Support to Girls

No matter how successful a program or resource, the results are time-limited if we don't provide the girls with ongoing support. We need to continue to teach skills, help reinforce those skills and support girls as they try them out. Otherwise, it is hard for girls not to succumb to the *body thieves*—to the tyranny of kind and nice and perfect, the pressures to be thin, and the prejudice towards fat.

We need to support girls as they move through developmental transitions. The girls in one grade six group that I facilitated talked about smoking. One girl summed up this transition very clearly. She said "Right now I think that smoking is yucky and I don't ever want to smoke. But I may change my mind when I am in high school. If my friends all smoke, I will smoke even though I don't want to so that I can be equal to my friends."

We mustn't make the mistake of believing that the skills we teach in elementary school will carry over into middle school or high school when girls confront a brand new set of pressures and expectations and when their peer groups are the most powerful socializing agents in their lives.

We're All Responsible

In the professional training workshops that I facilitate there is often a wide range of participants including parents, teachers, mentors, coaches, counselors, nutritionists, child care and youth workers, youth group leaders, fitness instructors, public health nurses and sometimes even high school students. One of the most valuable outcomes for the participants is the realization that there is no one person or organization that is totally responsible for fighting the *body thieves*.

We all have different roles to play and we approach from different perspectives. Many of us may be involved with prevention on an individual basis. Using the skills and strategies presented in this book we can work directly with the girls in our lives, seize memorable moments to teach skills in the context of a particular issue, do presentations and facilitate groups. Existing school programs can address some of the issues or topics in the prevention model outlined in this chapter such as conflict resolution and bullying. Parks and recreation facilities can provide girls with opportunities for physical activity. Organizations can help girls develop and maintain their voice. Parents must be included in prevention efforts because they reinforce the skills that are being taught.

While there is no one way that is the right way, for me the most important part of prevention is teaching girls about their *grungies* and helping them develop healthy relationships by giving them skills for communication and self expression. I then redirect the emphasis on appearance and encourage girls to use their bodies. Finally I work with girls to explore their relationship with food and provide them with skills for media awareness and activism.

The following chapters address the different elements of prevention. At the end of each chapter I have outlined Feature

Resources that you might find helpful. You can find information about how to obtain these resources in the Resource section at the end of the book. You might want to mix and match resources depending upon your own orientation, skills and interests. Just make sure that they address the changes in girls' bodies and changes in their lives.

Endnotes

1. Friedman, S. (2000), *Just for Girls Program Manual.* Vancouver: Salal Books
2. Irving, L. M. & D. Neumark-Sztainer. (2002) "Integrating the prevention of eating disorders and obesity: Feasible or futile?" Preventive Medicine
3. Berg, F. M. (September/October 1999) "Integrated approach: Health at any size," *Healthy Weight Journal,* p. 74
4. Friedman, S. (2000) *Nurturing girlpower: Integrating Eating Disorder Prevention/Intervention Skills into your Practice.* Vancouver: Salal Books
5. Adapted from Shisslak, C.M., Crago, M., Estes, L. S. & N. Gray (1996) "Content and method of developmentally appropriate prevention programs," in Smolak, M. P. & R. Streigel-Moore (Eds) *The Developmental Psychopathology of Eating Disorders.* New Jersey: Lawrence Erlbaum Associates
6. O'dea, J. (2000) 'School-based interventions to prevent eating problems: First do no harm," *Eating Disorders: Journal of Treatment and Prevention*, 8: 123-130
7. Ibid
8. Killen, J.D., Taylor, C.B., Hammer, L.D., Litt, I., Wilson, D.M., Rich, T., Hayward, C., Simmons, B., Karemer, H. & A. Varady (1993) "An attempt to modify unhealthful eating attitudes and weight regulation practices of young adolescent girls," *International Journal of Eating Disorders*, 13:369-78
9. Paxton, S.J. (1993) "A prevention program for disturbed eating and body dissatisfaction in adolescent girls: A one year follow-up," *Health Education Research*, 8:43-51
10. Neumark-Sztainer, D., Butler, R. and H. Palti (1995) "Eating disturbances among adolescent girls: Evaluation of a school-based primary prevention program," *Journal of Nutrition Education,* 27:24-3
11. O'Dea, J. and S. (2000) "Improving the body image, eating attitudes and behaviors of young male and female adolescents: A new educational approach that focuses on self-esteem," *International Journal of Eating Disorders,* 28: 43-57
12. Gordon-Larson, P. (2001) "Obesity-related knowledge, attitudes and behaviors in obese and non-obese urban Philadephia female adolescents," *Obes Res*, Feb: 9(2):112-118

8

∞

Translating Fat Talk

"Whenever my boyfriend puts his arm around my waist, like, I feel fat?"   Nicole, 15 years old

"When I sit in class I feel self-conscious about whether or not my thighs are flattened out or whether my sides are sticking out."   Brie, 10 years old

"What do you do when you feel fat because you are fat?"
     Michelle, 12 years old

It's hard to grow up female without learning to speak 'fat.' Fat talk has become a widely-used and accepted shorthand for communication by women and girls in our society. Even before girls are able to identify the full spectrum of their feelings they are able to speak *fat*, to say 'look at my thighs' or 'if only I was thinner' in place of talking about something real.

Take the members of a group that I facilitated, for instance. When I asked the girls at the beginning of a session how their week had gone one fifteen year old girl replied "Hard, I've been feeling fat a lot. I feel so gross." "What's going on underneath this?" I responded. "Do you think it has anything to do with your friend Tara?" knowing that she was having difficulty in her relationship with her best friend.

After several more moments of fat talk, she admitted that maybe she was feeling fat because she was angry at Tara for not showing up when they were supposed to go for a bike ride. "Isn't it lucky that we here are all bilingual," I said to the girls at the end of the session, "You individually speak in fat and the rest of us translate into English—and we all know what each of us is talking about!"

Because most of us are not bilingual in this way, we respond to the content when girls speak fat and get caught in a well-known, much dreaded ritual that goes like this:

Lisa: "I feel fat. I feel so gross!"

Us: "You're not fat. You look really good."

Lisa: "Yes, I am."

Us: "No, you're not!"

Lisa: Yes I am, just look at my thighs."

Us: "Your thighs look fine. You're not fat!!!"

Lisa: "Yes I am!"

After a while we become frustrated because we have reached a dead end. We continue to tell her she's not fat—which goes nowhere, or we give into our frustration and tell her that if she feels so fat why doesn't she lay off the chips. She also feels frustrated. She feels that we can't help her because we are not listening to her and we just don't understand—and in a way she's right because we don't.

When Girls Feel Fat

When girls talk about 'feeling fat' they are not referring to the size or amount of flesh on their bodies. Thin girls feel fat and fat girls feel fat. Nobody feels fat all the time. If at two o'clock, for example, you felt fine and at two-thirty you felt fat, the chances are that you didn't swallow a watermelon. The change that took place was not physical. It was emotional.

Every time girls 'feel fat' it is in response to an emotional trigger tied to a feeling that is unfamiliar to them or difficult to express or is labeled bad by our society. It is also a response to an experience that girls can't talk about either because they lack the necessary language or because they stop themselves because they are afraid of hurting someone else.

The Grungies—Understanding Fat Talk

As described in previous chapters, girls are socialized to repress their feelings and internalize their distress—to draw their pain into themselves. They ask "What's wrong with me? What did I do?" They talk about being angry with themselves. They worry about what people think about them, and seek to accommodate others at their own expense. When girls can't deal directly with what's bothering them, they learn to do so indirectly by redirecting their negative voice back onto themselves.

When I was developing the *Just for Girls* program we called this negative voice the *grungies*. We explained that girls 'hit themselves with a grungie' whenever they tell themselves something that makes them feel badly about themselves. Because girls are socialized to value themselves according to how they look, and because fat is considered bad by our society, the most popular grungie is 'feeling fat.'

Girls deflect the feelings that they cannot express onto their bodies and encode them in a *language of fat*. When girls are not able to translate their fat talk (the grungie) into the real experiences or stories that lie underneath, they act on their anxiety and discomfort by focusing on the fat. They diet in an attempt to feel better and to gain control of their lives.

Grungies

Grungies are our negative voice. They are the things we say that make us feel badly about ourselves.

The most common grungies are 'fat,' 'ugly' and 'stupid.'

Underneath every grungie is the story of a real feeling or experience waiting to find expression.

As adults we all have our own grungies. When I ask the participants in my professional training workshops if any of them felt fat in the previous week, almost everyone nods her head. The same thing happens when I ask them if they felt stupid or ugly—the other two most popular grungies. Before you can help girls identify their grungies, take a few moments to become aware of your own.

If I had my way the 'grungie' concept would be in every English language dictionary. Dealing with the grungies would be a part of every prevention program and part of everyone's repertoire of skills. Every time a girl felt fat, we would help her become aware of her grungie and encourage her to translate the fat talk into English so that she could express what was really going on.

I can just see those of you who are familiar with my work and are probably grungied out by now nodding your heads and thinking, here she goes again!

The Grungie Thoughts Test

Use this test repeatedly to establish the pattern of grungie thoughts.

0	1	2	3	4
Never	Sometimes	Moderately often	Often	Almost always

"How often in the last week have you had these thoughts?"

1.___My life is lousy because of how I look.

2.___If I was thinner I would feel more confident in my work.

3.___I feel fat.

4.___Why can't I ever look good?

5.___Other people look like they are 'together.'

6.___I can never do anything right.

7.___I must lose weight.

8.___People won't like me because I'm fat.

9.___Other people are more articulate, talented, compassionate, etc.

10.___When things don't work out for me I feel stupid.

11.___If I was more interesting I would have more friends.

12.___If I was thinner I would do things I've always wanted to do.

13.___I'll never be attractive.

14.___I hate my body.

15.___Everyone here knows more than I do.

16.___Everybody else is thinner than me.

17.___I feel fat when I am with people who are thinner than me.

18.___I'm so boring. I never have anything interesting to say.

19.___When I make a mistake I feel stupid.

20.___Whenever I'm in a new situation I feel fat or stupid.

If you score between 1-26 *grungies* are probably not an issue for you. Between 27-60 sounds like the beginnings of a problem. Between 61-80 looks like you might need help.

In my professional training workshops I often facilitate a simulated 'grungie group' with four or five brave women who volunteer to form a semi-circle in front of the larger group. I ask them to remember their own grungies and encourage them to tell the stories that are underneath. Workshop participants find this very valuable because it gives them an opportunity to identify and experience their own grungies and to understand the relationship between feeling fat and the fact that there is a real story that lies underneath.

The women speak about issues in their lives that are familiar to all of us: their feelings of inadequacy mothering teenage girls, their difficulties in setting boundaries at home and at work, their need to please other people, their inability to express their anger, their guilt in wanting time alone for themselves, problems they are having in their relationships, their grief over the breakdown of relationships and the loss of parents. In the telling of their stories, these women validate their life experiences both for themselves and for others.

You might find it helpful to practice identifying your own grungies as a way of learning how to do this with girls. Remember there is no right or wrong, that awareness comes with patience and curiosity, and that you don't need to be perfect yourself in order to help girls.

When a Girl has been 'Hit by a Grungie'

• Help her pay attention to what she is explaining about herself. Girls use grungies in different ways. Some say 'I feel fat.' Others say things like 'If I were smarter or thinner...' or 'I'm so unattractive....' or 'I'm such a loser....'or 'I suck....' When girls are younger they use anything that makes them different from their friends to give themselves a grungie—such as 'I'm too tall (or too short...)' 'My hair is too straight (or too curly....)'. Some girls give themselves a grungie when they constantly feel guilty, blaming themselves for things that are beyond their control. The first step is helping girls recognize which grungies are truly theirs.

• Begin by saying to her "I know that you feel fat, but most of the time when you feel fat, it is usually about something else, even if right now you don't know what it is." We have to take the focus off fat (and ugly and stupid, etc.) before girls can discover what they are really feeling. Even when girls don't know what lies underneath their grungies, the very fact that they are aware of and curious about them takes away the grungie's power—because it stops girls from hitting at themselves and engaging with the idea of 'fat' and encourages them to redirect their focus onto what is real.

• Help her look at the context. Be as specific as you can. Ask her what time of the day it was when she was hit by the grungie. What was she doing? What was she thinking about? Was there anything that she didn't want to do but felt she had to? Was she feeling angry, disappointed, insecure or lonely? Was she having conflict with any of her friends? These are feelings and situations that most girls have difficulty dealing with. One fourteen year old girl volunteered to talk about her grungie even though she was sure there was nothing underneath. We discovered that she had it in the mornings when she was at home. When I asked who was there she told me she was alone. Then when I asked how she felt about that, she said "Lonely," and quickly added "Then I felt fat."

• Ask her to describe the circumstances when she felt fat, ugly or stupid—but this time leave out the grungie. Ask her to replace it with a real feeling, something other people can relate to. For example, the first time she might say "I woke up in the morning and felt fat." Now ask her what she would feel if she didn't feel fat. Stupid, awful, confused, depressed are not allowed! Ask her what she was thinking about and encourage her to insert a real feeling, thought or description such as "I woke up in the morning and felt anxious because I didn't want to go to school." Or "I woke up in the morning and the first thing I thought about was my math test."

• At first she may not know what's underneath her grungie. Encourage her not to give up. Let her know there is no right or wrong. Remind her it takes time to make the connection between feeling fat or ugly or stupid and something else that is lurking underneath. One girl shared that she had her grungie when she was on the field playing soccer. This was her first game since she was away sick. When she looked at what was under her grungie she found that she was afraid that she wouldn't be able to play as well as she usually did and would let the team down. She had redirected her fears into fat thoughts.

• Sometimes girls say they feel fat but there isn't anything underneath. They say it's because their clothes don't fit or they ate too much. I ask them how they feel about the fact that their clothes don't fit. Does it make them scared that they may not stop gaining weight? Do they feel like a failure for having to get bigger clothes? I ask girls what feeling full feels like. What is scary or uncomfortable about it?

• Even if someone is fat, they may not feel fat. When they do feel fat, talking about how they feel about being fat allows for engagement—for the possibility of schmoozing. Getting caught up in the feeling fat ritual is a dead end street. Remember that feeling fat always has a negative connotation and is always used as a way of putting ourselves down. Every time a girl says she feels fat, what she is really saying is "I don't like my body" which means that "I don't like myself"—and that is learned behavior. It's also a way of speaking in code. Ask her what happened to make her feel fat when she didn't feel fat twenty minutes ago.

• If girls tell you they feel fat all of the time (and many girls do), just focus on one or two specific incidents. Don't give up. Girls who are very preoccupied with food and weight are so out of touch with themselves that having them acknowledge just one real thing is progress. Remember that the reason girls speak fat is because some things are just too difficult or scary to say directly—even to themselves.

• Girls need a lot of support in helping to identify and then deal with their grungies. Be patient. It takes time and experience to elicit the kind of information that is usually underneath—it's like peeling back the layers of an onion. If they can't figure it out right away, it's not because you've done something wrong, but because they don't have enough practice. Remember that the process is just as valuable as the goal. Just thinking about grungies and what may be underneath breaks the obsessive cycle that happens when girls feel fat.

• When girls have a sense of what's underneath their grungie it's important for them to know they don't have to do anything directly about it. Lots of times it is just too scary to contemplate and perhaps even inappropriate. They don't have to confront their teacher or yell at their best friend. Because our society is so focused on 'instant' solutions, girls sometimes think that they have to act immediately every time they have a feeling. We cannot expect girls to take action when they are not ready, or don't have the proper skills or support, or are really scared. But we must guard against their silencing what they know and feel.

Dealing with Grungies—Translating Fat Talk

• Become aware of the grungie.

• Be curious about it.

• Be specific as to the time and place that it occurred.

• Ask yourself what you were thinking and feeling at the time.

• Tell the story but leave out the grungie.

• Don't swallow your feelings—do a *Dead Flower Ceremony* to get rid of the emotional intensity (see page 89).

• Give the other person feedback symbolically to tell them how their behavior makes you feel.

• Decide whether or not you will tell them in real life.

• Clarify your feelings and reactions.

• Resolve the issue in a way that is safe for you.

Helping Girls Express their Feelings

Once girls are aware of their grungies, we need to help them identify and express the feelings that lie underneath. At the beginning this can be hard for girls to do because they have already learned to express some feelings and to repress others. For example, girls and women are encouraged to feel only positive feelings, and then only those feelings which have to do with the caring side of their relationships with others.

Good feelings are compassion, love and empathy. Bad feelings are greed, jealousy and competition. Disappointment is a difficult feeling, because girls are taught that if they are disappointed they shouldn't have wanted whatever it is in the first place. Insecurity is also difficult to handle—especially for girls who associate the 'perfect' girl with being not only thin but also confident all of the time.

While anger and hurt are different sides of the same coin, girls learn to express the hurt but to repress the anger. The taboo against expressing anger is so strong that sometimes they don't even realize when they are angry—the best they can do is know that they are a tiny bit annoyed. Sometimes when girls cry in response to a situation it's not because they are feeling hurt but because they are feeling angry.

'Liquid' anger through tears is acceptable but verbal anger is not. Because girls are raised to be 'nice,' instead of feeling angry with someone else they say that they are angry with themselves. This is learned behavior. I tell girls that my cat Theodora will swat you if you touch her the wrong way. However, I've never seen her hitting herself and meowing 'bad cat'. Because girls don't learn the skills to express their anger directly in a healthy way they do so indirectly through sarcasm, hostility, by withdrawing from other people and by gossiping and putting the other person down behind her back.

Sometimes the anger boils over and girls attack verbally or physically. Because girls have difficulty with their own anger, they can't handle the anger of others. They believe that if someone is angry with them it must be because they are a bad person and the other person doesn't care for them anymore.

Anger is an emotion that warns us that something is not right in our lives. We may get angry when someone is mean to us, when we can't do something that we really wanted to do, or when we think something is unfair. It can be a gift when it is expressed respectfully—as a way of telling people that you care enough about the relationship between you that you want to set things right.

It's hard to have a relationship with someone if the moment you say something that could be taken negatively, they shrivel up or if they deal with their own anger and hurt by retaliating indirectly. According to Carolyn Heilbrun, author of *Writing a Woman's Life*, "when [girls] are not permitted to express anger or even to recognize it within themselves they are refused both power and control in their own lives."[1]

Dealing with the Emotional Intensity of Feelings

It helps to think of feelings—especially anger—as water boiling in a kettle. The steam that pours off is the immediate reaction, the urgency and emotional energy that we experience first. Imagine a situation where you felt so angry or frustrated you wanted to hit someone, or a situation where you felt so disappointed or hurt you wanted to curl up in a ball and die.

During adolescence girls experience their feelings with such intensity that they are convinced the feelings will last forever—they will never go away. Often girls deal with the discomfort of this intensity by reacting and hitting out, or by redirecting the feelings onto their bodies and against themselves. The first step in dealing with feelings in a constructive way is to discharge the emotional intensity or burn off the steam. The best way to do this is symbolically, without the other person there.

Girls can find a private place and just talk out loud or rant about what is bothering them. They can imagine that the person is right there in front of them (or on the other side of the room if that feels safer). They can say things like "I'm so angry with Sally because she talked about me behind my back. I just want to…" They can be as mean as they like.

Girls can be physical. They can stomp on the floor, kick a pillow or hit their bed with a towel and say just how angry or disappointed or hurt they feel. This is a good way to discharge emotional energy and often is necessary before girls are ready to express how they feel.

Girls can hold a *Dead Flower Ceremony*. When girls are able to express their feelings symbolically they don't have to censor them or worry about the other person's reaction and response. In the initial reaction they can be as mean as they want to, because they don't have to be afraid that they are going to hurt the other person or feel guilty for having experienced the feelings in the first place.

Sometimes girls have to spend a lot of time dealing over and over again with the intensity of their feelings symbolically before they take the next steps to resolve the situation. Girls have to be reminded to take baby steps and then only when they feel ready.

THE DEAD FLOWER CEREMONY

[Materials: dead flowers (or tissues) / pens / garbage can]

We often give people live flowers to show our love and appreciation of them. Why not send them dead flowers (symbolically) when we feel angry, hurt or disappointed!

Have the girl (or girls if you are doing this with a group) think of someone that they are angry with. If anger is hard for some girls, then use words such as annoyed, just a little bit upset, etc. Ask them to think about what they would like to say to the person if they were not afraid of hurting him/her or being hurt themselves. [You can use real dead flowers or make the flowers out of tissues or other paper.] If you are using tissues, have them write what they would like to say on the tissue.

Place a garbage can in the center of the room. Have the girl stand in front of the garbage can, say out loud what she would like to say to the other person and then throw the flower *and her feelings* into the can. Once she has said what she needs to, she can let the feelings go.

If you are doing this exercise with a large group have the girls simultaneously and silently say what they need to say and then throw away the flowers and feelings.

One grade 9 group I facilitated was held into the month of June so the girls were able to bring real dead flowers. The ceremony went over so well that the next week each girl came to the group carrying a full bag of dead flowers! The garbage can over-flowed that day with feelings that would otherwise have remained inside.

Once girls have discharged the intensity, the feelings now simmer—just like the water in the kettle that has been unplugged or removed from the stove. Girls are still angry. But with the emotional intensity lessened they can now practice what they want to say to the other person about how that person's behavior made them feel.

They can speak to the person symbolically without that person being there, by imagining that he or she is sitting on a chair. They can also draw a picture of that person, put it in front of them and say "I'm so angry with you, Sally because..."

In a grade nine group the girls drew a picture of their soccer coach and put it on a chair. They took turns telling her how they felt about her behavior. After they expressed their feelings they decided that they didn't need to talk to her in person. They found that expressing their feelings in this way helped them move past the intensity. Once the girls were able to express and validate their feelings as well as their right to those feelings they could let go of them. Talking to a chair or to a picture may initially feel silly but when you can express the feelings directly you can get them out and let go of them.

Telling Someone How You Feel

When girls tell someone how that person's behavior made them feel they need to do it in a way that allows the other person to understand how and why they felt the way they did. They need to be prepared for the person's response and for their initial hurt or defensiveness. Telling someone how his or her behavior made you feel doesn't mean the person has to agree or change the behavior, but it opens the door for negotiation and leaves the connection intact.

Giving Feedback

• Be specific. Talk about just the one incident.

• Let the other person know that you are not trying to criticize or blame her for anything but want to tell her about a situation where you felt uncomfortable.

• Describe the behavior so that the other person has an idea of what she did that made you react.

- Describe the feelings that you had.
- Use "I" statements.
- Describe the outcome or effect that this behavior had on you.
- Let the person know what you want from them

> The acronym **WIN** helps us remember
> how to give feedback. It stands for:
> **W**hen you...
> **I** feel...
> I **N**eed...

Example: Your friend keeps borrowing your rollerblades. She promises to return them next day but that never happens. She usually keeps them for weeks. You can tell her:

"WHEN YOU borrow my rollerblades and don't return them right away, I FEEL that I don't have many choices as to when I want to use them. I NEED you to give them back promptly."

Dealing with the Response to Feedback

After we have given someone feedback, we need to deal with the response. The person may not see things in the same way we do. She may feel hurt or angry. Her first reaction may be to feel blamed or criticized. It's important that we don't try to make her feel better and take back our own feelings because we feel we have caused her to be hurt.

If we can listen to the other person without feeling criticized, without feeling that we did a 'bad' thing, we can then let her know we understand how she feels even if our reality is different from hers. We can reiterate how her behavior made us feel and ask her if she can understand why we felt the way we did.

- Listen with curiosity. Don't plan your response in advance.

- Ask yourself if there are any parts to her story or to her response where you can see how she might have felt the way that she did.

- Acknowledge her feelings. If she feels hurt or angry, don't try to take her feelings away from her. Your guilt doesn't do her any good.

- Let her know that you can see how she feels the way she does. You might not have felt the same way, but you can respect how she feels.
- Use "I" statements.

Making Ourselves Heard—"Yes, but…"

Whenever we give someone feedback we need to be prepared for the possibility the other person will become defensive and respond with "Yes, but…" When this happens, the person deflects the message that we are trying to put across. She responds to the words and loses sight of the content—the idea we want her to hear. In order to keep us from losing our own focus it helps to respond by repeating our message over again word for word. We may have to do this several times until the other person begins to hear us. We can acknowledge that she also may have an issue, but we can only deal with hers after we have resolved ours.

Understanding and Clarifying Our Reactions to Others

Our reactions to other people often have more to do with us than with the other person. If we enter a room full of strangers and have to interact with them, chances are we would be drawn to some of these people and would want to move away from others—even though we don't know them. This is because every time we have such interactions, we bring with us our whole train of relationship baggage. If you remind me of my Aunt Tessie who constantly criticized me, I will move away from you even though I've never met you before. If you remind me of my Aunt Jennie who always thought I was wonderful, my initial response will be to move towards you.

Girls grow up thinking that their responses to people are their direct responsibility. If their intuitive response is to pull away from somebody, girls blame themselves and believe they are unkind and pulling away is somehow wrong. Then the guilt/shame makes them feel fat. We need to help girls clarify their responses to other people so they can be aware of and trust their own instincts. We also need to give them language to do that. We need to let girls know they don't have to like or be liked by everybody. The more self-knowledge girls possess the more choices they have in structuring relationships with others.

FEATURE RESOURCE
The *Just for Girls* program

Just for Girls is an open discussion group program that I developed for preadolescent and adolescent girls. The program is based upon relational theory and addresses what happens to girls in the process of growing up female that silences them and encourages them to define themselves by the numbers on the bathroom scale. It teaches girls about the grungies by helping them become aware of their fat talk and it encourages them to tell the stories and express the feelings that lie underneath.

The *Just for Girls* program is made up of ten to twelve weekly sessions. At the beginning of the each session the facilitator holds a grungie circle where girls are encouraged to remember and talk about their grungies of the past week and tell the stories that are underneath. Girls have the opportunity to address their specific concerns through art work, role play, group discussion and other activities.

Just for Girls validates girls' feelings and helps them understand the societal pressures that they face during adolescence and the physical and emotional changes they are experiencing. It provides them with an awareness of their own bodies that goes beyond relating to them solely in terms of how they look. It teaches girls how to strengthen their friendships and support one another.

The *Just for Girls* program was developed to be used by a wide variety of women who are comfortable forming relationships with girls. The *Just for Girls* manual contains the complete blueprint for the program, a context for the issues that concern preadolescent and adolescent girls, 18 structured session plans and 25 reproducible handouts.

Endnotes

1. Heilbrun, C. (1988) *Writing A Woman's Life*. New York: Ballantine Books

9

∞

Celebrating Girls' Bodies

"Why are girls so ashamed about their bodies — like hiding their bodies under big loose shirts and pants?"
Morgan, 12 years old

"How can I convince myself that I am fine the way I am? I know that I don't have to change for people to like me, but I just can't think of my physical appearance without finding fault."
Elise, 13 years old

"When my male friends talk about girl's bodies, they emphasize how great skinny bodies and huge breasts are. How can they realize that most girls cannot have big boobs without the big body to match — unless they have surgery?"
Georgia, 17 years old

"The very first relationship we have is with our bodies. It is the foundation of our relationship to our selves. To be *embodied* is to experience the body as the center of existence–as a reference point for being in the world. It is to feel alive, to perceive bodily states as they change from pleasure to pain, from hunger to satiety, from energy to fatigue, from vitality to excitement to calm and tranquility. To be aware of our bodies helps us perceive the changes that signal emotional shifts that form the basis of our intuition." [1]

Everything we think, feel or do registers in our bodies through subtle changes in our musculature and in our bodily functions. Try walking around as if you have just won the lottery. How do you hold your body? How do you feel? Now try walking around as if you are really depressed. What difference do you notice?

Imagine a situation where you are annoyed or angry with someone. Trying telling that person symbolically with your shoulders hunched. Now straighten up and pull your shoulders back. What kind of change has taken place? What kind of sensations do you experience in your body when you feel angry? Do you clench your jaw? Does your heart beat faster? What changes happen in your breathing? What happens when you feel nervous or afraid?

If we could feel 'at home' in our bodies we could have a relationship with them that would allow us to celebrate them at whatever size and shape we are. Instead of experiencing our bodies from the inside, however, we learn to evaluate them in terms of what's on the outside. This robs us of our kinesthetic experience of our bodies and of the body knowledge that makes up an integral part of our sense of self.

Body Image

...consists of a collection of factors that influence how you perceive and feel about your body. Body image involves:

• How you see or picture your body

• How you feel others perceive your body

• What you believe about your physical appearance

• How you feel about your body

• How you feel in your body

• What you say to yourself about your body

• How your body feels when you are moving.

...other factors that affect how you perceive your body:

• Physical changes—puberty, menopause and pregnancy

• Injuries or disabilities

• Sexual and physical abuse

• Sexual harassment, racism and homophobia

When we speak of our body image we are not speaking about our actual body but rather an image that is a product of our imagination—one that is influenced by our physical and psychological experiences of our body and by the process of our socialization and our experience in the world. Translating from the physical body to the image that represents it is a complex process—one that is distorted by attitudes in our society towards women and therefore towards women's bodies.[2] For example, while the literature points to more negative body-image experiences among overweight or fat+plus women,[3] many fat women have a positive experience of the sensuality, softness and comfort of their physical bodies. It is our culture that gets in the way and turns what feels good into something that is perceived as negative.

Factors that Influence Body Image[4]

Internalization—is a process in which your interactions with others and with the outside world become a part of how you perceive yourself. For example, if your body is accepted, loved and praised, you will feel good about it and your body image will be positive. If other kids tease you, or your parents criticize how you look, you tell yourself negative things about your body and as a result your body image will be negative. If you have been abused or have had surgery or injuries, these traumatic life experiences can be frozen into your body image.

Projection—is a process whereby your body becomes a screen onto which you project feelings that you have been taught are negative. *Grungies* are projections. Instead of feeling angry, for example, you redirect or project the anger onto your body and focus on feeling fat instead of on resolving the feeling. Every time you have a grungie you have projected a negative image onto your body.

Identification—is a process whereby you incorporate the feelings your parents have about their own bodies into how you see yourself. If your mother goes around giving herself grungies you will learn how to give yourself grungies, too. If your mother diets and is critical of her body, then chances are you will feel the same way about your own body. If your father makes negative comments about your mother's body or makes comments about women on TV you will evaluate your own body in terms of how you think he feels women's bodies should be.

Culture—is a powerful influence on body image in terms of how girls and women are socialized (i.e., devaluing women and the pressure to be thin).

The Power of Thin

Repeated exposure to a particular image teaches us to like that image and reject what is different. Just think about how car companies redefine our definitions of what is 'in' by constantly changing their designs. The same thing happens with our bodies. We have become so used to seeing extremely thin women defined as cultural icons that we have learned to define this image as beautiful and to describe as fat anyone of a larger size.

Girls are taught from birth to value themselves in terms of their appearance and that to be thin is to be considered attractive. Even when they are toddlers we evaluate girls with very strict criteria and worry about what they will look like when they grow up. When I proudly showed pictures of my two year niece doing yoga to other members of my family, the response that I received was "Oh no! She has her mother's thighs."

When girls are as young as seven, they are already concerned with weight and body image.[5] These concerns are intensified when they reach puberty and are socialized to reject their changing bodies. Girls are initiated into an anorexic culture that promotes a waif-like image and where the accumulation of body fat during puberty is judged abnormal by adult society—though it is biologically normal and necessary to female development. Girls measure themselves against each other which reinforces the message that regardless of how they feel about their bodies they must be seen as constantly trying to change them in order to fit into the culture.

Adolescent girls feel a great deal of ambivalence towards their bodies. Boys make sexual comments and try to grab their breasts. Adult men and women make comments about how they look. Girls are taught by television and magazines that they should look good enough to be noticed and therefore valued. But when that happens they feel uncomfortable because that kind of attention objectifies their bodies instead of validating them.

The Ideal Body—an Historical Perspective

The obsession with body shape and size is not a new phenomenon. Throughout history, society has worshipped a variety of 'ideal' images of the female body. While women themselves were relegated to second-class or inferior status, those who came closest to the physical ideal were revered and given elevated status—just because of how they looked.

In prehistoric times, goddess figures were both fat and pregnant, linking rotundity with sexuality and fertility.[6] In the 1890s, the ideal woman was large. Fat was seen as alluring—as women's silken layer. It was regarded as a stored-up force, equated with reserves of energy and strength.[7] It was a sign of health—in contrast with thinness as a sign of tuberculosis and influenza, the two great fatal diseases of the time.

In the early 20th century, voluptuousness was definitely 'in' as represented by the corseted hourglass figure of the popular Gibson Girl. Plumpness was deemed a sign of emotional well-being, a good temperament, and disciplined habits.[8]

During the 1920s, the positive view of body fat that prevailed for so much of history gave way to fat aversion. While the suffragists struggled to obtain the rights of women, the beauty ideal shifted to the flapper who was flat-chested, slim-hipped, and androgynous.[9] The emphasis was on her cosmetically decorated face—a mask that prevented and protected her from showing who she really was. With World War II, society's image of the female changed once again. The ideal woman was now full-bodied, and had big shoulders that made her strong enough to take her place in the work-force as men entered the armed forces. She had the actress Betty Grable's shapely legs.

In the 1950s, men returned from the armed forces and women were pressured to give up their jobs to stay at home and have babies. Marilyn Monroe became the ideal because her voluptuous and curvaceous body and her big breasts represented motherhood. For this brief period of time women's natural fullness was enjoyed. The price, however, was women's seclusion and isolation in the suburbs and their rising use of alcohol and tranquilizers.

In the 60s and 70s, the second wave of the women's movement came into being. Twiggy—a thin waif-like model who looked anorexic—became the ideal. Society's current obsession with thinness began when she replaced Elizabeth Taylor, Kim Novak and Marilyn Monroe as the body-type for women to emulate. The average weight of Miss America (as well as the Playboy Playmate) soon dropped below the national average. The average model, dancer or actress was—and continues to be—thinner than the rest of the female population.[10]

What is defined as beautiful is not really about appearance but is about manipulating female behavior so that it conforms to what is considered desirable at a particular time.[11] Fluctuations in the body ideal tell us about women's place in society and about the economics of different times. When life was precarious and resources were scarce, fat was highly desirable because it represented health and wealth. A man with a fat wife was seen to be rich and therefore respected. In *Fiddler on the Roof,* Tevya sings that if he were a rich man, his wife Goldie would have double chins.

In times of prosperity, thinness was associated with idleness. The less a woman did and therefore the more powerless she was, the more it reflected on a man's ability to provide for her. The 'trophy' wives of today are visible tokens of men's financial success. They must be young, have ideal bodies and their surfaces must be plastic-perfect because their role in life is to flaunt their husbands' wealth (hence, his power) on their backs.[12]

The more economic opportunity there is for women, the smaller or thinner (and therefore more insubstantial and invisible) woman are supposed to be. The Antifat Crusaders reinforce this social control of women's weight through the Body Mass Index and the mythology that obesity shortens women's lives. When women are portrayed as strong and become strong, they become sexualized which then neutralizes their personal power. Just look at athletes such as women who play international volleyball—especially beach volleyball. Because of the skimpy uniforms that they are required to wear the emphasis is placed on their breasts and buttocks rather than on their physical agility and strength.

The more women obsess about their bodies, the less likely they are to get off the scale and on with their lives, and the easier it becomes to keep them silent. The more energy required to achieve an ideal body, the less time women have to be productive and take their place in the world. In a support group that I facilitated, one woman said that she had spent her whole life waiting to be thin. She was 50 years old. Is this what we want for ourselves or for the girls in our lives?

Clothing Creates the Ideal Body Shape

Until the late 1960s, fashion and accessories helped women achieve the ideal body shape. For women who were thin when fat was in vogue there were inflated rubber garments replete with dimples for the back, calves, shoulders and hips.[13] Think about Scarlett O'Hara lacing up her corsets in *Gone With the Wind*. Remember the bustles that women wore? or those brassieres that pushed up your breasts and that have now come back into style as bustiers?

In *Storm Clouds Over Party Shoes: Etiquette Problems for the Ill-Bred Woman* the artist, satirist and author Sheila Norgate offers us these dictates of fashion through the years that were designed to help women cover up their 'flaws.'[14]

> "For the thin woman, an easy, graceful manner is most important. When she develops such a manner, and combines it with the fluffiest and most frilly of feminine fashions, one will see how very charming she can be. The too-stout woman faces a more difficult problem. She must carefully consider each detail of her dress, making sure that it does not in any way accentuate her fleshiness…" (1923)

> "The over-plump girl looks more slender in dull fabrics and quiet colors…the butterfly looks very dashing in brilliant shades, but gray is, no doubt, more becoming to an elephant." Fat prejudice was alive and well in 1935!

> "The thin woman has a great friend in taffeta." (1941)

Those of us who grew up in the late 1950s were raised by similar fashion rules. We knew that horizontal stripes made you look fat and that vertical stripes made you look thin. Beginning in the late 1960s, however, there was a shift in the way that women were expected to achieve the ideal body. Whereas women once bought magazines to look at clothes that could camouflage their 'faults,' advertisers changed their message so the focus was now on having the perfect body to fit the clothes.[15] By promoting and reinforcing insecurity magazines boosted their declining readership and along with dieting, women turned to plastic surgery to drastically alter their body shape.

Girls Under the Knife

A British couple made headlines around the world by announcing that for their daughter's 16th birthday they would give her a bust boost. When doctors warned the surgery would be physically and psychologically harmful, the mother responded that her daughter had wanted breast implants since she was 12. "Jenna is lovely looking, but she's not confident," the newspapers quoted the mother—who herself had two breast enlargements and other cosmetic work on her nose, teeth and hips.[16]

Jenna's mother is not alone in her choice of gift. She is part of a tide of 40-something baby boomer parents who are being tucked, peeled and augmented as never before. And they are passing their practices onto a growing army of teenagers who believe that their lives will be transformed through the acquisition of perfect breasts, a new chin or whiter teeth.

An Internet site aimed at teenagers <wowgo.com> found that 75% of female visitors aged 12 to 17 said they would like cosmetic surgery. More than 35% wanted an operation to remove excess fat from their stomach and hips and 24% wanted breast implants. According to the American Society of Plastic Surgeons there were 24,623 cosmetic-surgery procedures on teens in the U.S. in 1998—an 85% jump since 1992. The statistics are similar in Canada. Nose shaping is most common, followed by breast reduction, breast augmentation, ear surgery and liposuction. The more extreme procedures include microsuction which can remove baby fat from their cheeks, and injections of botox (a muscle toxin) that can relax frown or squint lines or even paralyze sweat glands in the armpits for four to five months.[17]

Girls can't just have a normal natural body anymore. It has to be a perfect body or a *perfected* body. Because so many surgically-altered bodies are reflected back at them by the media, many girls feel flawed. They feel that something about them is intrinsically wrong or broken and has to be fixed.

According to Carla Rice who runs the *Body Image Project* at the Sunnybrook and Women's College Health Sciences Centre in Toronto: "Cosmetic surgery is too accepted as a quick-fix solution to poor self-esteem. If you don't have the body you want, you simply go out and change it."[18] Yet most girls feel unhappy with themselves even after surgery, because changing the outside doesn't begin to address what is really going on underneath.

With adolescent girls, their ideas about their bodies change as fast as their bodies do. Just as with the grungies, their insecurities about their bodies means that there are other triggers in play in their lives. [Try the Body Image Test on page 109 to see how your perception measures up.]

Helping Girls Reclaim their Natural Bodies

There are many things that we can do to teach body awareness and to help girls reclaim their natural bodies and feel good about themselves. Chose the activities here that you yourself feel connected to and feel comfortable doing. Later on you might want to come back and try the rest.

Teach Girls about Different Body Types[19]

Bodies come in three basic shapes (somatypes) that are genetically determined. They are based on the embryonic layers from which each type is supposed to have developed. *Endo* means inside, as in the gut. *Meso* means muscle. *Ecto* refers to the outer layer–skin, for example, hence skinny. Although we tend towards one body type we all have characteristics of each in varying degrees.

Endomorph:

• Soft, round body, larger in thighs.

• Average to large frame with shorter limbs in proprtion to the body. Tends to gain weight more easily than other body types because their metabolism is usually lower and body fat is stored more easily.

- More muscle mass means they excel in sports that require strength. A fair number of baseball catchers and pitchers, football players, hockey players, weight lifters and golfers are endomorphs.

Mesomorph:

- Most common body type. Tends towards muscularity with broad shoulders, narrow hips, large bones and heavy muscles, higher body weights.
- Many swimmers and skaters tend to be mesomorphs.

Ectomorph:

- Tends towards being very lean with little muscle or fat. Body type is thin, straight up and down with few curves.
- High metabolism means they are able to eat a lot with little weight gain.
- Long distance runners and basketball players tend to be ectomorphs.

You can't change your body type and/or natural weight because it is mainly determined by genetics. Most adolescents don't develop their natural body type until they are about 18 to 21 years old. Some people grow tall and bulk out later. Others bulk up first and grow taller later. Ectomorphs represent roughly 10% of the population—yet the rest of us keep trying to make ourselves fit into this type.

Teaching girls about different body types lets them know why they are different from their friends and why some girls are naturally thin and others are naturally fat. This helps take the stigma off fat and normalize it. It also gives us a context for size and takes the prejudice away from fat.

Look at Family Members

Look at pictures from your family album and/or encourage girls to bring family pictures to your class or group. Discuss who they most resemble. Try to identify the predominant body type of each person. If both parents are large, girls have an 80% chance of being large. If one parent is large, girls have a 50% chance of being large. If someone looks like their Aunt Tessie and Aunt Tessie has big hips, their chances of looking like Tyra Banks are pretty slim (pardon the pun!). Look at how many different family members live on genetically in a person's body.

Trace Your Dieting History

Do a time line with your dieting history. Go back into your memory as far as you can. What events are associated with each weight loss and weight gain? [Note: You can do this history together with or separately from the next two. These are wonderful awareness exercises for you to do for yourself, but they may need to be adapted for the age range of your girls.]

Trace Your Body History

Do a time line that traces your body history. Go back into memory as far as you can. What events can you associate with your body?

• Did you have any operations or break bones?

• Were you a victim of violence or abuse?

• Did you have any major illnesses?

• What are the good memories that you have of your body such as being hugged, being physically active, dressing up for Halloween or performing in a dance recital?

• How does your body history affect how you experience your body today?

Trace Your Body Image History

Do a time line with your body image history. Go back as far as you can into your memory. What events are associated with body image? What messages did you receive from:

• Your mother, your father?

• Your school?

• The media?

• A religious institution?

• How does your body image history affect how you experience your body today?

Take the *Body Image Test*

adapted from *(oxygen)thriveonline*
<http://www.thriveonline.com/shape/wgames/gen/shape.bodyimage.html>

How healthy is your image of your body?
Take the test yourself before you use it with girls:

0	1	2	3
Never	Sometimes	Often	Always

_____1. When I look in the mirror, the image reflected back to me is not who I want to be.

_____2. I'd rather shop for pet food than for clothing.

_____3. I go through at least three outfit changes when I get dressed and I'm still not happy.

_____4. I never exercise or participate in sports unless I can wear baggy sweats.

_____5. I think my body is ugly and I'm sure that others think so too.

_____6. When I'm out with friends I feel that everyone else is more attractive than I am.

_____7. When I go out with my family, I can't help wondering if people think I missed out on the 'good-looking' genes.

_____8. I compare myself with others to see if they are heavier than I am. It's all I can think about when I'm with another person.

_____9. I am so self-conscious about how I look that it's hard to enjoy activities like going out to dinner or to the movies with friends.

_____10. Being unhappy with my appearance preoccupies my mind.

_____11. I know that my thoughts about my body and appearance are negative, but I can't stop them.

_____12. I believe that dieting will change my life forever.

If you score between 0-12, body image is not an issue with you, 12-18 sounds like the beginning of a problem, 19-24 means that body image concerns and grungies are taking up a big part of your life, 25-36 looks like you might need help.

Teach Girls How to Take Care of their Bodies

By the time girls reach adolescence they have learned that taking care of their bodies means 'looking good.' What are the other ways we take care of our bodies? (Rest, sleep, good food, physical activity, protection from physical harm, etc.)

Encourage girls to be kind to their bodies and therefore-themselves. Encourage them to indulge themselves—take long hot baths, light candles, use lotions and bath salts that smell good.

Encourage girls to see clothes as costumes instead of as a way of measuring themselves against an ideal. Who are they? What mood do they want to portray? A *Just for Girls* group for grade six girls was held in a daycare center. The girls loved borrowing the kids' costumes and dressing up.

Teach Girls How to Talk about their Bodies

Along with giving ourselves grungies, we constantly talk judgmentally about our bodies. We say we'd never tell someone what we weigh, be seen in that bathing suit or this pair of shorts, or constantly make comments about our size. Once girls become aware of how they talk about their bodies they realize they have the choice of changing what they say—so they can talk about themselves as being strong, tall, short, quick, and using other positive descriptions.

Teach Girls to Challenge Others about their Body Talk

Girls can't control what others have said in the past about their bodies. But they can control what they say now. We need to teach girls that when someone makes a critical comment about their body they can say things such as "I don't like what you are saying" and that they can deflect the comment back onto the other person by asking "Why is my weight, size, hair, etc. an issue for you?"

Give Girls Permission to Love their Bodies

Often the feelings girls have about their bodies have more to do with the messages they receive about how they should look than how they actually feel. Girls need to know that it is all right to love their body even when it doesn't fit into the cultural ideal. We can give them that permission by giving them positive feedback about their bodies—by commenting on their strength, their functionality, their softness and their beauty and refraining from saying negative things about our own. When girls know that we value their bodies it's easier for them to start valuing them, too.

BODY DRAWINGS

[Materials: roll of heavy brown or white paper / felt pens]

Girls in our society are socialized to disregard their internal emotional and kinesthetic sense of their bodies and to experience their bodies solely in terms of how they look. This exercise is designed to help girls develop body awareness. You can do it with a group of girls as I have described it here, or with just one girl. [It's a great mother/daughter activity.]

Have girls draw an outline of each other's body:

Part 1: Have the girls use different colors to indicate:

• Those parts that they use a lot.

• Those parts that they really like.

• Those body parts that are the strongest, those that are the weakest.

• Those parts that they have confidence in—that work when they want them to.

• Those parts that give them pain.

• Those parts that make them feel embarrassed.

Part 2: Have the girls walk around as if they were alone in the room and act as if:

• They were feeling angry. Where would they feel anger in their bodies?

• They were feeling sad. Where would they feel sadness in their bodies?

• They were feeling hurt. Where would they feel hurt in their bodies?

• They were feeling disappointed. Where would they feel disappointment in their bodies?

Using different colored felt pens, ask the girls to color in those places in their bodies where they feel those feelings. Before you do each one, have the girls imagine what it felt like when they walked around the room. Ask them to imagine a situation where they felt the feeling. If they don't know where the feeling is in their bodies, have them guess. Remind the girls that there is no right or wrong way to do this activity. [You can do Part 1 or Part 2 separately or together.]

Redirecting the Power of Appearance

Let's face it. We all have moments when we get up in the morning, face the mirror with our eyes closed and fervently hope "Please, please let me look like Cindy Crawford, Tyra Banks, Britney Spears or whoever is the current celebrity of the month." No surprise, when we open our eyes Cindy, Tyra or Britney isn't there. They are probably looking in their own mirrors wishing that they, too, looked like someone else. Most of us are not model material and even if we were we could probably still find something to criticize about our bodies.

We need to help girls redirect the power of appearance onto ways of making them feel good about themselves. We need to teach girls to focus on something else other than how they look. I have given you some activities in this chapter. Others such as dealing with the grungies, encouraging girls to use their bodies to participate in physical activity and sport, helping girls enjoy their food and becoming media activists are covered in other chapters in this book.

Provide Girls with Role Models

• Bring in pictures of girls and women of different body types. The magazines listed in the resource section feature a variety of body types and sizes. So do pictures of athletes. For example, look at a photograph of a women's soccer or hockey team. Collect pictures of people from the newspaper. Hang the pictures in girls' bedrooms, in classrooms and in the halls of your school.

• Encourage girls to name their heroes. Have them collect pictures of women they admire, look up to, or who have been positive influences in their lives. Try to stay away from rock stars or movie stars. Each week have the girls place a different picture on the family fridge or bring it into class for the bulletin board. Ask the girls to introduce the women and talk about why they admire them. Point out that when girls talk about great people and their achievements their looks are generally irrelevant.

• Choose a hero of the month and have the girls do research about her.

• Visit an art gallery or museum and/or examine a number of art books and look at the pictures of women to see how women's bodies have been depicted throughout the ages. Talk about the function of these bodies and the messages that the pictures are trying to convey.[20]

Build a 'Bank Account' of Self-Esteem Points

Help girls build a 'bank account' of self-esteem points that they can refer back to when they become overly concerned with their appearance. Give them specific feedback about their skills, qualities and talents. Tell them the things that you appreciate about them. Help them to describe each other in the same way. Encourage girls to throw away empty descriptions such as 'pretty' and 'nice'.

Build a Sense-Of-Self Mobile[21]
Reprinted with permission of National Eating Disorders Association

Materials (for each participant)

One 8¾" paper plate	Eighteen paper clips
10" piece of string	Eight 8" pieces of string
Hole punch (optional)	Two 3x5 cards cut in quarters (8 pieces)

This exercise helps girls develop a balanced sense of self.

Before starting the activity, punch 8 holes around the perimeter of the pie plate and one in the center. Punch a hole in each piece of index card (or pass the hole punch around to the girls and let them prepare the pieces themselves).

Have the girls write one positive quality, characteristic, skill, role, interest or talent that she knows to be true about herself on each card.

Attach paper clips to both ends of the 8" pieces of string.

Hook one end of the string into each card and the other into the edge of the pie plate.

Attach paper clips to both ends of the 10" piece of string. Slip one paper clip through the hole in the center of the pie plate. Hang mobile. [The pie plate hangs better turned upside down.]

You can also use this exercise to encourage girls to give each other feedback by passing the cards around for written comments.

This is a great family exercise, because it gives everyone an opportunity to recognize and acknowledge each other's skills, talents and positive characteristics.

Help Girls Find a Passion

Introduce girls to and encourage them to participate in activities that make them feel good about themselves. Help them find a passion and become involved with it. It can be physical activities, sports and dance, drama, volunteering, or taking care of pets for the SPCA.

Having a passion has tremendous benefits for girls:

• It takes girls out of themselves.
• It provides them with another peer group outside of their friends at school.
• It let's them excel at something.
• It helps center and ground them.
• It broadens their experiences and exposure to things.
• It focuses them on something they do, rather than on how they look.

Give girls positive feedback about what they are doing. We tend to take our accomplishments for granted and focus only on the things that we can't do.

FEATURE RESOURCES

Everybody's Different program

The *Everybody's Different* program was developed by Jennifer A. O'Dea for use by classroom teachers in Australia to improve body image by building general self-esteem in secondary school girls and boys.

The *Everybody's Different Program* evolved out of the first controlled study to successfully demonstrate that an interactive program can change behavior. In this case, improving self-esteem can improve the body image and eating attitudes of adolescent girls and boys, including those that are considered to be at risk of developing an eating disorder.

The program consists of nine consecutive weekly lessons of fifty to eighty minutes each with additional home-based activities such as family discussion and positive parental input. The lessons engage the students through the use of group work, teamwork, games, play, drama and a 'content-free' curriculum.

The program fosters a positive sense of self, involvement in vicarious learning, exchange of feedback and a positive environment in which the students feel that they cannot fail. The program deals with the following topics:

Lesson 1 Dealing with stress

Lesson 2 Building a positive sense of self

Lessons 3, 4 and 5 Address different stereotypes in our society. Includes discussion on being a responsible individual and learning to accept and value differences.

Lesson 6 Positive self-evaluation, individuality, uniqueness

Lesson 7 Involving significant others by learning to receive positive feedback

Lesson 8 Relationship skills

Lesson 9 Communication skills

Liking the Me I See in the Mirror

Liking the Me I See in the Mirror is an educational resource manual on body image and self-esteem developed by Suzanne Hare and Dianne Drummond in Edmonton, Alberta. It is intended for use by teachers with girls and boys in grades 4 and higher. Each of the six lessons includes an introduction, rationale, expected outcomes, background information, handouts and activities. The program deals with the following topics:

Lesson 1 What is Body Image? (An Introduction)

Lesson 2 It's in the Genes (The Physical Self)

Lesson 3 Who am I, What am I Like? (The Physical Self)

Lesson 4 Learning to Accept My Inner and Outer Self (Self- esteem/Body Image)

Lesson 5 The Quest for Health (Self-care)

Lesson 6 Accepting Me at My Best
(Perfection versus Excellence)

Endnotes

1. Hutchinson, M. G. "Imagine ourselves whole: A feminist approach to treating body image disorders," in Fallon, P., Katzman, M.A. & S. C. Wooley (1994) *Feminist Perspectives on Eating Disorders.* New York Guilford Press, p. 153

2. Ibid

3. Cash, T. and F. (May 17, 2001) "Beyond body image as a trait: The Development and Validation of the Body Image States Scale," *Eating Disorders: The Journal of Treatment and Prevention,*

4. Anne Kearney-Cook Workshop in Vancouver Washington, February 28, 2001

5. Thelen, M.H., Powell, A.L., Lawrence, C. and M.E. Kuhnert (1992) "Eating and body image concerns among children," *Journal of Clinical Child Psychology,* 21: 41-46

6. Seid, R. P. "Too 'close to the bone:' The historical context for women's obsessions with slenderness," In Fallon et al, p.5

7. Ibid

8. Rothblum, E. "I'll die for the revolution but don't ask me to diet.: Feminism and the continuing stigmatization of obesity," In Fallon et al, p. 61

9. Ibid

10. Wolf, Naomi (1991) *The Beauty Myth: How Images of Beauty are Used Against Women.* New York: Morrow, p. 185

11. Ibid, pp. 12-15

12. Landsberg, M. (1989) *'This is New York, Honey:' A Homage to Manhattan, with Love and Rage.* Toronto: McClelland & Stewart, Inc., p. 95

13. Seid, p. 5

14. Norgate, S. (1997) *Storm Clouds Over Party Shoes: Etiquette Problems for the Ill-Bred Woman."* Vancouver: Press Gang, pp. 26-27

15. Wolf

16. MacDonald, Gayle "Girls Under the Knife," *The Globe and Mail,* Saturday, January 13, 2001

17. Ibid

18. Ibid

19. Omichinski, L. (1995) "No Weigh: Teens and Diets," in Parent Guide, HUGS International Ltd.

20. Thanks to Mary Pabst and Brenda Sigall

21. Adapted from Kathy J. Kater (1998) *Healthy Body Image: Teaching Kids to Eat and Love their Bodies Too.* Seattle: EDAP

10

∽

Getting Girls Off Diets

"On your first real day of camp you take a 'before' picture. And later, they take an 'after' picture. This is my third summer here but I'm still embarrassed standing there...No one here is comfortable with the way they look in their bathing suit. We're all here for the same reason: to lose weight and come back to be with friends.

"My parents were trying to help me and put me on a diet, but also I think they were embarrassed if I didn't look good in something—even more embarrassed than me. My parents have my 'before' and 'after' pictures. When I get home they say, look how thin you are, look how fat you were and I think 'now you think I look good because I lost the weight.' I want to believe that I looked good all along. I just want to believe that."

14 year old camper who attended a weight-loss camp.
New York Times Magazine August 26, 2001

The fourteen year old camper is not alone in her attempts to lose weight. Dieting today has become a normalized part of the female culture, something most girls and women are expected to do—especially if they want to fit in with their friends. Like any cult it has its own identifiable system of ideas, methods, values, beliefs and norms that constrain and shape our thoughts and actions around our bodies and around food.[1] It is the biggest *body thief*.

As adult women, most of us have been on diets. We usually go on one during stressful periods in our lives. When we feel we can't control what goes on in our lives, we try to control our food. Every time we start a diet we know that this diet is going to be *the* diet—the one that finally works. We count the pounds that we are going to lose and envision ourselves in the dress one size too small that has been hanging in our closet forever. We imagine ourselves doing all of the things that we have put off doing once we lose weight.

There is such a feeling of cleansing and purity that goes with beginning the diet. We throw out all the 'bad' food and replace it with the 'good' food required by our current diet (the one that will change our lives). For the first few days (even weeks) we feel in control. Sometimes we even feel righteous. Look at all those other people eating pizza and ice cream! [I remember my surprise during my early dieting years when I found out that ice cream had an expiry date. I couldn't imagine anyone having ice cream long enough to let it get stale.] Think how healthy we will be! Friends comment on our weight loss and we feel so good about ourselves. How can life get any better?

Alas, there comes a time in every diet when we begin to feel the effects of the deprivation and we hear the sound of the Oreo cookies calling our name. When that happens, we eat as if our grocery store is going to go out of business. As we eat the 'forbidden' foods we feel guilty and beat up on ourselves. We're such failures. Can't we do anything right? When we recover from making ourselves feel badly we begin the next diet that is going to be the diet that will change our lives forever.[2]

Most women began dieting in the 60s and 70s when Twiggy first arrived on the scene and the ideal body type was not as narrowly defined as it is today. As one of those women, I went up the scale and down the scale. I tried high fat, low fat, lots of water, grapefruit, all the dieting doctors and attended three different Weight Watchers. When I failed one diet, I went on to the next. Had there been an Olympic medal for dieting and for weight lost and gained, I would have been right up there with the best of them contending for the gold. Despite all my efforts I only succeeded once in becoming a size ten—a size that was considered slim at the time—and even then I felt I was fat.

The daughters of my generation were the first to be raised by chronic dieters, by—women like myself who counted calories and defined themselves by the numbers on the bathroom scale. These young women elevated weight-loss to new heights as the definition of thinness was revised and they became more serious about their dieting practices.

Laboring under perverse notions of food and appetite, some women today believe permanent dieting and chronic hunger are healthy 'lifestyles' and that food does not nourish but instead kills.[3] They have a fear of being full and an obsession with counting grams of fat. The motto today is "Don't eat or you'll be sorry." And if anyone finds herself with unbridled appetite, it is because there is something wrong with her—she is *addicted* to food. The fact that she is just plain hungry would never cross her mind.

Dieting Begins When Girls Are Young

Girls begin to restrict their food intake when they are as young as five.[4] Forty-five percent of children in grades 3 to 6 want to be thinner.[5] One six year old little girl said to me, "I never eat more than one slice of bread. My mother says that it's fattening." Most young girls have not yet integrated beliefs about dieting and thinness with beliefs about attractiveness. They are dieting not because they believe it will make them thinner, but because they are responding to the cultural norms as every woman does.[6]

As girls go through puberty, 14% of 11 to 12 year old girls have significant concerns about weight and shape[7] and 61% of adolescents and college-age women are dieting[8] in an attempt to combat their natural bodies. Eighty per cent of girls of normal height and weight want to lose weight.[9] During adolescence, peer groups reinforce the importance of thinness with fat talk (grungies) and the need to engage in weight-loss behaviors. The rejection of fatness becomes a shared value in the group.

Talking about dieting serves not only as a means of giving and receiving information about weight control but also as a means of reinforcing the cultural obsession with weight and the prejudice towards fat.[10] Disordered eating practices are so common that in order to fit in, girls have to be preoccupied with losing weight even when they feel good about their bodies. If you want to know what a girl is doing to manage her weight just look at her friends' attitudes towards their own bodies and their weight management practices and dieting behaviors.[11]

Passing the Dieting Torch

As adults we pass the dieting torch on to our girls. We do this when we make comments about girls' bodies or about our own, and when we practice fat prejudice. We do this when we insist that our daughters reflect well upon us with an acceptable body size and shape and when we encourage girls to lose weight to fit in with their friends, or to swim faster, do a higher triple lutz or gain a position on the swimming team. We do this when we try to restrict their food. We become *body thieves*. By encouraging girls to change their body shape we rob them of their natural bodies and make them hostages to the tyranny of the bathroom scale.

We are part of the same culture that our girls grow up in. As women many of us, if not most, have some form of unhealthy relationship with food and with our bodies and some form of disordered eating. We may be in a constant state of semi-starvation from chronic dieting, under-eating, fasting or skipping meals. We may never know when we are hungry or when we are full. We may obsessively over-exercise on a regular basis.

The most powerful lessons that girls learn about dieting are those from their mothers. Little girls constantly watch their mothers. They pay attention to what their mothers wear and how they act and to their attitudes, beliefs, roles and struggles. They emulate what they see. A mother who diets is likely to have a daughter who has learned to deal with stressors in her own life by dieting, too. A mother who diets ten times a year is likely to raise a daughter who diets more than ten times a year. A mother who is preoccupied with weight is likely to bring up her daughter to be preoccupied with weight.[12] In our own personal battle with food and weight issues we put our girls at tremendous risk.

The Effects of Dieting

The effects of dieting are far-reaching. In Chapter 5 we learned about 'set point' theory–which suggests that diets do not work as we suppose and, in fact, make us fat! The 'set point' theory holds that everyone has a genetically determined weight range that our body attempts to maintain. When you diet, your body cannot tell the difference between a deliberately constructed low-calorie diet and an actual famine. Once you reduce your caloric intake, your body tries to protect itself from starvation by gradually burning fewer and fewer calories, making weight-loss ineffective. When you go off the diet, your body will work not only to regain the weight that you have lost, but also to store extra pounds in the event that you will try to starve it again. The set point is thus raised to a higher weight range and we eventually gain that additional poundage.

When girls diet during adolescence they stimulate the reproduction, growth and concentration of fat cells and fat storage enzymes in their buttocks, hips and thighs. When they go off their diet their bodies become efficient in storing calories in those fat cells.[13] Not only does dieting make girls fat but yo-yo dieting (the repeated cycle of weight-loss and regain) contributes to an increased risk of cardiovascular disease and high blood pressure later on in life.

Learning from the Minnesota Experiment

In the late 1940s Dr. Ancel Keys conducted what has become a classic study of starvation for the U.S. government.[14] In the *Minnesota Experiment* men with no previous history of weight problems were put on a restricted diet of 1,570 calories a day—about half of what they normally consumed. Their eating patterns and personalities were then studied over a three-month period.

Men who previously had no particular interest in eating and cooking became fascinated with food. Many started collecting recipes and studying cookbooks and menus. About a third of the men expressed an interest in taking up a career that involved food after the study was over. Many began to snack between meals, and others developed odd food cravings. Men who originally seemed to be comfortable with their appearance began to view their bodies negatively. Despite having lost weight, several complained about feeling overweight, and others became quite critical of their body shape and size.

In addition to the preoccupation with food, irritability and fatigue and depression set in. One man in the study developed major personality disturbances after just 10 weeks on a diet of about 1,500 calories. Mentally and emotionally he was in starvation mode, though he had lost only 10 pounds or 7% of his body weight. His diet was less strict than many of the weight loss programs advocated today, and his weight loss was less than that now being recommended by the National Institutes of Health for everyone with a Body Mass Index above 30.

Many in the program continued to be preoccupied with food and reported a loss of control over their eating behaviors even after they were reintroduced to normal eating patterns through a three-month rehabilitation program. Mood changes related to starvation—such as depression, irritability, anxiety, pessimism and frequent anger—persisted through this period.

Dieting puts us at risk of starvation and its effects. By denying themselves, dieters experience the same affects as the men in Keys' study. They are more likely than nondieters to turn to food when they are anxious or depressed (such moods are typically a side effect of the diet itself).

The result of self-imposed food deprivation becomes chronic obsession with food. The study demonstrates that overeating is a normal physiological and psychological response to food deprivation, rather than a lack of willpower. It also shows us what happens when food is restricted over a period of time and people are in starvation mode.

The Paradox of Dieting

There is a fundamental paradox in our professional and societal beliefs and attitudes about dieting: what is diagnosed as disordered eating in thin people is what is purposely prescribed for fat people.[15]

Dieting is the most important predictor of eating disorders in girls[16] and the pursuit of thinness is a growing social problem and public health threat. Most programs that address eating disorders include the promotion of size acceptance and discourage girls from dieting—up to a point.

Size acceptance breaks down as girls move away from what is considered to be the ideal weight. Girls who are fat or 'over' weight are encouraged to use the very same diets to lose the 'extra' weight that thin girls are discouraged from using. Dieting makes our girls sick however we look at it, whether we are dealing with anorexia nervosa or weight-loss/regain. It can kill them—all in the name of health.

Breaking the Dieting Cycle

Dieting is the biggest *body thief* and the most potent political sedative in women's history. It creates passivity, low self-esteem and anxiety and ensures that we remain focused on our weight instead of on our lives, on changing our natural bodies instead of creating social change. Dieting robs girls of their relationship with their bodies and contributes to silencing their voices. If we want to prevent girls from going on diets, we need to get off of our own—something that can be very difficult to do.

In 1978 I read Susie Orbach's revolutionary book *Fat is a Feminist Issue.*[17]   Light bulbs went on and bells started to peal when I read that women didn't have to be on diets. My first reaction was to view the book as heresy. How could she even suggest such a thing? My second reaction was incredible relief! Getting off my diet was more difficult.

If I didn't have to diet, how was I going to know what to eat? How would I gauge what was too much without my Weight Watcher scale? If I could eat anything I wanted, wouldn't my weight shoot up? If I wasn't dieting, then how would I deal with the issues in my life that had been deflected onto my preoccupation with food? How could I give up my dream of being thin—of being someone other than myself?

Dieting has been a way for women to create structure in their lives for such a very long time. It is a familiar if painful way of interacting with the world. When life becomes stressful and we feel out of control we can always start another diet. After all, we may not be able to control the events in our lives but there is always the illusion that we can control our food and our bodies. In the fleeting moments of weight-loss, we feel good about ourselves. How do we get our daughters or the girls we work with off diets when they are such an integral part of our own lives?

The more we ourselves have invested in being thin the more damage we do. We endow thinness with such magical qualities that it becomes much harder for us to accept our daughter's body or the bodies of girls we work with if they don't fit into our vision of the ideal. In one survey, 55% of daughters said that their mothers were critical of their weight when they were children, 64% when they were teens and 57% currently as adults. Some mothers are so critical of their daughters' bodies that they rate their daughters as being even less attractive than their daughters rate themselves.[18] Some mothers cannot acknowledge that their daughters are at risk or have an eating disorder unless they are hospitalized for self-starvation or self-induced vomiting. It's hard for them to hear the expressions of concern from teachers, doctors and their daughters' friends.

Getting Girls Off Diets

Giving up dieting is like quitting smoking. Sometimes you have to think about it a whole lot and try to quit many times before you can finally do it. If you can't seem to get off your diet just yet, it doesn't mean you can't help girls get off theirs. Just be honest about your own struggles and be really careful to monitor the messages that you give to girls. It's a lot more important to girls if you can be honest with them than if you are perfect and do everything right.

Help Girls Explore the Myths About Dieting

The first step in getting girls off their diets is to explore their beliefs with them. The true or false test Exploring the Myths about Dieting on page 125 is a good way to do this. All of these items have already been covered in this book. Answers:

1 – False	4 – False	7 – False	10 – True	13 – True
2 – True	5 – False	8 – True	11 – False	14 – True
3 – False	6 – False	9 – True	12 – False	

Talk About What Really Happens When You Diet

Girls need accurate up-to-date information about food and how food restriction affects their weight, their energy and their moods. The chart on page 123 provides you with information about all of the reasons why girls diet and what really happens.

When girls are younger you might need to explain concepts such as metabolism. You might also need to adapt the chart so that it is appropriate for their level of understanding and includes only the facts that are relevant for them right now.

TOP TEN REASONS TO GIVE UP DIETING

#10 Diets don't work. Even if you lose weight, you will probably gain it all back and you might gain back more.

#9 Diets are expensive. If you did not buy special diet products, you could save enough to get new clothes, which would improve your outlook right now.

#8 Diets are boring. People on diets talk and think about food and practically nothing else. There's a lot more to life.

#7 Diets don't necessarily improve your health. Like the weight loss, health improvement is temporary. Dieting can actually cause health problems.

#6 Diets don't make you beautiful. Very few people will ever look like models. Glamour is a look, not a size. You don't have to be thin to be attractive.

#5 Diets are not sexy. If you want to feel and be more attractive, take care of your body and your appearance. Feeling healthy makes you look your best.

#4 Diets can turn into eating disorders. The obsession to be thin can lead to anorexia, bulimia bingeing and compulsive exercise.

#3 Diets can make you afraid of food. Food nourishes and comforts us, and gives us pleasure. Dieting can make food seem like your enemy, and can deprive you of all the positive things about food.

#2 Diets can rob you of energy. If you want to lead a full and active life, you need good nutrition, and enough food to meet your body's needs.

#1 Learning to love and accept yourself just as you are will give you self-confidence, better health and a sense of well-being that will last a lifetime.

WHAT *REALLY* HAPPENS WHEN WE DIET*

HOW WE DIET	THIS IS WHAT *REALLY* HAPPENS
Skipping meals or decreasing calories	This lowers metabolism so we store fat more easily from fewer calories. The brain's and muscle's demand for fuel causes rebound "munchies," usually for high fat and high sugar items. Poor attention span, irritability, fatigue. Muscle tissue may be lost.
Cut out starchy foods	Your body loses its best source of stable energy. You'll be more likely to feel moody and tired. You'll end up eating higher fat and sugary foods to satisfy munchies.
Go on preplanned meal replacement diet or liquid diet	You have a 95% chance of regaining any weight you lose in 1 to 3 years You give away control to the plan, which lowers your self-esteem. You often lose muscle mass along with fat. This lowers your metabolism, making it easier to store fat on fewer calories. Habits are replaced temporarily, not changed permanently. Also, it's expensive.
Fasting	Most of the weight lost is water. Muscle mass decreases-which lowers metabolism. Subsequent fat gain. Can be medically dangerous for some individuals.

WHY WE DIET	THIS IS WHAT *REALLY* HAPPENS
To be slim	Slimness is temporary. Over the long run, 95% of dieters regain the weight. Many women get fatter, so they diet again, with similar poor results. This is called diet cycling and it can lead to obesity.
To be healthier	Diet cycling increases health risks more than being fat. There is no evidence that being fat is unhealthy. There is evidence to show that being too thin is unhealthy. Most dieting decreases muscle mass. Muscles are needed for good health. Your body and mind don't run well when you restrict calories. Dieting makes you moody and irritable, and makes you obsessed with food. This feels like failure, but in fact it is physiological response and has nothing to do with will power. 30 minutes of physical activity a day will make you healthier and help you feel good about your body.
To be more attractive	What attracts you to someone else? Do you want your friends to like you for your body or yourself? What are long term relationships based upon? If you are dieting, are you any fun to be around?

*Adapted from material developed by Cathy Richards
for the British Columbia Interior Health Region

Support Girls Through the Grieving Process

One of the major steps in giving up dieting is dealing with our sense of loss and feelings of grief—especially so for long-time dieters. We need to let go of *what might have been* before we can move on to *what is*. Girls need to understand it's not the diet that they mourn but the letting go of all the dreams and hopes and fantasies that are attached to being thin.[19]

Being thin means being beautiful, intelligent, loved, accepted and sexy. It means being perfect and feeling confident all the time. It means having a boyfriend now and a successful career later on. We can support girls through the grieving process by validating their feelings and their right to have these dreams. We can explore what being thin means to them and help them find other ways of feeling good about themselves.

Change the Way Girls Think

Getting off a diet means giving up counting calories and fat grams. It means normalizing food and learning how to listen to your body. It also means moving from weight loss to healthy living and changing how you think. Use the chart on the next page that was developed by dietician Linda Omichinski[20] to help girls become aware of how they think about food, exercise and their bodies. Help them reframe their thoughts so they can take the necessary steps in redefining their goals and moving away from dieting to a different way of being in the world.

Get Rid of the Scale

Colleagues of mine organize a scale-smashing event in Vancouver every year during *Eating Disorder Awareness Week*. It's usually a great success. There is something very liberating about swinging a mallet on a metal symbol of oppression. Over in Victoria, BC, they convert the pieces of the scale into artwork to express how they feel about dieting and about their bodies.

We need scales to weigh babies so we can monitor their growth and ensure they are getting enough to eat. Grocery stores need scales to measure the amount of bulk food you buy. Hospitals need scales to determine the amount of anesthetics patients require since dosage is often dependent upon weight.

There is absolutely no reason why we as individuals need scales. Getting off the diet also means getting rid of the scale and finding another measure of self-worth.

Beware of Diets in Disguise

Because diets have been getting such bad press recently, those people who make tons of money getting us to participate in the continuous cycle of weight-loss/weight-gain have had to find other ways to keep their hands in our money pockets. One way of doing this is through promoting 'lifestyle changes.' Calories are controlled implicitly by dividing foods into portion sizes, thus promoting the perception that this is not dieting—while at the same time celebrating weight-loss.[21] Concepts such has 'healthy eating' have also been co-opted by the diet industry. Where 'healthy eating' once referred to nutritious food, today it has come to describe low-calorie and low-fat foods. We need to be aware that these are diets in disguise and help our girls become aware of them, too.

EXPLORING THE MYTHS ABOUT DIETING

True or False?

Read each statement and check the box you think is correct:

True?	False?	
_____	_____	1. Dieting always leads to permanent weight loss.
_____	_____	2. Each person has her own natural weight.
_____	_____	3. It's easy to lose weight!
_____	_____	4. All fat people are fat because they overeat.
_____	_____	5. All fat people are unhealthy.
_____	_____	6. Thin people are healthier than fat people.
_____	_____	7. Eating normally means eating only diet foods.
_____	_____	8. Dieting may cause weight gain.
_____	_____	9. Most diets don't work.
_____	_____	10. Normal eating means eating a variety of foods.
_____	_____	11. It's easy for everyone to gain weight.
_____	_____	12. Everyone can change their body type.
_____	_____	13. Dieting can lead to an eating disorder.
_____	_____	14. Exercise always makes you lose weight.

Adapted from Teacher's Resource Kit
National Eating Disorder Information Centre, Toronto, Ontario, Canada

FEATURE RESOURCE

Teens and Diets—No Weigh

Teens and Diets—No Weigh: Building the road to healthier living is an empowerment program developed by Linda Omichinski of HUGS International for adolescents 12 to 17 years old. Putting teens in the 'driver's seat' of this non-diet program builds self-confidence needed to make safe decisions based upon personal and emotional needs. The facilitator's manual includes dialogue guidance scripts, games, brainstorming questions and role plays. The program also provides many support materials such as a parent guide, teen journal/workbook and a cookbook.

HUGS also supports adults seeking a lifestyle without diets. It provides information, workshops, professional training and resources about non-dieting. Their vision is to challenge the myths of the diet industry by shifting attitudes and beliefs away from the preoccupation with weight and size to an acceptance and appreciation of healthier living.

DIET VS NON-DIET THINKING		
Printed with permission of Linda Omichinski, HUGS International		
ISSUE	DIET THINKING	NON-DIET THINKING
Goal	Weight loss	Confidence in ability to make choices for better health
Progress	Any weight loss	Gradual lifestyle changes
Self-acceptance	Only after weight loss is achieved	Starts the natural self- nurturingcycle
Success	Goal weight	Energetic daily living, increased self-esteem
Exercise	No pain, no gain should/shouldn't	Get hooked on increasing activity, fun & energy
Food	Food is the enemy, deprivation, willpower	Food is the friend celebrate,enjoy, savor
Language	Should I have it?	Do I want it?
Thinking	All-or-nothing	I can have it if I want it.
Attitude	Perfectionistic	Flexible, goes with the flow
Choice	No choice / Diet in control	Person in charge, decides what to eat
Hunger	Out of touch with physical hunger	In tune with body's internal cues of physical hunger

Endnotes

1. Waterhouse, D. (1997) *Like Mother, Like Daughter: How Women are Influenced by Their Mothers' Relationship with Food—and How to Break the Pattern*. New York: Hyperion Books, p. 10

2. Friedman, S. (1997, 2001) *When Girls Feel Fat: Helping Girls Through Adolescence*. Toronto: HarperCollins, Firefly, p. 155

3. Seid, R. P. (1994) "Too 'close to the bone': The historical context for women's obsession with slenderness," in Fallon et al. (eds.) *Feminist Perspectives on Eating Disorders*, New York: The Guilford Press, p. 8

4. Feldman, W.F., Feldman, E. & J. Goodman. (1986) "Health concerns and health related behaviors of adolescents," *CMAJ*, No. 134: 489-493

5. Maloney, M.J., McGuire, J., Daniels, S.R. & B. Specker. (1990) "Dieting behavior and eating attitudes in children," *Pediatrics*, May; 85(5): 714

6. Smolak, L., Levine, M.P. & F. Schermer. (1998) "A controlled evaluation of an elementary school primary prevention program for eating problems," *Journal of Psychosomatic Research*, 44:339-354

7. Cooper, P.J. &I. Goodyer. (1997) "Prevalence and significance of weight and shape concerns in girls aged 11-16 years old," *Br J Psychiatry,* Dec: 171:542-544

8. Berg, F. (May/June 1992) "Who is dieting in the United States?" pp. 48-49

9. Jones, J. M., Bennett, S., Olmsted, M.P., Lawson, M.L. & G.Rodin, (2001) "Disordered eating attitudes and behaviours in teenaged girls: a school-based study," *CMAJ*; 165(5):547-52

10. Paxton, S. J. (1999) "Peer relations, body image, and disordered eating in adolescent girls: Implications for prevention," in Piran, N. and M.P.Levine and C. Steiner-Adair (Eds.) *Preventing Eating Disorders: A Handbook of Interventions and Special Challenges*, Philadelphia: Brunner/Mazel, p. 91

11. Levine, M. P., Smolak, L., Moodey, A.F., Shuman, M.D. & L.D. Hessen. (1994) "Normative developmental challenges and dieting and eating disturbance in middle school girls," *International Journal of Eating Disorders*, 15: 11-20

12. Waterhouse, pp. 2-3

13. Ibid, pp. 48-49

14. LeCrone, H. (1950) "How preoccupation with food leads to loss of control," in Ancel Keys et al *The Biology of Human Starvation*, Minneapolis: University of Minnesota Press

15. Lyons, P. (2000, Fall) "Challenging the 'war on obesity'" *Perspective: A Professional Journal of the Renfrew Center Foundation*, 6(1): 10

16. Patton, G.C., Selzer, R., Coffey, C., Carlin, J.B. & R. Wolfe. (1999) "Onset of adolescent eating disorders: population based cohort study," *BMJ*, March 20: 318(7186):765-768

17. Orbach, S. (1978, 1998) *Fat is a Feminist Issue*. New York: Galahad Books

18. Fleming, A.T "Daughters of Dieters," *Glamour Magazine*, November, 1994, p. 222

19. Siegler, A. (1993) "Grieving the lost dreams of thinness," in Brown, C. and K. Jasper, (Eds.) *Consuming Passions: Feminist Approaches to Weight Preoccupation and Eating Disorders*. Toronto: Second Storey Press, pp. 152-154

20. Omichinski, L. (May/June 1993) "A paradigm shift from weight loss to healthy living," *Healthy Weight Journal*
21. Stinson, K. M. (2001) *Women And Dieting Culture: Inside A Commercial Weight Loss Group.* New Brunswick, New Jersey: Rutgers University Press

11

∽∞∽

Food, Glorious Food

It used to be that when we said we sinned last night, every-one knew we had sex. Today if we say we sinned last night, people immediately think about chocolate and other food we 'shouldn't' really have.

"When we eat lunch everybody watches what everybody else eats. They say 'oh, are you eating that? That's so gross. That will make you fat.'"   Caleigh, 14 year old girl

Most women grow up with an uneasy relationship with food and eating. For those of us who have been chronic dieters, eating is often accompanied by shame and by guilt for being or thinking we are overweight. Eating with gusto and without apology is sometimes seen as breaking the female rule of dieting and deprivation. On a recent trip the flight attendant came by with a tray of soft drinks, asked the men what they wanted and automatically handed the women a diet cola.

Most of us with disordered eating patterns have learned to categorize what we eat into foods that we really want but can't have, foods we should have but don't want, foods we think are healthy, and foods we think will make us fat. We don't know when we're hungry or when we are full. Since our knowledge of nutrition comes mainly from counting calories or grams of fat, we rarely consider fueling our bodies to make ourselves strong. We worry so much about food, but often don't eat enough to sustain ourselves.

Food is an important part of our social life. Many of us are born into cultures that are identified by unique customs focusing upon food. What we eat and how we select food is influenced by the availability of certain foods, by how much money we have (or lack), and by our individual tastes. Sometimes we eat for psychological reasons—as a way of dealing with feelings that are difficult to express.

Girls' Erratic Relationship to Food

Girls' erratic relationship to food often begins when they are born. Some mothers, harboring a great fear of fat, are known to wean their babies onto skim milk to ensure that they will be thin when they grow up. In the process they stunt their growth.

As girls grow up they tend to adopt the eating style of their parents because the foods that are available in the home are those that the parents enjoy.[1] Their early exposure to foods such as fruits, vegetables and foods high in sugar and fat dictate what foods girls will accept and prefer.[2] Parents who don't trust their own relationship with food often over-feed or under-feed their children—which destroys their hunger mechanism and their ability to regulate their food intake.

In an Illinois study, preschool children were given a snack of pudding a few minutes before their meal. They were then allowed to eat as much or as little of the meal as they wanted. Some of the children got pudding snacks that were high in calories and some got low-calorie pudding. Most of the children compensated at lunch for the calories in the snack. If the pudding was low in calories, they ate more lunch. If it was high in calories they ate less lunch.

But some of the children failed to compensate. They ate the same amount of lunch whether they had the high or low-calorie pudding. Researchers found that those children could not gauge their hunger because their parents managed the amount of food those children ate. They just ate everything put before them.[3] Another study that rewarded children for eating everything on their plates found that children could be taught to ignore how full they were and eat for the reward.[4] When children and parents struggle early over feeding, the kids are more likely to be fat as teenagers.[5]

By the time girls are 10, many are already skipping breakfast. Sometimes this is because there is no food in the house. Sometimes there is nobody home to prepare it, or to socialize with while they are eating. Some girls are responsible for younger children (either their siblings or their neighbor's children) and have no time to eat themselves. One of the consequences of not eating is being malnourished, constantly feeling tired and 'spaced out.' This means not being able to concentrate in class.

Girls need to eat more during puberty because they are growing, but they often see their need to eat as abnormal (as do we) and restrict their food intake because they are afraid of gaining weight. One girl said to me, "I eat and eat and think that I am not normal. My mother says that I am going through a growth spurt. Is that really true?"

During adolescence girls alternate between 'pigging out' and feeling guilty, and then dieting and feeling in control. Girls constantly juggle their desire for 'junk' foods against 'healthy' foods. 'Healthy' foods are seen as good because they are high in nutritional value and don't contain 'bad' ingredients such as fat, sugar and cholesterol. 'Junk' foods are affordable, convenient, taste good and part of the teen culture. Because they are often eaten outside the home they are associated with freedom— with walking to the store with friends or hanging out at a certain restaurant.[5]

Normalizing Girls' Relationship With Food

It takes a long time for those of us who are getting off diets (or are diet drop-outs) to develop a comfortable relationship with food. We don't eat enough at some times and overeat at others. We may not be counting calories but we are still conscious of grams of fat. We try to transform our dieting behavior into a restrictive definition of what we consider to be normal eating: eating only when we are hungry and always stopping when we are full; replacing the 'good' foods and 'bad' foods of dieting with the foods of 'healthy' eating. This only works for a short time because it is artificial and has nothing to do with the actual needs of our bodies.

According to Ellyn Satter, nutritionist and author of *Secrets of Feeding a Healthy Family,* normal eating is a flexible, positive and joyous experience rather than the punitive one that most of us practice.[6]

NORMAL EATING

• Normal eating is going to the table hungry and eating until you are satisfied.

• Normal eating is being able to choose food you like and to eat it and truly get enough of it—not just stopping because you think you should.

• Normal eating is being able to give some thought to your food selection so you get nutritious food, but not being so wary and restrictive that you miss out on enjoyable food.

• Normal eating is sometimes giving yourself permission to eat because you are happy, sad, or bored, or just because it feels good.

• Normal eating is three meals a day—or four or five—or it can be choosing to munch along the way.

• Normal eating is trusting your body to make up for your mistakes in eating.

• Normal eating is leaving some cookies on the plate because you know you can have some again tomorrow, or eating more now because they taste so wonderful.

• Normal eating is overeating at times; feeling stuffed and uncomfortable. And it can be under eating at times and wishing you had more.

• Normal eating takes up some of your time and attention but keeps its place as only one important area of your life.

• Normal eating is flexible. It varies in response to your hunger, your schedule, your proximity to food and your feelings.

It takes practice and awareness for all of us to learn to eat normally. Many women and girls have tremendous anxiety around eating because of our fears of getting fat. The idea of 'forbidden' food is so ingrained that it takes time for us to get beyond it. As well as being obsessed with 'good' food to control our weight, we also feel tremendous responsibility for our health. This is because we are constantly bombarded with new studies that show that certain foods prevent cancer and others prevent heart disease and still others prevent osteoarthritis—all of which are caused by something else that we eat. Food and drink manufacturers capitalize on our guilt by advertising special 'healthy' ingredients that are added to their products. Viewing food as medicine takes the joy and pleasure out of food and out of the social process of eating.[7]

Teach Girls to Eat with Awareness and Sensuality

Years ago I co-facilitated a group for women called *Learning to Love Yourself.* At the last follow-up session we would do a food ritual with the women. We would ask them to bring some food to share with the rest of the group. At the end of the evening we would gather quietly around the table where we placed the food. Each woman took a turn coming up to the table and selecting a food. She smelled the food, looked at its color and texture and then put it in her mouth. She ran her tongue over the food and paid attention to the taste and to the feeling of the food in her mouth. She paid attention to what it felt like as she swallowed the food. Throughout the ritual she voiced her thoughts and feelings out loud. When she was finished another woman took her place.

After all the women had a turn, they talked about what the exercise was like for them. For many, the food ritual was the highlight of the program. Because so many women relate to food as an enemy, it began a process of helping them eat with awareness and bringing back the sensuality.

We can teach girls in groups or individually to eat with awareness and to bring back sensuality—not just as a one-time exercise but on a continuous basis:

• Help girls pay attention to their hunger signals by paying attention to what they feel and what they are telling themselves when they want to eat. This will help them distinguish between stomach hunger, emotional eating, eating for distraction and eating because everybody else is.

• Get rid of distractions. Find a quiet place and turn off the television or the music while you are eating.

• Have the girls spend some quiet time before they eat. Five minutes of sitting with their eyes closed and concentrating on their breathing helps them bring the focus from outside back inside themselves. This may be difficult at first with girls who are always on the go or think it is silly but don't give up. Suggest they think of a quiet place, a sunny place, a comforting place or anything else that can make this into a friendly ritual.

• Have girls pay attention to the smell, color and texture of a particular food. Have them put food into their mouths and pay attention to the taste and how it feels when they swallow.

• Talk about what the experience was like. Some girls will find this easy to do. Others take longer to get over the fear—especially of eating in public and 'forbidden' foods.

The Debate About Fat Consumption

The attitudes that we develop towards foods that contain fat are similar to the attitudes that we have towards fat people. According to nutritionist Frances M. Berg, studies began to appear in the late 1980's linking high-fat diets to obesity and heart disease. People were advised to cut down on their fat consumption so the maximum amount of fat they ate was no more than 30% of their diet and only 10% unsaturated fat.

'Cut down' was transformed by many into 'eliminate.' As a result, many teenage girls—already the most poorly nourished of any group in North America—don't drink milk or eat meat in their extreme fear of fat. Many university students strive to eat zero fat. As many as 81% of 10 year old girls in a California study were afraid to eat fat and felt guilty if they did so.

While low-fat diets may benefit some people, they harm others. According to Berg, health problems related to low dietary fat intake are now beginning to surface. Low-fat diets have been shown to lower 'good' HDL cholesterol levels. There is also confusion over what exactly is good fat. In an attempt to lower their fat, people have turned to high-sugar, calorie-dense, low fiber, highly-processed food and have increased their daily energy intake of calories.[8]

There are differing views in the United States and Canada about the fat intake recommended for children. Nutritionists and pediatricians in the United States recommend that children adopt the restriction of 30% fat/10% unsaturated fat when they are between the ages of 2 and 5. In Canada, however, there is a call for a gradual transition that begins at age 2 and lasts through the growth period until adult height is achieved. The belief here is that if you restrict fat intake—especially from the dairy and meat groups—this results in reduced access to other important nutrients. As a result, lower fat intake can compromise nutrition and growth. As well, children with low-fat diets tend to have deficient intakes of energy, protein, calcium and other nutrients and also tend to be smaller in stature.[9]

A nutritionist on a daytime TV show elegantly summed up her suspicion of low-fat food by stating she wouldn't eat something if she couldn't pronounce the names of its ingredients.

Fat is a necessary part of our diet, regardless of how we feel about it. Fat supports normal body growth and the development of healthy cells in the brain. It gives food flavor. It provides the extra energy that the body needs to support growth spurts. Having fat in your diet doesn't mean eating three bags of chips a day. It means that we encourage girls to have the fat requirements that they need.

Providing Appropriate Nutrition Education

While nutrition education is an important part of prevention, we need to think carefully about how we provide it. According to Ellyn Satter, "the best nutrition education at school helps young girls support and extend their intuitive eating capabilities and reinforces their trust in themselves and in their relationship with food. For older girls it reinforces their trust in their own ability to eat what is right for them." [10]

The information that we give girls should teach them what the different categories of food groups do and about the relationship that carbohydrates, protein and fat have to their well-being. This will help girls make informed choices instead of reactive decisions. We also need to help girls explore the latest myths around food. For example, one young client of mine who is struggling with bulimia feels guilty eating carbohydrates because her father who is a devotee of the latest 'truth' keeps telling her that they are bad.

The traditional way of giving girls information about healthy foods does little to change behavior. We need to rethink our tendency to use the *Food Guide Pyramid* or the *Canada Food Rules* to teach children about food and nutrition. According to Ellyn Satter, this just confuses them because they are not able to apply the nutrition rules which stress negativity and restraint and avoidance instead of exploration, adventure and trust.[11]

We need to be careful that school health education and health promotion messages are positive. Using negative language and focusing on problem-based messages perpetuate the myth that foods such as sugar and fat are 'bad' and that other foods are 'good.' These messages also produce an atmosphere of fear and apprehension around food and eating that not only reduces the enjoyment of food but may also contribute to eating problems.[12]

Putting Nutrition Education into Practice

When girls are young, expose them to a wide variety of foods and let them decide what to eat and how much. We have a tendency to follow toddlers and young children around to make sure they get enough nutrients. Yet even if they eat a lot of one food group and none of another, over time they do eat balanced diet because they are listening to their bodies and not to their heads. It is only when girls start school that they stop listening to their stomachs and start becoming defined by the world around them.

• Avoid labels such as 'healthy eating' or 'junk foods' because they promote an either/or approach to food. Instead, place the focus on achieving a balance.

• Recognize that what we label as 'junk' food is seen as normal eating behavior by adolescents. Girls who eat only 'healthy' food are seen as weird.

• When girls do eat fast food, encourage them to limit the servings that they receive. Many restaurants today offer more fries and bigger drinks for just a little bit more money. It's always hard to resist a bargain.

• Talk about food as energy. Discuss what happens when your body doesn't have enough fuel.

• Allow teens to have input into their meals. Find creative ways of compromising around food. Share your feelings about what you want and help them plan what they want.

• Do not use food as a punishment or a reward.

• Don't restrict access to food that is in the house. When food is restricted girls will seek it out in greater quantities.

• Any changes in family meal choices should focus on healthy food for everyone and not single out one person.

• Have dinner with your children. Children who eat with their families are more likely to eat the five or more recommended servings of fruit and vegetables and are less likely to eat fried foods away from home or drink soft drinks.

• Don't make meals a battleground. Agree to resolve your conflicts in a more neutral place.

• Encourage girls to build strong bodies. Girls who eat foods with calcium and participate in weight-bearing physical activities develop stronger, denser bones. The National Bone Health Campaign (NBHC) *"Powerful Bones, Powerful Girls,"* is a multi-year national campaign to promote optimal bone health in girls 9-12 years old and thus reduce their risk of osteoporosis later on. It features a web site for girls <www.cdc.gov/powrfulbones>.

• Encourage girls to eat breakfast. Skipping breakfast regularly gets their body attuned to not being hungry until close to suppertime and causes them to overeat at supper and all night long. As they get used to eating breakfast, they will notice in a few weeks that they are eating less later on because they are fuelling their body regularly with the energy it needs to do the daily activities. Eating breakfast allows girls to be hungry more often so that they fuel their bodies and give them food when they need it.[13]

• Encourage girls to cut down on caffeine. Many girls consume the equivalent in caffeinated sodas of three to five cups of coffee a day. Girls are constantly bombarded with advertising and many high schools raise money by signing exclusive deals with companies like Pepsi or Coke. Drinks such as Coke, Pepsi and Mountain Dew contain phosphorus which can impede the body's ability to utilize dietary calcium when calcium is low.[14] Ten per cent of 13 to 18 year old girls drink five cans or more of soft drinks a day and 25% of them drink 3½ cans a day. They do so at the expense of their milk intake.[15]

• Encourage your school to serve nutritious meals in the cafeteria and to limit high fat / high sugar snacks in vending machines. Many school cafeterias feature fast food while rejecting foods high in calcium such as milk and yogurt.

• Encourage girls to eat more carbohydrates. This causes them to crave less sugar because carbohydrates are a natural source of sugar and give them immediate energy as they break down in the body. If girls don't get this energy source naturally, it will cause them to crave sources of high sugar foods such as candies, cakes and cookies.[16]

• Teach girls to not eat candy or chocolate or drink cola, root beer or chocolate milk on an empty stomach. An overproduction of insulin by the pancreas causes their blood sugar to rise and drop quickly which gives them a boost of energy and then wipes them out.

• Teach girls that if they eat quickly, they don't taste their food. Moreover, they will be hungry sooner.

• Teach girls that if they eat more regularly they can begin to taste the food and the texture of the food. This is a satisfying and sensual experience.

• Encourage girls to eat more during the day. This decreases binges later on. When girls have access to food energy they are more alert, can function better in school and have more energy for physical activity.

FEATURE RESOURCE

Healthy Body Image: Teaching Kids to Eat and Love Their Bodies Too!

Healthy Body Image was developed by Kathy J. Kater for use with girls and boys in grades four to six. It consists of eleven classroom lessons that challenge prevailing cultural norms about body size and shape; address the purpose of healthy eating and physical activity; and examines the role of the mass media in the perception of body image. Each lesson outlines the goals and describes the desired outcomes for students.

The lessons also provide the teacher (or other facilitator) with background material, a suggested lesson script, concepts needed to teach the lesson and suggestions for group discussion. Activities that are imaginative and engage and hold the attention reinforce the concepts being taught. The lessons include:

Growth and Change in Appearance

The Development of Unrealistic and Negative Body Images in Western Society

Identity and Competency

How Your Appearance Will Change in Puberty

Genetics

Understanding the Internal Weight Regulatory System

Sold on Looks

Hunger and Eating, Eating Well for Confidence in Body Weight

Physical Activity for Health and Confidence in Body Weight

Compared to Whom

Endnotes

1. Oliveria, S.A., Ellison, R.C., Moore, L.L., Gillman, M.E., Garrahie, E.J.,& Singer, M.R., (1992) "Parent-child relationships in nutrient intake: the Framingham children's study," American Journal of Clinical Nutrition, 63: 593-598
2. Birch, L.L. (1992) "Children's preferences for high fat food," Nutrition Review, 50:249-255
3. Johnson, S.L. & L.L. Birch (1994) "Parents' and children's adiposity and eating style," Pediatrics, 94:653-661
4. Birch, LL, McPhee, L, & Shoba B. C. et al, (1987) "Clean up your plate: effects of child feeding practices on the conditioning of meal size," Learning and Motivation: 18:301-317
5. Crawford, P.B. & L.R. Shapiro (1991) "How obesity develops: A new look at nature and nurture," in Obesity and Health, F.M. Berg (ed.) Hettinger, N.D. Healthy Living Institute, pp. 40-41
6. Chapman, G. & H. MacLean (1993) "Junk food and healthy food: Means of food in adolescent women's culture," Journal of Nutritional Education, No. 2
7. Satter, E. (1999) Secrets of Feeding a Healthy Family. Kelcy Press, Madison, WI, p. 5
8. Ibid
9. Berg, F.M. (July/August 1998) "Rethinking low-fat advice," Healthy Weight Journal, Vol. 12. No. 4
10. Nutrition Recommendations Update: Dietary Fat and Children, Report of the joint working group of the Canadian Pediatric Society and Health Canada
11. Satter, p. 181
12. Ibid
13. Center for Science in the Public Interest (March/April 2000) in Healthy Weight Journal, Vol. 14, No. 2
14. Ibid
15. Ibid
16. Brody, Jane E., "Added Sugars are Taking a toll on Health," New York Times, September 12, 2000
17. Omichinski, L. (1995) Teens and Diets No Weigh HUGS for Teens & Diets: Parent Guide IV, p. 15

12

∞

Becoming Physically Active

"I used to be really good at soccer. Before grade 6 the guys and girls would play on the same soccer team and the guys actually accepted that I was good and let me play net and stuff. But as soon as grade 6 it was like 'you're a girl,' 'you can't do anything,' so I stopped playing."

Amy, a fourteen year old girl

"PE teachers should take a poll of what the kids want to do. Make sure that through the course of the year they cover the things that the class wants to do. Make sure that people will actually have fun in PE."

Amelia, a fourteen year old girl

"I've always been a big girl. People misinterpret my body and its abilities. They assume that I'm terrible in sports and have no coordination whatsoever...There are a lot of us so-called fat people that can move. My playing field of choice is the dance floor. I may not have Barbie's body but my skills as a dancer continue to get recognition and I'm proud of what I've accomplished. For someone to take one look at my weight and dismiss my abilities is someone that needs to expand their narrow mind."

Debbie Litonjua, Promotion Plus Network News
Vol. 12, No. 1, Spring 2001

Tremendous benefits come from being physically active. Regular physical activity makes us stronger. It improves our concentration, our posture, our breathing and our digestion and helps us sleep better. It helps us deal with tiredness and stress. It lowers our cholesterol and blood pressure and can reduce the risk of coronary heart disease by 50%.[1] Physical activity contributes to the building of maximum bone mass before we are 35 and to maintaining it during the rest of our life cycle, thus preventing osteoporosis.[2] Regular physical activity can reduce our risk of breast cancer by a third or more–postmenopausal women who do the equivalent of a 30 minute brisk walk daily (in addition to regular daily activities) see their risk of developing breast cancer fall by 30 per cent.[3] It ensures we are healthy regardless of whether we are fat or thin.[4] As we get older, regular aerobic exercise improves our cardiovascular system to nourish our brain which improves our memory.[5]

Physical activity is a major component in the prevention of eating disorders and fat+plus in children. Girls who participate in physical activity on a regular basis are more able to remain connected to their bodies during adolescence. They are more able to experience them kinesthetically from the inside instead of focusing on how their different body parts look on the outside. By having a secure relationship with their bodies and experiencing them as functional rather than decorative, girls are more likely to feel positive about them regardless of their size.

There are many other health and social benefits derived from being physically active. Girls who participate in a daily 30 minutes of regular physical activity benefit from improved health, fitness and motor skills and have increased aerobic capacity, strength and endurance. Physical activity can buffer the effects of anxiety and depression.[6] It has a positive effect on how girls do in school in terms of memory, observation and problem solving as well as making a significant improvement in attitude, discipline, behavior and creativity.[7]

Even though girls are biologically capable of being physically equal to boys when they are young there are some differences in performance and fitness levels between the genders.[8] By the time girls are six, they have lower fitness levels and less skill competence than boys of the same age.[9] At 12, their involvement in physical activity begins to decline steadily—until only 11% of them are still active when they are 16 and 17.[10] If girls don't have a history of physical activity during childhood and adolescence, they are less likely to be physically active as adults.[11]

In this chapter we will look at a broad definition of physical activity that includes but does not focus upon sports. The next chapter will specifically address girls and organized sports.

The Crisis in Physical Education

There was a time when being physically active was a natural part of play and of growing up. Those were the days when it didn't require two salaries just to survive, when parents weren't always exhausted from juggling family and work, when personal computers hadn't been invented, when cable TV didn't exist, when everybody kept an eye out for each other's children and the fear of abduction or molestation rarely entered anyone's mind.

Today, structural and social changes in our living arrangements and our lives limit girls' ability to play informally. Because of the changing demands on their lives, adults have patterned their kids' lives away from their natural tendency to play actively. Fewer than one in four children get 20 minutes of vigorous activity daily (or half an hour of any type of physical activity every day of the week).

The only opportunity that many girls get to participate in physical activity is in school. Despite recommendations that schools provide 30 minutes of daily physical education for every grade level,[12] this is available to only 36% of Canadian children in grades one to twelve.[13] At recess and at lunch time girls tend to huddle together talking and playing quiet games on the sidelines while boys take up most of the space in the schoolyard. Nearly 50% of young people ages 12 to 21 (and over one-third of high school students) do not participate in vigorous physical activity on a regular basis.[14]

Every province in Canada requires mandatory physical education in grade seven, eight and nine–except for Ontario where it is not required in grade nine. Although physical education is offered in grades ten and eleven it is usually one of several elective courses the student can chose from. In the United States only Illinois requires mandatory physical education for all students in grades K to 12. In schools that do offer physical education, there are often barriers that stand in the way of girls fully participating and learning the skills that they need.

The Experiences of Nine to Twelve Year Old Girls

Few elementary schools have qualified physical education teachers. Most often these classes are run by classroom teachers who have little training and are not provided with support by the school nor by the educational system. While there are teachers who are active themselves and committed to making physical education a priority, most teachers feel a lack of self-confidence that limits their use of equipment and activities in the gym. Sometimes teachers withdraw physical education in order to punish students for misbehaving in class or pre-empt it for subjects that are considered more important.

Sometimes teachers have to deal with a class that includes children with physical disabilities, children with behavior problems and children with developmental challenges. Funding for teachers' aids or support personnel is often lacking and teachers are reluctant or feel unqualified to teach these classes by themselves. Most of these teachers are women who bring with them their own negative experiences in physical education and pass these attitudes onto the girls.[15]

According to Myra and David Sadker, authors of *Failing at Fairness: How Our Schools Cheat Girls*, boys receive most of the attention in the classroom.[16] Unlike girls, who mature earlier than them, when boys enter elementary school they move into a world that is out of synch with their cognitive and physical development. Their need for physical activity makes it difficult for many of them to adapt to the restricted environment of the classroom. Female teachers spend a great deal of time trying to dampen and diffuse the energy of the boys because of their fear that its eruption will cause chaos in the classroom. They leave girls to their own resources or use the girls to quiet down and socialize the boys.

Many teachers interact differently with boys than they do with girls. They praise boys on their skills and correct their mistakes. They help them and encourage them. They give them specific feedback. Girls receive less time, less help and fewer challenges. They are praised on their efforts, but too often their achievements are attributed not to skill but to luck.[17] When this dynamic plays itself out in the gym, girls fail to learn the motor skills necessary for them to participate in and enjoy physical activity and sport. They don't learn to perform basic bodily movements confidently or develop skills such as throwing catching, hitting and kicking. They begin to undervalue and underestimate their own capacity and potential for competency in physical activity and to fall further behind boys in skill development.[18]

Girls believe that it should be fun to participate in physical education. Grade four girls explain that gym class is fun and classroom activities are work. Fun is associated with having more strength and energy and with feeling good. It is the balance between skill and challenge—something that should be applied to teaching all subjects not just physical education. Girls have fun when games and activities are geared towards their skill level. For example, girls who feel confident passing a ball to a teammate or skipping to a double-Dutch sequence will have fun because they experience challenge, excitement and success.[19] Girls also have fun when they are able to play their favorite activities and games and when they are able to socialize with their friends.

Even at the age of nine girls see boys as the main barrier to their being able to have fun and are uncomfortable participating in physical activities with them.[20] This is because boys bring a different kind of energy and very different goals to physical education classes. In the male developmental schema competition is seen as necessary to prepare boys to take their place in the larger world. Organized sports (which make up most of the physical education curriculum) socialize boys by providing them with the attributes society sees as necessary for developing a masculine identity—such as aggression, competitive spirit and athletic skills.[21]

Many boys don't want to play with girls, especially girls who are less skilled than they are. They place them on the bottom of the hierarchy (with boys who are relatively unskilled and therefore suffer the same fate as girls). They tease them and make disparaging comments about their efforts and abilities. They exclude them from their games and rarely pass the ball to them.

They intimidate them by pushing and shoving them and calling them names. As one grade four girl said "Sometimes when you can't do it, they say bad things. If we don't hit it right, we don't get a point and then they get mad." "I want to try out for the basketball team," says one grade six girl, "but I'm not that good. The boys won't let me play with them because I'm not as good as they are. Even when they do let me play they push and shove me and won't throw the ball."

Girls who are skilled in sports silence themselves and tend to hold back when playing with boys. In grade four girls refuse to be the leader or the shooter and defer to a boy, often assuming that he will go first. In grade five girls back down in discussions about game situations. They won't try to control the play in a game as the boys do by calling out instructions. By grade six they hold back when playing on teams with boys. They pass rather than attempt to score a basket or a goal. When these same girls participate in all-girl situations they don't defer to anyone, are clear in their explanations and are uninhibited in the play.[22]

Girls see boys as being stronger and more physically skilled than they are. Often the teacher reinforces this belief by placing boys in leadership positions such as making them team captains and having them coach the girls. When girls feel that they can't keep up or be as good as the boys or fear that they will be overwhelmed by them, many remove themselves from sporting activities. Can you imagine as an adult being repeatedly put in a situation where you are belittled and ineffectual and made to feel totally self-conscious and a failure? You'd leave—which is what most girls do as soon as they can.

Girls experience a lot of fear about getting hurt when they don't have the skills to play the games. This limits their ability to have fun. They talk about sprains, scrapes and getting hit on the head with the ball. Because they don't have much knowledge about their bodies, some girls get scared when they feel their heart beating heavily or when they sweat as a result of aerobic activity.[23]

The Experiences of Adolescent Girls

Many girls drop out of physical education after grade nine when it is no longer mandatory for them to take it. Just as in elementary school, a large percentage of the high school curriculum is based on team sports and is competition-oriented. Many girls simply don't want to repeat the negative experiences that they have already had.

Some girls drop out of physical education because they are self-conscious about their changing bodies. Body image concerns make them reluctant to change their clothes in front of other girls or be scrutinized wearing shorts during class. Some girls have to run around the gym without the support of athletic bras because they have not been made aware of their existence. Often there is not enough time after PE classes for girls to shower or change so that they must go around sweaty for the rest of the day.

Adolescent girls cite competition. lack of fun and harassment by boys as the main reasons they stay away.[24] Grade nine girls talk about not having the skills to feel confident or to derive enjoyment from playing sports. They compare themselves to others who are on organized teams outside of class and thus have more opportunity to practice. They talk about feeling self-conscious about being watched when they compete. One girl says "I try hard but usually I lack the skills and feel like a fool." "I hate the way they look at you," says another. "It puts your confidence down. Like, you're going to feel bad if someone thinks you're not good enough for the team. It puts you down."[25]

Girls who have the option of taking PE in the latter part of high school decide not to take it because of the boys who cut them down, exclude them, ridicule them and hurt their feelings.[26] Boys make comments about their skill level. Says one girl "You never get the ball. The boys make comments—'oh, you're too slow, you couldn't have caught it'." Says another "If you're playing with the boys, you'll always get picked last. The team captains will always be boys because the teachers assume they know more about the sport and they'll pick their friends and then the girls they know or popular girls can play and if you're not their friend you'll get picked last."

Physical education class is a time when girls' bodies feel really exposed to the boys and their comments. Says one girl "If there is a bigger girl running around the gym and they are running a little bit slow and the guys are dashing by thinking they are so good, then they say something like 'thump, thump, thump, there must be an earthquake.'" Often their comments are sexual. Says one girl "Guys are pigs. If they are standing there where you are doing jumping jacks they will say 'oh, baby.'"

Girls limit their opportunities by learning to accept boys' hassles. Rather than demanding that they stop, they usually try to ignore the boys because they feel that if they do something, they will just make it worse by drawing attention to themselves. Girls come to believe that physical education is more important for the boys than for them—'because everything in PE is made for guys.' Eventually they lose interest and drop out, bored and discouraged.[27]

Some girls drop out of physical education because it is not valued in their schools. In many schools physical education tends to be seen as a luxury or a non-academic subject—a 'throw away' course. It is usually the first subject to be eliminated when schools are threatened with cuts to education.[28] Girls are told by administrators and teachers to concentrate first on academics, especially if they want to get into college or university.[29] Rarely are girls told about the benefits of physical activity to their lives, their health and their sense of well-being—especially how being physically active can help them do better in school.

Shifting the Emphasis Away from Sport

Girls surveyed about this subject want a variety of personal fitness activities such as aerobics, weight training and self-defense. They want extra-curricular outdoor activities such as hiking and canoeing as well as opportunities to use community recreation facilities. They see physical education as providing an opportunity to socialize with their friends that is not offered in other classes.

In Canada and in the United States changes are already in the works to move the focus in physical education away from competitive sports to physical activity and fitness. Many provinces have revised or are in the process of revising their physical education curriculum to integrate PE with health and to encourage active living and lifelong physical activity. In Spokane, Washington, students in one school use heart-rate monitors, exercise bands and other equipment to help them learn to stay in shape. The plan is to have all schools in Washington State onboard in the next five years. While it seems exciting that changes are in the works and that personal health, active living and fitness will become a part of any quality physical education program they should not totally replace sports. We need to ensure that we don't take an either/or approach for in so doing we just replace one group of kids whose needs are not getting met with another.

All over Canada and the United States there are creative physical education teachers developing innovative programs to meet the needs of their students. Yet these creative teachers work mostly in isolation with little support from their educational system and their attempts are often sporadic. In many places changes are happening at the same time that education budgets are being cut, placing more pressure on teachers who are already overloaded.

While changes in the curriculum are needed and welcome, they are of no value if they remain at the policy level because there is no money for training and supporting the teachers who have to implement them. We need to make sure that good balanced programs are implemented and that teachers are supported. We need to look at how sustainable these programs are in terms of changing attitudes and instilling in kids a lifelong desire to use their bodies. While we develop new curriculums and programs to be implemented in all of our schools, we need to improve the existing ones.

What You Can Do

Regardless of where your school is in the process of change, you might find the following suggestions useful. You can adapt them to elementary and secondary school students and to your own interests and abilities. They can be valuable not only to teachers but also for those of you who otherwise work with girls and want to increase their participation in physical activity. Parents will find these useful as a basis for negotiating girl-friendly programs in schools.

Be Aware of Your Own Beliefs and Behavior

• How important is physical activity in your own life? How often do you participate? What stands in your way?

• Think about your own experiences with physical education. What were the things that made you want to participate? What did you hate?

• What were the barriers that stood in your way? Are you replicating them or helping prevent them today in your interactions with girls?

• What are your beliefs about the differing physical abilities of girls and boys?

Pay attention to how you treat the girls and the boys. Most of us want to treat them fairly and equally and believe that we do. Often we are surprised when we find out how much we placate the boys and ignore the girls or encourage the boys and discount the girls. One of the most eye-opening experiences I had was in a workshop I facilitated for a group of teachers. During the break, one woman pointed out to me that I paid more attention to the men, answering all their questions and praising them for their input. To my chagrin, she was right. Whenever I became annoyed at the men for interrupting I placated them instead of asking them to wait. This incident generated a teachable moment and a really good discussion when I brought it up with the group after the break.

Consider the Importance of Gender

Ensure that attention is paid to the importance of gender in your school. When we develop generic programs for 'youth,' as most organizations tend to do, we do a disservice to both girls and boys by making the programs the same and not addressing their particular developmental and gender needs.

Make the Program and Activities Student Driven

Include girls in the planning. Ask them what they want to do and give them realistic choices. If we are going to design and implement programs that will encourage girls to be physically active, then we need to be prepared to listen to them and to act upon the information that they share with us.

Teach Skills[30]

Why would anyone want to participate in something that makes her feel lousy? If we want girls to be active then we have to begin by teaching them skills:

• Provide a range of activities that reflect the various movements that you want to teach such as hitting, catching, throwing, running, pivoting and jumping. This will provide girls with the opportunity to develop a wide range of skills.

• Provide a lot of practice time for skill development and improvement in girl-only groups. This way girls don't feel embarrassed when they make a mistake.

• Use small groups such as pairs, groups of three, two against two—and keep mixing them around. This gives everybody fair chances and increases their opportunity to practice. It also ensures participants are active, rather than waiting for a turn and makes it a lot safer for girls to learn. It also helps to pair girls with their friends because they can provide each other with support.

• Modify the equipment and rules to suit the size and skill level of the girls. You can use a beach ball instead of a volleyball, play soccer in a smaller area and designate a target on the wall for basketball until girls are ready to move onto the regulation field and court. This will help them experience more success and therefore be fun and will increase participation.

• Ask girls to make up their own games using the skills that you are teaching and have them teach these games to small girls-only groups. If you are teaching dancing, girls can also make up dances with different steps and sequences and teach them to their friends.

Give Everyone a Chance to Play and Develop

• Find creative ways to include everyone. When 100 boys and 8 girls showed up for intramural basketball in a middle school, the teacher assigned four points to baskets scored by the girls and by the grade 6 boys who were also being left out. This gave more aggressive boys a good reason to pass the ball more often.

• Try to avoid games and activities where kids are eliminated. If elimination is part of your game or activity make sure that everyone has a way of getting back into the activity very quickly and change the rules so that more kids stay involved.

• Keep games and activities short. Girls will participate even if this is not their favorite activity because they know it will soon be over. Having a variety of activities ensures that everybody gets a chance to do something that they can succeed at, that they want to do and that they are interested in.

• When playing games and sports, change the players and teams around on a regular basis so that the focus is on participation and skill development and fun instead of on scoring and winning.

Vary the Activities and Provide More Choice

Girls need to be aware that physical activity is not just about basketball and baseball. They need to understand that their needs are important and that there is something for them.

• Try to move beyond the traditional sports program and introduce a variety of non-traditional activities such as skipping rope, different types of dancing, rollerblading, yoga, gymnastics, skating, hockey and martial arts.

• Encourage girls to develop life-long activities such as walking, curling, cycling and orienteering. Take these opportunities to teach related subjects such as physiology, anatomy, geography, map reading and safety.

• Establish close contact with community programs and recreation centers. Bowling is again becoming a favorite activity of teenage girls because it is paced so they can socialize with their friends and also be physically active.

Plan Activities to Suit Different Body Types and Sizes

Girls come in all shapes and sizes and we need to plan accordingly for them. Girls who are good at track and field may not have the endurance necessary for swimming or hiking. Most likely the hockey goalie is not the girl who will become an elite gymnast. If you vary your activities you can accommodate the needs of all girls, including the ones who are fat.

In one elementary school, an eleven year old girl of above average weight was excited when she entered grade six because this teacher was going to teach regular physical education classes. When she discovered that the activities were focused primarily on running she was very disappointed. Even though she played soccer after school and rode a horse, she still questioned her competence and felt badly about herself.

In one secondary school, the girls had to complete a certain amount of laps around the track. If one girl stopped, everyone had to complete extra laps. One fat girl just couldn't keep up—earning the anger of the rest of the students. When her parents complained they were told that she could skip physical education if she produced a note from her doctor. But the girl wanted to participate in physical education. She loved playing basketball and riding the exercise bike. She just couldn't run laps.

Don't Link Physical Activity to Weight

It is important that we don't define the goal of physical activity as weight-loss or weight-control and that we don't equate fitness with being thin. Girls who are concerned with weight and body shape often select fitness programs as a means of losing weight, putting themselves at risk of developing an eating disorder. Advocating weight-loss as a way of dealing with childhood obesity only increases the fat prejudice these children already experience and turns them off using their bodies. The goal of physical activity should be to help kids become and remain strong and healthy regardless of their size.

Examine How You Do Assessment

Take a balanced approach to assessment. Instead of focusing either on skill acquisition or participation, assess students on the following:

Skill acquisition—including improvement and how hard someone tries

Knowledge—such as understanding the rules and set-up of the
game or sport

Sporty Spirit—such as cooperation and being a good sport[31]

Allow for Girls-only Activities

Provide girls with opportunities where they can learn new
skills and participate in activities without the boys. Not only do
girls need a safe place to learn, they are also underrepresented
in organized sport outside the school and may need more time
and opportunity to learn and practice their skills.

Set aside girls-only gym time at lunch and after school.
Don't be discouraged if it takes time for girls to begin to make
use of it. Try not to bow to pressure to include the boys or turn
the gym over to them if the attendance initially is small.

Create a Welcoming Environment for Girls

Ensure that school bulletins, notice boards and newspapers
devote an equal amount of time to girls and boys in the amount
of coverage and pictures. Check posters to ensure that there is
an equal portrayal of girls and boys and female and male athletes. Make sure photographs include girls and women of different sizes, shapes and body types. The physical education
teacher in one secondary school invited me to talk to the grade
nine girls because she was concerned about a number of girls
who were restricting their food. However, by only having photographs of girls doing gymnastics visible she reinforced the
message that only girls of a certain body type can successfully
participate in physical activity and sport.

After School Activities

It's not that adolescent girls don't value the importance of
physical activity in their lives, it's just that there are other things
they consider more important or more pressing. Teen girls are
often the ones who look after their brothers and sisters. They
are expected to help out with domestic chores at home. Some
girls have after-school jobs. Many want to hang out with their
friends. Watching boys play sports, especially a boyfriend, is a

lot more important to them than playing sports themselves.

Girls generally have fewer opportunities and are less encouraged to be physically active than boys.[32] Even if they did want to participate in team sport it would be hard for many of them to attend regular practices and games. This is different from boys who set aside time in their daily lives to participate in physical activity and sport. Many families still consider sports to be a male activity and see the participation of their sons as more important than it is for their daughters.

When one high school team was going off to participate in a volleyball tournament, one of the athletes couldn't go because her parents had to take her brother to hockey and she had to baby-sit. The coach said "This is your only volleyball tournament of the year. How many hockey games does your brother play?" He played about 30 games, but she had still had to miss the volleyball tournament because in her family he was the priority.[33]

Many girls don't include physical activity as part of their social practice—unless you consider the amount of time they spend walking up and down the mall with their friends. Unlike boys who get together with their friends specifically to play sports, adolescent girls just like to hang out with their friends. Physical activity doesn't enter into their socializing unless someone else initiates it and even then they have to work hard at keeping up their commitment to it. Says one girl "About two months ago my friend and I talked about working out. At first it was hard to make it happen. We were always busy with school or our social life and everything. Then we made this pact that we are going to run at least once a week and it worked out for a while. For the past 2 months we have been going rollerblading or jogging twice a week and it has really been fun because you have someone else who is trying it and we motivate each other."

Girls undervalue the importance of physical activity to their own well-being. Because of the societal pressure on girls to be thin, they have a more negative view of their bodies than boys both in terms of physical appearance and competence. They diet and worry about their weight instead of using physical activity as a means of coping with stress and anxiety. Even when they are very young many girls are conscious of how different their bodies are from those of their friends. In one baseball league the managers sewed labels with the size of the uniforms on the outside of the shirts in order to make uniforms easier to distribute to their ten year old girls. This caused excruciating discomfort for both the girls with the XS and the XL shirts who had to constantly display how different they were from the other girls every time they played.[34]

What Community/Recreation Centers and Other Organizations Can Do

Offer Girl-only Programs and Activities

One of the major ways for girls to be physically active is through after-school programs that are structured just for girls. Girls-only activities provide girls with a safe environment to learn and practice skills, to make mistakes and then try again without having to feel that they have failed, and to build their confidence and their competency to feel comfortable exercising. One of the really strong motivators in participation is the social aspect. Girls will continue coming to an activity if their friends are also there.

Combine Physical Activity with Prevention

The best kinds of after-school activities are those that combine physical activity with an opportunity for girls to talk about issues and concerns of importance to them. These programs offer girls a way to define themselves other than in terms of how they look and allow girls to develop additional interests, interact with other girls and learn about themselves. Social activities provide an incentive for girls who are inactive to come to a program. Once they are there they will try the physical activities. If they have fun, they will come back.

Mix and Match Resources

Mix and match programs from the Featured Resources of this chapter and the Resources detailed at the end of the book. For example use the *Just for Girls* program to teach girls about the grungies and for facilitating your group and use the *Teaching the Basics Resource Manuals* to teach skills. Use the *On the Move Handbook* to look at activities that others have already done and for help in recruiting girls. You don't have to start from scratch. You just have to modify and enrich what you are already doing. There is no right or wrong way. Just remember that girls want to have fun—which means teaching skills, providing social interaction and providing variety.

Consider the Format

Consider whether to offer a drop-in program or have fixed registration. Drop-in programs give girls a chance to come and try the program out without having to make a long-term commitment. They also allow them to bring their friends along to future sessions. This is important in getting girls to participate.

Pre-registration ensures that the same girls will be there all the time and therefore may make it easier to build trust. Most community and recreation centers and organizations insist on pre-registration because they need a certain number of girls in the group in order to make it financially viable.

Make Personal Contact with Adolescent Girls

Before girls reach adolescence it's easy to get them to participate in after-school activities. All you have to do is sign them up. If the activities are fun, the girls will return—especially if their friends are there. Such is not the case with adolescent girls who have more demands on their time, and are much more afraid of making a mistake and being seen as 'uncool' or as different from their friends. Girls this age also don't want to be imagined as having a 'problem' by attending a formal discussion group. As for physical activity, they don't make the connection between using their bodies and feeling good about themselves—they've already been burnt by PE.

Before adolescent girls will try out something new they need to know what the group/activity is about and what is expected of them. They also need to know that you will relate to them and not talk at them. Most of the time girls will try something new based on the connection that they have with you. When I was developing the *Just for Girls* program I would go into the schools with my co-facilitator and talk with girls. Then I would invite them to a group and encourage them to bring a friend.

Go Where the Girls Are

After you have made contact with girls you need to keep on reminding them of the program or activity. This means thinking like a girl and putting your notices up where the girls are–in the malls and in their favorite stores. If you have a program offered through a community or recreation centre, don't imagine that girls are actively looking for things to do in the sports or activity section of the community or recreation centre brochures.[35]

Share Yourself

Once your group gels take risks and try new things with the girls. Participate in the activities if you can instead of standing on the sidelines and watching. Make sure that you share yourself with the girls. You might want to review Chapter 3 which talks about schmoozing.

Make Activities Affordable and Accessible

Many girls don't participate in physical activity because they can't afford to. If the activity is some distance from their home, transportation may create a barrier for them. Try to keep the cost low by charging a small drop-in fee. If possible, subsidize the program for girls who can't afford it. Try to ensure that the activities are right after school or on the weekend. Many parents don't want their daughters to go out at night. Girls often feel the same way.

Provide a private space for the activities. If they are held in the gym, then make sure the doors are closed and people, especially boys, can't look in. Have staff members respect the girls' privacy by staying out of the gym or the room the group is in. A group in one school was held in the drama room. A well-meaning teacher kept going in and out as she planned her classes for the next day. This interfered with the group dynamics and made the girls feel self-conscious about their participation.

Don't Give Up

It often takes time to get a new activity established. After you invite girls and advertise the program, they need time to think about it and check it out with their friends. At the first session you may only get two girls. The next session these girls may bring their friends. The attendance builds up as word of mouth spreads that this is a fun place to be. This is what usually happens with *On the Move* programs.

Because community and recreation centers need to focus on the bottom line and because many municipalities are feeling a huge financial crunch, they often don't provide the time for their facilitators to recruit girls or for groups to run at a loss. Yet if community and recreation centers are serious about getting girls involved in physical activity, this is what we have to do. It's a matter of fairness. It's part of their mandate. And providing equal opportunity is also the law.

The Influence of Parents

Parents who are physically active tend to have daughters who are physically active. This is because they are role models for their daughters, provide them with opportunities for sports and physical activities, encourage them and teach them skills and include physical activity as an important part of their lives.

While this may sound good, and may apply to some parents and be something for others to strive for, this is often more easily said than done.[36] Fathers and mothers view and participate in sports and physical activity differently.

Because sports are part of the male culture many fathers consider their participation as part of their lifestyle. Sports are a way of having fun, enjoying the comradery of other men and being active. Fathers who are physically active tend to practice with their daughters and teach them sports skills. Too often, however, the demands of long work days prevent fathers from getting their daughters to practice as much as necessary to become proficient or to watch them play. In single-parent families, fathers may have little or time-limited contact with their daughters.

Mothers who are active can also teach their daughters skills and practice with them. However, mothers are generally a product of the same physical education system as their girls. Many lack the skills to participate in sports and feel that they don't have the skills necessary to play with or coach their daughters.

When women participate in physical activity it is usually in order to lose/maintain weight—something encouraged by our society. Activities such as aerobics, walking, swimming and bicycling are often perceived as punishment for what they have eaten or as insurance against what they are going to eat. Women who are above average weight often feel self-conscious joining physical activities. They may feel limited by their weight and self-conscious about what they can do.

Because women have been socialized to put the needs of others ahead of their own, many find it difficult to view physical activities as leisure—as something they are entitled to enjoy. Even if they were active before marriage, the idea of entitlement to leisure may seem like a joke to women whose workdays include paid employment, domestic work, childcare, part-time study, volunteer work and/or taking care of aging parents.[37]

What Parents Can Do

You don't have to be a superstar or be in top condition to be active with your daughter. Make a commitment to go for walks instead of watching television and support each other in keeping to it. Walking allows you to spend quality time together. You'd be surprised what people share when they are walking side by side and are not interrupted every few minutes. It also says you value physical activity in your life.

Check out local bike paths and other safe places and try bicycling together. Cycle to the video store or on other errands instead of taking the car. If it's been years since you've been on a bike, be gentle with yourself and give yourself time to relearn. Go hiking in the summer. Focus on having fun.

'Snack' on Exercise

You don't have to do all thirty minutes of activity a day at once. In the same way that you stop for food snacks during the day, you can stop for a ten minute exercise 'snack' three times a day. Go for a walk, park your car at the far end of the mall parking lot or take the stairs instead of the elevator. Explore with girls how they can incorporate exercise 'snacks' into their day.

Join an Activity Together

Join an activity together such as yoga or belly dancing or any other type of dancing. Practice the moves at home together. Go bowling. Lift weights together. Give each other permission to be beginners and make mistakes. Encourage each other when you feel too tired or too busy to go to the classes.

Make Physical Activity a Family Affair

Plan physical activities the entire family can participate in. The four-year-old son of a colleague of mine is so used to physical activity being a part of his life that he gets upset whenever she tries to take him somewhere in her car. Plan activities such as cycling, swimming and bowling with other families as family outings and make physical activity part of your social activity.

Actively Support Her Involvement in Physical Activity

Help her learn the fundamental skills of running, throwing, catching, kicking, swimming, rollerblading and whatever else she might be interested in. If you can't do this yourself, then find someone else who can teach her. Check out the *Premier's Sport Awards* program described at the end of this chapter. Wouldn't you get help for her if she was having difficulty with math or reading?[38]

Encourage Her to Try a Variety of New Activities

Help her find activities that suit her body type. Try to make her experiences with physical activity a success. It might take time until she finds an activity or sport that she feels passionate about. Don't give up when she gets discouraged. Don't equate physical fitness with being thin. This places limitations on girls who are fat who can and do participate in the same activities as thin girls. Remember you can be fat and fit.

Buy her equipment that fits instead of making do with her brother's hand-me-downs. Many communities have swap meets and second hand sports stores where you can get great bargains.

Share her interest in her activity. Talk to her and listen to her talk about her experiences, her hopes and her fears. Make sure she has time in her life for physical activity. Don't make her baby-sit or do housework instead of being active.

FEATURE RESOURCES

The *Premier's Sport Awards* program
(Teaching Children their Basic Sport Skills)

The *Premier's Sport Awards* program has been designed to be used by anyone, anywhere. It provides quality physical activity resources to help teachers, coaches and instructors teach children their basic sport skills. The program consists of various *Teaching the Basics Resource Manuals*, a personal goals-setting component and brightly illustrated posters.

The program's fourteen sport-specific resource manuals include badminton, basketball, curling, disc sports, field hockey, golf, gymnastics, ice skating, judo, orienteering, soccer, softball, track and field and volleyball. Each manual offers time-saving lesson plans, a brief history of the sport, skill breakdowns, head-to-toe warm-ups and cool downs, skills checklists, drills and games, and sound technical advice.

On the Move handbook

On the Move (OTM) is a national initiative across Canada designed to increase opportunities for non-active girls and young women ages 9–18 to participate in sport and physical activity. An innovative programming concept, *OTM* is designed for practitioners in the sport, physical activity, education and health sectors advocating for community-specific participant-driven programs. The *On the Move Handbook* outlines the *OTM* concept, discusses the issues and barriers surrounding girls and young women's participation, provides information about program design and implementation, leadership, promotion, and building community supports.

Coordinated by the Canadian Association for the Advancement of Women and Sport and Physical Activity (CAAWS) *OTM* has been successful across Canada. Because they are participant-driven, *OTM* programs have included almost every type of physical activity imaginable. There are several characteristics they have in common: the emphasis is on fun, participants have time to socialize, programs are female-only, and a safe and supportive environment is created.

New Moves program

New Moves is an alternative physical education program for inactive girls developed by Dr. Dianne Neumark-Sztainer and her research team at the University of Minnesota. While it was initially developed for girls who identified themselves as being overweight (and can still be used with them) it is now being used with all adolescent girls. The program is made up of three components: physical activity, nutrition and personal development (or obesity/eating disorder prevention).

The *New Moves* classes meet Monday to Friday for 90 minutes. Every class includes some kind of physical aerobic activity. At the core is non-competitive exercise that everyone can do daily like walking, swimming and yoga. Fun and offbeat activities are taught throughout the semester such as self-defense, funk aerobics and jump rope. Girls learn about nutrition and are encouraged to pay attention to what they eat. In small groups they talk about the issues that concern them (and most adolescent girls) and learn to support one another.

Endnotes

1. Heart Health Coalition (1997). British Columbia—Setting the Pace: A Plan To Improve The Health Of British Columbians Through Physical Activity, Vancouver, BC: Heart and Stroke Foundation of B.C. & Yukon

2. *American Journal of Health Promotion*, 1996, Vol. 10: 171-174

3. Globe and Mail, A1, September 27, 2001, citing research published in the *American Journal of Epidemiology* and the *Journal of Medicine and Science in Sports and Exercise*

4. Marlene Habib, "Study suggests exercise —not counting calories—the cornersone of health." *The Vancouver Province*, January 2, 2002

5. University of Ca., *Berkeley Wellness Letter*, Vol. 17, No. 7, April, 2001

6. The Presidents Council on Physical Fitness and Sports (1997) Physical Activity and Sport in the lives of Girls: Physical and Mental Health Dimensions from an Interdisciplinary Approach, Washington, D.C.: Department of Health and Human Services

7. Keays, J.J. & K.R. Allison (1995) "The effects of regular moderate to vigorous physical activity on student outcomes: A Review," *Canadian Journal of Public Health*, Vol. 86, No. 11

8. Greendorfer, S. (1987, June) "Hop, step and jump away: Socialization of females into sport," A presentation given at the New Agenda II Conference, Indianapolis, IN

9. Dahlgren, W. (1988) A Report of the National Task Force on Young Females and Physical Activity, Ottawa, ON: Department of Fitness and Amateur Sport

10. Hay J. & Donnelly, P. (1996) "Sorting out the boys from the girls: Teacher perception of student physical ability," *Avante*, Vol. 2, No.1: 36-52

11. Gibbons, S., Higgins, J.W., Gaul, C. & G. Van Gyn (1999) "Listening to female students in high school physical education," *Avante*, Vol. 5, No. 2: 1-20

12. Canadian Association for Health, Physical Education, Recreation and Dance (CAHPERD), *Girls and Boys in Elementary Education: Issues and Action*, 1999

13. "Did You Know?"(1996, January 30) *Parents*, 71, 30

14. National Association for Sport and Physical Education: Shape of the Nation Survey, 1997

15. Fenton, J.M. (1996). "Linking girls' experiences in physical activity to school culture and social and political contexts: Elements of an exemplary model," University of British Columbia unpublished Master's thesis

16. Sadker, M. & D. Sadker (1994) *Failing at Fairness: How Our Schools Cheat Girls*, New York: Simon and Schuster, pp. 5-8

17. Ibid

18. Dahlgren, W.

19. Mandigo, J.L. & R.T. Couture (1996) "An overview of the components of fun in physical education, organized sport and physical activity programs," *Avante*, Vol. 2, No. 3: 42-55

20. Fenton, J.M.

21. Cahn, S.K. (1993) "from the muscle moll to the butch ballplayer: Mannishness, lesbianism and homophobia," in *U.S. Women's Sport Feminist Studies*, p. 334

22. Snow, K. (1994, Fall) "Where are the role models: Exploring the invisibility of female athletes in the media," *Canadian Woman Studies: Women and Girls in Sport and Physical Activity*, Vol. 14, No. 4

23. Fenton, J.M.

24. Humbert, M.L. (1995). "On the sidelines: The Experiences of young women in physical education classes," *Avante*, Vol. 1, No. 2: 58-77

25. Canadian Association for Health, Physical Education, Recreation and Dance (CAHPERD), *Girls in Action Speaking Out*, 1997

26. Humbert, M.L.

27. Griffin, P.S. (1989) "Equity in the gym: What are the hurdles?" *Canadian Association for Health, Physical Education and Recreation Journal*, 55(2): 23-26

28. Hardman, K. & J. Marshall. (1999) "The world-wide survey of the state and status of physical education in schools," University of Manchester, England. http://www.icsspe.org/eng/forschung/hardman_eng.htm

29. Gibbons et al

30. Canadian Association for Health, Physical Education, Recreation and Dance (CAHPERD), *Girls and Boys in Elementary Education: Issues and Action*, 1999

31. Interview with Bryna Kopelow, Executive Director of JW Sporta and past chair of CAAWS and Promotion Plus: Girls and Women in Physical Activity and Sport

32. Dahlgren, W.

33. Interview with Sydney Millar, *On the Move* National Coordinator, Canadian Association for the Advancement of Women and Aport and Physical Activity (CAAWS)

34. Interview with Bryna Kopelow

35. Interview with Sydney Millar

36. Jaffee, L. & J. Rex. (Spring, 2000) "Parental encouragement and girls' participation in physical activity," *Melpomene*, Vol. 19, No. 1: 18-23

37. Lenskyj, H.J. (Fall, 1994) "What's sport got to do with it?" *Canadian Woman Studies: Women and Girls in Sport and Physical Activity*, Vol. 15, No. 4

38. Interview with Bryna Kopelow

13

⚭

SPORTS

"If you grew up female in North America you heard this: *sports are unfeminine*. Girls who play sports are tomboys or lesbians. Real women don't spend their free time sliding feet first into home plate or smacking their fists into soft leather gloves."
>   *The Stronger Women Get, the More Men Like Football*
>   by Mariah Burton Nelson[1]

"Some coaches are really great. They really know how to get to you. If you have a really good coach everyone gets to know each other and to motivate each other and you have so much more fun."   15 year old Zoe

"Some coaches get so caught up in the winning that they don't watch out for the players. Last year I sprained my ankle playing soccer but he still made me go out there and play. He wasn't concerned that there was an injury. He was more concerned with wanting the team to win."
>   16 year old Amanda

More girls are participating in sports today than ever before. Sports help girls and young women take charge of their bodies by making them aware of their physical capacity and by providing them with a sense of ownership. They provide girls with permission to challenge society's restrictive view of femininity and with the opportunity to rebel against societal pressures to assume a passive role.

Girls who participate in sports take up more space—both physically and on the field, ice rink and court. They extend their arms, they make themselves bigger, and they use their bodies aggressively and instrumentally. Often they make contact with other bodies.[2] Using their bodies in this way can initially be difficult for girls because they are socialized to not take up space—to make themselves small and invisible; and they don't like to feel tall, to seem wide, to make loud noises or to dominate a big space.

Sports teach girls how to listen to their own bodies for signs of fatigue, overexertion and pain. They offer girls a chance to enjoy their own physical natures—to experience their bodies as expansive, joyful and sensuous.

Adolescent girls who participate in sports develop greater cardiovascular capacity and greater strength and flexibility than girls who do not. They are less likely to engage in sex at a younger age, and if they are sexually active, are less likely to have unprotected sex.[3] They are also less likely to smoke,[4] and to get involved with drugs. They have a more positive body image and experience higher states of psychological well-being.[5]

Group activities and team sports offer girls the chance to make friends and develop meaningful relationships with peers and caring adults. They learn teamwork, cooperation, sharing and working towards a common goal—values that not only help girls in their personal and social lives but also later on, when they enter the world of work.

Ladies Don't Sweat

Although sports are central to many girls' lives today, it wasn't usually so. A hundred years ago girls and women were strongly discouraged from using their bodies for strength and enjoyment. Girls were taught that proper ladies didn't sweat. Doctors were afraid that women would adopt masculine mannerisms, deeper voices and overdeveloped bodies that would jeopardize their sexual identity.[6] They were afraid that women's reproductive organs could be damaged.

In the 1920s, for example, there was an outcry against women bicycling because their saddles were said to cause contracted vaginas and collapsed uteri and to induce menstruation. Even though female farmers and factory workers engaged in heavy work without male complaint[7] women's tennis matches were reduced from the best of five to best of three because of fear of female overexertion. By 1969 tests were still being conducted to measure the effect on the uterus of landing shock from jumping.[8]

The strongest objection to women participating in sport was that it was not compatible with women's traditional subordinate role in a society where sport functioned in an all-male domain. The idea of strong aggressive women was just too much to bear. If women became free to engage in athletic activity as they saw fit, what else might they do? And who would look after the kids when they hefted their equipment bags onto their shoulders, grabbed their skates and hockey sticks (or soccer balls or basketballs or baseball mitts) and went out the door?

Even if women did participate in sports their experiences were considered to be inferior to and much different from those of men. Until very recently this 'truth' has been perpetuated through the teaching of stereotypical gender roles in existing physical activity and sport structures.[9]

The Fight for Gender Equity

Women have been demanding sports for girls and women ever since the first wave of the feminist movement (1848 to 1920). The fight was taken up with even more fervor during the second wave in the nineteen-sixties and seventies. As a result the report of Canada's Royal Commission on the Status of Women in 1979 called for the provinces and territories to review their policies to ensure that school programs provided girls and boys with equal opportunities to participate. It also urged the establishment of policies and practices to motivate and encourage girls to be active.

The *Canadian Charter of Rights and Freedoms* in the Constitution Act of 1982 prohibits discrimination on the basis of gender and sets forth the fundamental freedoms which are guaranteed equally to men and women.[10] In 1981 the Canadian Association for the Advancement of Women and Sport and Physical Activity (CAAWS) was founded to advocate for progressive change within Canada's sport system leading to the enhanced presence of girls and women at all levels and in all areas—as athletes, participants, leaders, coaches and trainers. Its sister organization Promotion Plus: Girls and Women in Physical Activity and Sport was founded in British Columbia in 1990 to promote opportunities for girls and women and remains the only provincial organization of its kind.

In the United States *Title IX* of the Education Amendments was passed in 1972 prohibiting discrimination in schools (and other educational programs) that receive federal funds. It requires schools to offer male and female students equal opportunities to play sports, to treat male and female athletes fairly, and to give male and female athletes their fair shares of athletic scholarship money. Their federal funding can be withdrawn if they don't.[11] In 1974 the Women's Sports Foundation was founded by Billie Jean King and other athlete activists to serve as advocates for gender equity and as a clearinghouse for information about *Title IX*.[12]

The fight for gender equity is world-wide. In 1994 the historic first World Conference on Women and Sport entitled "Challenge of Change" was held in Brighton, England. It drafted the 'Brighton Declaration on Women in Sport' which was endorsed on May 8, 1994 by 280 delegates from 82 countries including the U.S. and Canada.[13]

In 1998, 400 delegates from 74 countries attended the second world conference entitled "Reaching Out for Change" in Windhoek, Namibia. The 'Windhoek Call for Action' promoted global action to further the development of equal opportunities for girls and women to participate fully in sport in its broadest sense.

The third world conference in 2002 entitled "Investing in Change" drew 550 people from 97 countries to Montreal, Quebec. This conference identified barriers still faced by women in sport and physical activity and celebrated the positive changes over the past four years. The 'Montreal Tool Kit' was developed to help delegates bring about change in their own organization, community, region and/or nation. As a delegate to that conference I can attest to the enthusiasm and commitment of women to sport. The energy generated was phenomenal!

The Gender Equity Fight Goes On

The battle for gender equity is on-going. Girls currently make up almost 40% of high school athletes yet take a back seat to the boys in terms of resources and space. In many places they receive fewer opportunities to participate, lower budgets for athletic teams, inferior coaching and equipment and practice facilities and competitive opportunities. Boys still get first shot at the playing fields and the ice rinks that have traditionally been considered their domain. Equity is not viewed as bringing fairness to the girls, but as taking something away from the boys.

In *Too Many Men on the Ice: Women's Hockey in North America,* Joanna Avery and Julie Stevens describe difficulties encountered by girls and women in Canada and the United States in their attempts to take their space on the rink.[14]

One such case began in 1982 when a group of girls on Long Island decided to play ice hockey. Ten years later the Island Waves (as they were called) tried to merge with an all-boys program. All they wanted was to be treated like the boys in the Arrows Hockey organization and receive the basic necessities that hockey programs provide their teams. Instead they came up with less ice time, fewer teams, inferior practice time and space, unequal time with instructors and no access to tournaments. Despite initial agreement, they were not allowed to keep their names or their uniforms. The Arrows withheld grants obtained from the Women's Sports Foundation and refused to sign papers for funding from the state of New York.

The Waves decided against taking the issue to court as many other organizations have done, but instead to separate from the Arrows and incorporate on their own. On April 15, 2001 the Long Island Waves successfully became a New York State Amateur Hockey Association sanctioned program.[15]

Gender equity is not just about team sports. In Coquitlam, British Columbia a non-profit gymnastics club with a predominately female membership made repeated requests to the City of Coquitlam for financial assistance to help pay for the privately owned gym it rented. The requests were made on the grounds that the City subsidized other facilities used by non-profit sport groups that were male. When the requests were denied the father of a gymnast filed a complaint with the British Columbia Human Rights Commission with the help of Promotion Plus: Girls and Women in Physical Activity and Sport. The complaint was based on the grounds that the denial constituted discrimination on the basis of gender. After mediated discussions on March 8,

1999 a five part *Gender Equity Program* was agreed upon, serving as a model for other municipal governments to follow in the future.[16] If you have questions about gender equity in your area, you can contact Promotion Plus or CAAWS in Canada and the Women's Sports Foundation in the United States. All of these organizations are listed in Resources.

Equity is Not The Same as Equality

In trying to provide girls with opportunities to participate in sport we need to make sure that we concentrate on equity and not solely on equality. Equality focuses on creating the same starting line for everyone. Equity has the goal of providing everyone with the same finish line. It recognizes that everyone does not start out the same and tries to provide them with what they need so that they can be equal but different.[17]

In our attempt to make sure that girls have the same opportunities as boys we sometimes try to treat them both the same. The rational is that if we have to increase the participation of girls in sports we should do a rugby program or a hockey program just because the boys have them. We then expect the girls to play and act like the boys. In focusing only on equality we run the risk of perpetuating the system and the structure and the behavior that has devalued and marginalized girls and women to begin with.[18]

We need to take into account the unique needs of girls and boys, the differences in their experiences, the role that sport plays in their lives, their different levels of skill and their interest in different activities. When we focus on gender equity we can look at how we can make the system better, what things we value about ourselves and the ways we interact, and how these things can be integrated into the system.

Organized Sports

When girls are between the ages of 6 and 9 they are as interested as boys in participating in sports activities. By the time girls are 14 years old, they drop out of sport at a significantly higher rate than boys.[19] The main reasons given are that they are not having enough fun (there being too much emphasis on winning), not learning the basic skills and how to improve, not getting enough playing time and constantly getting yelled at by coaches and parents.[20]

Girls don't receive the same positive reinforcement about their sports participation that boys do. Little boys receive balls, gloves and sports equipment by the age of two. They see their images on television as sportsmen. They see their photos in the sports reports. All of this gives them a sense of belonging and a feeling of entitlement. When girls see sports having the prefix 'women' before it such as 'women's' hockey or 'women's' soccer or when they are excluded from the media altogether, that sends them a clear message about the secondary position that women occupy and reinforces the belief that they are just visitors in a male domain.

Competition: How Much is Too Much?

It is one thing to revel in the victories of U.S. soccer player Mia Hamm, Australian track star Cathy Freeman or Canadian speed skater Catriona LeMay Doan. As our national anthem plays many of us look at our daughters and at the girls in our lives and think 'If only...' When we come back to reality we have to acknowledge that these women are the elite few of the very many in their sport. We have to ask ourselves, "Just what role does competition play in our girls' sports and how much is too much?"

The girls who join organized sports are a much more diverse group than the boys. The range of skill displayed is much greater. There are girls who initially join a sport because their friends are in it. They come just to have fun but may get hooked on the game when they grow confident participating. At age ten, it's too early to assess their future potential. If they are still physically active at 40 then the program has been a success, even if they never become stars. And there are girls who are naturally talented and show great promise. Trying to meet everyone's needs is difficult.

At soccer practice at one end of town a coach explains to the parents of a ten year old that the soccer association has raised the age at which girls can play in the competitive rep teams from eleven to twelve. "I don't think you understand how unfair that is," he says and goes on to explain how it isn't fair for girls who are very competitive to have to play with weaker or unmotivated girls for the next two years.

At the other end of town it's the soccer coach who supports that change in the rules and the parents who are up in arms because their daughters (who are really good at the sport) will now have to wait before they can show off their talents. "Some of these girls come out just to be with their friends and don't take the game seriously," says one parent. "We have to weed them out."[21]

Competition can be a lot of fun when girls are relatively skilled and experienced and when there is not a heavy emphasis on winning. It gives girls a chance to test themselves and to feel a sense of achievement. But 49% of girls don't have the minimum skills they need when they start to participate.[22] Although coaches and parents may expect girls to play with a certain level of competency, they often don't do enough to ensure that the girls learn the basic motor skills of catching, kicking, throwing and running that they need before they move on to finer motor skills and strategic play.

Waiting until girls are older before they are put into competitive leagues gives them more opportunity to learn skills and build their confidence. In the long run this produces better results because it provides girls with a solid foundation of being physically active. Girls also need to learn how to be a good sport, how to treat their teammates and their opponents with respect and how to receive and act upon feedback regardless of how well they play the game.

And how do the girls feel? Says one eleven year old soccer player "I don't mind when girls fool around during practice. I just wish they would take the actual game seriously."

What Parents Can Do

Know Your Child

Be realistic about the expectations being placed on your daughter for her stage of development. Remind yourself why she is in sports. When adults lose sight of what is important to girls, the girls often lose interest in the activity. Pay attention to the effort, the progress and the quality of the sport experience—not whether she is winning or losing. If you are more focused on fun, social interaction and skill development, the accomplishments will take place once the foundation is developed through instruction, practice and encouragement.

Get Involved in Sport Yourself

In Ottawa, a group of mothers decided to organize their own pick-up game after spending hours driving their kids to and from hockey. Everyone was invited to participate regardless of their skill and age. After one session when the men told them what to do and the children wanted attention, men and children were banished from the rink and no longer allowed to watch.

In Montclair, New Jersey, Lisa Ciardi conceived the idea of a mom's soccer league when she was standing on the side lines watching her kids play. Besides providing the women with an opportunity to be physically active these teams, like women's groups all over, provide them with an opportunity to share their experiences and support each other in their lives.[23]

Follow the 10 Point Game Plan

Adapted from *Parents Guide to Girls Sports* (Women's Sports Foundation)

✔ Encourage her to value the time she participates in sport. Let her know that her games and practices are just as important as her brothers'.

✔ Remember you are the parent—not the coach. Most parents think their daughter is a prodigy and are sure that only they know what's best for her, but too many coaches ruin the game.

✔ Don't relive your own sport experience through your daughter. She needs to follow her own path. Sometimes that even means pursuing a single-minded dream. It can also mean dropping out of the activity after all of the time and money that you have spent driving her and providing her with equipment.

✔ Make sure that you attend her practices and her games. If you only attend the games you are telling her that they are more important than the practices. If you can't go, ensure that someone else who is important to her is there. When you are at the game, watch it. Your daughter will notice if you are more focused on socializing than on watching her play. She will also want to talk about the practice/game after it is over.

✔ Don't compete with other parents. Your self-esteem should not depend on your daughter being better than someone else's.

✔ Acknowledge the individual contributions your daughter makes, but stress the teamwork aspect of sports as well. A win or loss can never be credited or blamed to one individual. It is the combination of everyone's output.

✔ Teach your daughter how to be a good sport. Congratulate the opponents and thank the referees. Never publicly criticize a coach or official's decision. Differences of opinion should be handled calmly and privately.

✔ Plan to meet with your daughter's coach at least once during the season. This will give you the opportunity to check on her progress, as well as discuss concerns that she has shared with you but has difficulty telling her coach.

✔ Expose her to other women in sports by attending school and college events, professional league games, watching women's sports events on TV and reading women's sports books and magazines.

✔ Encourage a balance of interests and responsibilities in her life. Family, friends, school and chores are still a part of her life even during the sports season.

Choose the Right Coach[24]

• Look for coaches who emphasize enjoyment, skill development and personal improvement over winning.

• Look for a team of kids who are having fun. See if everyone is getting into the game. Everyone should have the opportunity to play all positions.

• Ask the coach about his/her philosophy about sports.

• Check out the coach's attitudes towards body size.

Be An Activist

• Join together with other parents and encourage your local newspaper to include the sports that girls and women participate in. Hats off to media like the *Bergen Record* in northern New Jersey for making this a regular feature.

• Join organizations such as the Women's Sports Foundation, the National Association for Girls and Women in Sport, the Canadian Association for the Advancement of Women and Sport and Physical Activity (CAAWS) and Promotion Plus: Girls and Women in Physical Activity and Sport. Continue the quest for gender equity and help ensure that girls can take charge of their bodies through physical activity and sport.

• Write letters protesting inequity. The next chapter on Media will show you how to make yourself heard.

Coaching

The relationship a girl has with her coach is an important one. It can often be the deciding factor in whether she stays in a sport or drops out. While a female coach is a good role model for girls, chances are the coach will be male. In fact, some girls may spend their entire involvement in sports being coached only by men. While the number of girls and women involved in sports has increased over the past 20 years, the number of female coaches has decreased. As the demand and the pay for coaches increased, they attracted more men considered to be more experienced.[25]

Understand Gender and Gender Differences

Coaching girls is different from coaching boys even though the sport may be the same. The coach of a mixed high school paddling team described how the boys used to come to practice relying on their strength while the girls came to learn skills. Boys regard the showing of interest in learning as a loss of face-an admission that they somehow lack confidence in their skills. While boys will do what the coach tells them, girls visualize and focus on what they need and then offer it to the team-thereby empowering other players.

According to Danielle Sauvageau, coach of the Olympic gold-medal Canadian Women's Hockey Team you have to lead men but must convince women. Assistant coach Karen Hughes says coaching guys is about managing egos while coaching girls is about managing emotions. You might want to reread Chapters 1 and 2 to refresh your understanding of gender and socialization and think about the following:

• Unlike boys who use conflict to gain personal power, girls are socialized to minimize differences among their friends. While girls know who the more talented players are they don't develop a 'star' system but tend to share in the ups and downs as a team. Often girls will downplay their expertise in order to fit in. Let the girls know that they can be competitive, excel at their sport and still be liked and appreciated by their team.[26]

• Girls strive for connectedness and closeness in their lives. They are just as concerned (sometimes even more so) with being liked as they are with competing. Pay attention to the group dynamics, be sensitive to and deal with interpersonal issues as they arise. If you don't, the conflicts will fragment your team.

• Friends are very important to girls. However, you need to create a balance on the team. If girls make no friends on the team that pretty much ensures that they will not continue to show up. On the other hand, too many friends can make things difficult. On one soccer team, seventeen girls came from the same school and same social circle and recreated their interpersonal dynamics making the team next to impossible to coach effectively.

• Don't compare the girls on your team in terms of who is more competitive, who tries harder or any other criteria. That only splits your team or isolates a particular girl from her teammates and creates conflict.[27]

• Unlike boys, girls tend to take things personally. Let the girls on your team know that performance in sports is not about self-worth and that it is all right to make a mistake.

• Many girls ask questions indirectly. Don't make assumptions about what someone is saying or what you think she needs to know. Clarify what she is asking and be clear in your communication. As you build trust the girls may become more direct.

• Remember that giving feedback is a two-step process that involves 'roses and onions'—saying something positive first and then critiquing the problem or issue. Because girls tend to be self-critical it is important to check with them what they are actually hearing and taking in.

Be Approachable

Some girls may want to talk about issues going on in their lives. You may be the only person they can trust. Remember that you don't have to fix things; you just need to listen to them and validate them. When it's appropriate you may also want to refer them to local resources. If a girl tells you she is being or has been sexually abused or you think she is in danger, you **must by law** report this to your local child welfare authorities.

Allow Girls To Develop At Their Own Pace

Respect that everyone is different and allow them to develop at their own pace. Provide opportunities for girls to practice in small groups so that everyone gets a chance. Vary your groups according to skill level so that girls who are just learning don't become discouraged and girls who are skilled don't get bored. Focus on personal goals.

Value Girls of All Shapes and Sizes

Don't make comments about girls' bodies or their weight. Never suggest that someone can lose a few pounds. Create a warm, accepting environment for girls who are fat. Your job is to ensure that girls are active and healthy, not thin. Reread the warning signs for eating disorders in Chapter 6 and keep an eye on girls who you think are at risk. If you have any concerns, speak to the parents.

Know Where to Draw the Line[28]

Even though we wish otherwise, harassment happens in sport. There are different degrees of abuse. They all provide serious setbacks to girls' enjoyment of sport and to how they feel about themselves. Understanding about harassment will help you draw the line so that even well-intentioned behavior is not misunderstood.

Physical harassment is when a person is intentionally targeted or made to do excessive exercises as punishment—such as running extra laps.

Sexual harassment is where adults misuse their positions of authority and sexualize touch (such as fondling instead of a friendly hug or a long passionate kiss on the lips) or romanticize a relationship by flirting. Coaches need to understand that if a girl has a crush on you, you are the one to set the boundaries. Harassment also happens when spectators initiate sexual contact, make comments or engage in behaviors that are offensive, uninvited or unwelcome.[28]

Emotional harassment exists when a girl is made fun of, criticized, discriminated against or put under unrealistic pressure to perform. Girls don't learn through fear but by feeling supported.

Neglect is when a girl is not provided an appropriate level of care or supervision—such as leaving her to wait alone for her parent after the game is over and everyone else has gone.

The Dark Side of Sport

While sport can be a positive experience for many girls, it also has a dark side because of the pressure it can put on girls and women to achieve a low body weight. For example, a female runner cuts down on her caloric intake in order to lose just a few pounds to improve her race time, a soccer player wants to run a little faster and play a little better and cuts down on her eating or throws up after every meal, a national-class distance runner goes more than ten years without having a regular menstrual cycle and a figure skater begins to suffer from painful stress factures. What all of these women have in common is they are at risk or already affected by the Female Athlete Triad which can affect both recreational and elite athletes.

The Female Athlete Triad is made up of disordered eating, amenorrhea (not menstruating) and osteoporosis. When girls severely restrict the number of calories they are consuming or use other ways to restrict the amount of food they take in, they are at high risk of developing an eating disorder. Their performance is affected as well because of dehydration and/or muscle weakness.

When girls exercise they expend more energy. When they fail to take in enough calories or lose a lot of weight their body enters a state of constant energy depletion. Amenorrhea, the medical term for no periods, then develops because the hypothalamus (which is a part of the brain involved with periods and fertility) is unable to function properly and responds by signaling the ovaries to produce less hormones—especially estrogen.

When estrogen is low the body loses its ability to absorb calcium and to use it for bone growth/maintenance. This puts girls at risk of developing stress fractures and breaking bones through non-traumatic injuries. If the process of bone development is interrupted when girls are in their teens their bones may never reach their maximum density putting them at risk of osteoporosis when they are older. If estrogen levels come back up, bone loss can be halted and actually rebuilt—although there is still concern that the bones may never regain their full strength.[29]

Girls who participate in gymnastics, figure skating and competitive running have the highest risk of eating disorders because of the tremendous pressures to maintain little body fat and low weight. Girls who are encouraged by their coach to lose weight in order to increase their competitive edge or who are required to wear revealing uniforms such as volleyball and beach volleyball players are also at risk because of the emphasis placed on their body shape.

It is important to emphasize strength and health rather than thinness and perfection. If you think your daughter or a girl you are working with might be in danger, don't hesitate to share your concerns with her, with her parents, her coach and her physician. The organizations listed in the Resource section will provide information and guidance.

Feature Resource
GoGirlsGo Project

GoGirlsGo Project is a program developed by the Women's Sports Foundation to help girls ages 10 to 14 to begin to talk about challenging issues such as body image, drugs, peer pressure, smoking, depression, anger, self-esteem and stress. Eventually there will be four main areas of material including the *GoGirls Guide to Life*, the *Journal*, the *Coaches and Group Leaders Guide* and the *Peer Leader Guide*. The *Coaches and Peer Group Leaders Guide* contains all the stories, questions and helpful hints for coaches to run the program.

Endnotes

1. Nelson, M.B. (1994) *The Stronger Women Get, The More Men Like Football: Sexism and the American Culture of Sport*, New York: Avon Books, p. 1
2. Ibid, p. 34
3. Erkut, Sumru, (Spring, 1999) Research Report, Wellesley College Center for Research on Women
4. Edwards, P. *Evening the Odds: Adolescent Women: Tobacco and Physical Activity*, Gloucester, ON: Canadian Association for the Advancement of Women in Sport and Physical Activity
5. Women's Sports Foundation, "Health Risks and the Teenage Athlete," <www.womenssportfoundation.org>
6. Lenskyj, H. (1986) *Out of Bounds: Women, Sports and Sexuality*, Toronto: The Women's Press
7. Ibid
8. Scott, C. (Spring, 1997) "Billie Jean King: A force for change in women's sports," *Melpomene*, Vol. 16, No. 1, p. 11
9. Vertinsky, P. (1992) "Reclaiming space, revisioning the body: The quest for gender-sensitive physical education," *Quest*, 44: 373-396
10. Robertson, S. (Fall, 1995) "The life and time of CAAWS," *Canadian Woman Studies: Women and Girls in Sport and Physical Activity*, Vol. 15, No. 4, pp. 16-21
11. National Women's Law Center <www.nwlc.org>
12. Nelson, p. 22
13. Robertson, p. 20
14. Avery, J. & J. Stevens, (1998) *Too Many Men on the Ice: Women's Hockey in North America*, Vancouver: Polestar Books
15. "Arrows Can't Strike Down the Waves," (Fall, 2001) *The Women's Sports Experience: A Newsletter for the Supporters of the Women's Sports Foundation*, Vol. 10, No. 3, pp. 9-10

16. "Gender Equity," (September, 1999) *Communique*, British Columbia Recreation and Parks Association (BCRPA) and Canadian Parks and Recreation Association (CPRA)
17. Fenton, J.M.
18. Interview with Sydney Millar, *On the Move* National Coordinator, Canadian Association for the Advancement of Women and Sport and Physical Activity (CAAWS)
19. Women's Sports Foundation website
20. Anderson, C. (Summer, 1997) "Are kids having enough fun?" *Melpomene*, Vol. 16, No. 2, pp. 4-8
21. Interview with Bryna Kopelow, Executive Director of JW Sporta and past chair of CAAWS and Promotion Plus and with Lynn Sackville, mother of eleven year old Clea.
22. Anderson, C.
23. Araton, H. (2002) *Alive and Kicking: When Soccer Moms Take the Field and Change their Lives Forever*, New York: Simon and Schuster
24. Adapted from *Melpomene On the Move Newsletter*, Autumn, 1997
25. Acosta, R.V. & Carpenter, L.J. (1985) "Women in athletics—A status report," *Journal of Physical Education, Recreation and Dance* 56: 42-43
26. Werthner, P. (May, 2001) "Understanding the differences between how women and men communicate," *Canadian Journal for Women in Coaching*, Vol. 1, No.5
27. Ibid
28. *Coaches' Game Plan* developed by the Sport and Community Development Branch of the British Columbia government
29. Anderson, C.
30. Dr. Krista Cooper, "Ask the doctor," CAAWS website <www.caaws.ca>

14

∞

Defusing the Messages of the Media

"The media gives us pictures of people we will never be and crushes our dreams under piles of magazines. Television and movies show us 'perfection.' Why can't everybody be perfect? But we are either too heavy or too plain; too quiet or too loud. These are just some of the rules dished out in piles of beauty magazines and romance movies.

Girls become anorexic so that they can be models and be liked. We cringe at how skinny these moneymaking girls are, but underneath we long to be like that, too. Girls cry themselves to sleep at night after being teased about their weight. If a show came out with actors and actresses in a variety of shapes and sizes, it could change the definition of pretty."

a 14 year old girl's Letter to the Editor

Electronic media shape the way girls are reared and socialized and the way they learn to manage their lives. By selecting and manipulating reality, the media defines what is normal and acceptable and ideal, and emphasizes and reinforces the values and images of those who create the advertising messages and own the means by which these messages are disseminated.

The Media and Gender Stereotypes

An advertisement in the *New York Times Magazine* for Oprah Winfrey's cable television station *Oxygen* sums up the clichéd roles for women reinforced as stereotypes in the media. These include: the girl next door, the victim, the vamp, the blonde airhead, the wise-cracking neighbor chick, the spinster librarian, the sassy, head-bobbin', finger-waggin' African American girl, the ball-buster, the hooker with a heart of gold, the spooky Asian woman with a knack for erotic massage and kung fu, the shrew, the co-dependent, the trophy wife with the body by Mattel, the butt-inski mother-in-law and the butch lesbian.[1]

Men outnumber women two to one in prime-time television. Nine out of ten women who appear on TV are under the age of 46. As women age they are portrayed as sexless and more evil. When both men and women reach 60, they begin to disappear altogether from our screens.[2] Advertising for children is incredibly sexist. Girls are shown as being endlessly preoccupied by their appearance and fascinated primarily by dolls and jewellery, while boys are encouraged to play sports and become engrossed by war play and technology.[3] Most television programs for children are filled with active boys and passive girls, brought to them by action products for boys and beauty products for girls.[4]

Children's cartoons feature helpless girls being rescued by male superheroes. When girls have problems, they try to solve them with kindness and love, using rainbows and butterflies to overwhelm their opponents. When boys have problems they are clever and use trickery or problem solving skills to resolve a situation. They are also far more likely to use violence.[5]

While some shows such as *Recess, Arthur, Kratt's Creatures* and *Zoom* have strong female characters (and *Recess* also has a fat boy as one of its main characters), shows such as the *Flintstones* and the *Jetsons* show ridiculous portrayals of both women and men.

The more children watch television the more likely they are to form opinions about male and female roles. If the programs they watch are sexist, then these are the beliefs and values that they will internalize and the more likely it becomes that girls will focus on their body shape.[6] The students in Cambridge Massachusetts teacher Amy Purcell Vorenberg's grade three class watched television as part of a project on media literacy. The girls "talked about how girls were portrayed unfairly in the media, how girls on television were unrealistic and never allowed to do anything interesting. They shared stories with recurring themes of exclusion, helplessness, striving for boys' attention, stereotypic female roles and vanity."[7] It was already clear to these 8 and 9 year old girls that by watching these shows girls are taught that it is important for them to cultivate skills for changing their bodies and for developing roles in order to influence their future desirability.

The Media and Body Image

The media are *body thieves* because they play a negative role in shaping girls' feelings, thoughts and behaviors and have long been considered a key socio-cultural factor contributing to the development of disordered eating and fat prejudice. Media has a considerable impact on body image and self-esteem because it creates the context within which girls learn to place a value on their own bodies.[8]

As girls make the transition into adolescence they are bombarded by articles on exercise and dieting in teen magazines such as *Seventeen, YM* and *Teen* which teach them that they can attain self-definition, power and control by changing their bodies. (Only 5% of girls and women can attain the 'ideal' body type—even if they starve themselves!) Showing the same image over and over normalizes it. Because girls rarely see photos of average-sized, or full-bodied, or fat girls and women they come to believe that there is something abnormal about them.

Adolescent girls compare themselves to women in the media and feel tremendous pressure to be like them. Yet the images the media offer are often not even real. Beauty today is a product of technology. Computer imagery alters the size and shape of women's legs, breasts and facial features. Props create illusions. Airbrushing takes away any lines or blemishes. Photographs of body parts from one individual are superimposed on the photographs of another. In the movie *Pretty Woman,* for example, a model's legs were superimposed on Julia Roberts' body because Roberts' own legs were considered too short. Tyra Banks' hips were judged to be 'too large' for the 1998 cover of *Sports Illustrated Swimsuit Edition* and so they were retouched. By focusing on specific body parts, the media dissects women's bodies and encourages the dissociation from their bodies that most women feel.

When girls don't see themselves in the media, they think that there is something wrong with them, and then try to change themselves. They want wider eyes, longer legs, smaller feet, firmer thighs, longer nails and bigger breasts. Most of all, they want to be thin. The media reinforces a cultural message that disrespects, dismisses and disempowers girls and women.

The images, texts and practices selected for use by the media encourage girls and women to be overly concerned with their appearance (and to require all those advertisers' products) and less concerned with their own values, qualities, characteristics, skills and talents. While the media doesn't cause eating disorders or childhood obesity, it does intensify the existing preoccupation with weight and body image. According to Margo Maine, author of *Body Wars,* as long as girls are preoccupied with waging war against their bodies they cannot get on with their lives.[9]

Media and Fat Prejudice

The media reinforces societal attitudes towards fat by the way it portrays fat people and by their absence in leading roles. Fat women are usually character actors—somebody's mother, the stalwart friends or objects of derision. Aside from Camryn Manheim on *The Practice*, fat women rarely have important jobs and are never seen as sexual. Fat women never anchor the evening news.

The recent trend to portray 'glamorous' movie stars as fat characters or caricatures reinforces the myth that it is only alright to pretend to be fat if in real life you are thin. In *America's Sweethearts,* Julia Roberts gained 60 pounds by donning a designer fat suit for some scenes. Although she was willing to be seen on screen as temporarily overweight she drew the line at having any photographs published of her as a fat person.

Courteney Cox appeared in a fat suit in the television comedy *Friends* for an episode containing flashbacks to her character Monica's high-school years as an overweight teen. In the television show *Primetime Glick,* comedian Martin Short transforms himself into an overweight dimwit to portray the host of a fictitious television talk show and to garner more laughs.

In the movie *Shallow Hal* Gwyneth Paltrow donned a prosthetic to play a fat+plus woman. Every time that Hal saw her he was 'cursed' to only see the thin woman inside, implying that even in her personality, a woman must be thin. The centerpiece of *Shallow Hal* consists of jokes about women of size and about their weight. By laughing at the jokes, movie viewers help to perpetuate established stereotypes of people of size as inferior and thus deserving of mistreatment.

Media Literacy

When we watch television, read magazines and newspapers, and surf the net we need to know how to 'read' the messages in these visual images just as we need to know how to read the words on a page. Media literacy is a way of teaching using the media and their messages to help girls learn basic skills such as critical thinking, evaluating information, and detecting bias and persuasion so that they can better understand and navigate our viewing culture. A media literate person doesn't need to know all the answers, but knows how to ask the right questions.

Media literacy is also about knowing how media messages are created (whether it's a newsletter, a video or any other format) so that girls can understand how the media organize information to produce meaning and how they reconstruct reality. When girls learn what goes into making a message, they also learn what's left out of the product that the audience sees, and that helps them realize that all media messages are constructs. Somebody made them. They didn't just happen.[10]

How Media Literacy Works

All media productions present a point of view about the world. When making a production, the creators deal with the following choices:

• What story will be told or reported?

• From whose perspective will it be presented?

• How will it be filmed? (camera, placement, lighting, framing)

• What sort of music will be used, if any?

• Whose voice will we hear?

• What will the intended message be?

To understand the media's point of view we need to ask:

• Who has created the images?

• Who is doing the speaking?

• Whose viewpoint is *not* being heard?

• From whose perspective does the camera frame the events?

• Who owns the medium?

• What is our role as spectators in identifying with or questioning what we see and hear?

Media Literacy Programs and Body Image

Media literacy programs provide girls with the skills to think critically about media content in order to identify, analyze and challenge the beliefs around thinness, body shape and fat prejudice that the media continually reinforce. This reduces the risk of girls internalizing the media's most cherished myths and helps them develop a sense of self-worth that is based on internal rather than external characteristics.[11]

THE MEDIA'S MOST CHERISHED BODY MYTHS

√ Beauty is a woman's principal project in life.

√ Thinness is necessary for success and goodness.

√ It is not enough to be successful in life; you also have to be beautiful.

√ It is natural and acceptable for a woman to be self-conscious, anxious and ashamed of her body.

√ Fat is a sign of personal responsibility for weakness, failure and helplessness.

√ A winner can and should control, transform and renew herself through the technology of fashion, dieting and exercise.

Media literacy programs need to be taught on an ongoing basis throughout elementary, middle and high school. They need to be part of the curricula and part of teachable moments such as spontaneous discussions that arise out of students' concerns, questions and experiences. Like all other prevention programs, media literacy programs need to be tailored to the developmental stage of the students. They cannot be solely informational, no matter how good the information is or how well it is presented. They must be interactive, teach skills, engage the students in activities and be set in the context of their lives and experiences and concerns.

Becoming Media Literate

Whenever we watch TV or read magazines or newspapers, it is important to be able to assess them critically in order to understand the messages they trying to give us. The following exercises and activities teach media literacy skills. You can use them at home, in the classroom or with groups.

Critiquing Television Programs

Have girls choose a TV show they really like. Have them answer the questions listed below as they watch the program. They might have to watch the show more than once so it is a good idea to tape the program. Discuss the answers.

Part I

• Do you like the program? If so, what is it that you like or dislike about it?

• How do you think it is going to end? How do you know?

• How does it make you feel? What about the program makes you feel that way?

• Could the same events or story happen in real life? Could it happen here?

• How would you solve whatever problem the show addresses? Would your way be the same or different?

Part II

• What is the name of the show?

• What is the show about?

• Who are the main characters?

• What does the male character tell us about how men are supposed to be?

• What does the female character tell us about how women are supposed to be?

• What messages does the show give us about being male and being female?

• What messages does the show give us about how our bodies are supposed to look? How many people do you know that look like this?

- Does the show include any characters of different races?
- If so, how are they portrayed?
- Does the show include any fat or disabled characters?
- If so, how are they portrayed?
- If you were the director, how would you portray the women in the show?
- If you were the director, how would your show include a wide range of people?

Critiquing How Gender is Portrayed

Select pictures from newspapers and magazines that show the difference between posed and natural photographs of boys and girls, men and women. Describe what is emphasized in each.

Have girls physically imitate the ways in which men and women are positioned in fashion advertisements and features.

- How does this make them feel?
- Do the poses help or hinder the messages?
- Who is being targeted?
- Are there consistent differences between male and female poses? If so, why? What messages are women and men likely or supposed to get from these differences?

Cut and paste pictures of families from magazines and newspapers. Collect photographs of real families. Compare the family structures and the activities of each member. Discuss if the media portray families differently from real life families. What are the differences?

View clips from popular cartoons. Classify the cartoons as violent and nonviolent. Focus on the behavior of the characters:

- Why and how is violence used?
- Are the characters male or female?
- Who is the victim?
- How would the character react if the sex were reversed?
- Can the same situation be solved in a non-violent way?

Select several commercials:

• Identify whether certain commercials appeal to boys or girls and determine why.

• What does the advertisement tell you about each sex? Is this true?

• Is the voice of authority in the background male or female? Why?

• Make a list of things boys and girls like to do. Compare this list with what is shown in commercials.

• Do commercial children participate in the same activities as real children? Are boys and girls shown playing together?

• Try the same thing with magazines.

Critiquing How Different People are Portrayed

Ask girls to bring in images of women, men, youths, teens, the elderly, minorities and people with disabilities. Each week choose one of these groups. Have students bring in examples from magazines, film, TV, bumper stickers, newspapers, fiction, billboards and the internet.

• What are the prevailing media messages surrounding and reinforcing these stereotypes?

• What, if any, are the alternatives to the prevailing images?

Critiquing How Body Image is Portrayed

Using television or video clips and magazine and/or newspaper pictures:

• Make a chart of the similarities and differences in appearance and body size of the 'good' characters and the 'bad' characters.

• Make note of the type of camera shots used for the 'good' and 'bad' characters.

• Compare these characters with yourselves, your peers and your family members.

Examine magazines geared to 'larger' women.

• Are these women portrayed the same or differently from women in regular magazines?

• How many of these women are engaged in physical activities?

• How 'large' are the women who represent 'larger' women?

How Would You Be Portrayed?[12]

Ask girls to create a word portrait that reflects as accurately as possible the way they see themselves. Use the following outline:

Title   Your name (first, middle, last or nickname) in capital letters

Line 1   Four characteristics that best describe you

Line 2   You are the sister, daughter, foster child, etc. of parent, relative or guardian... (Give name)

Line 3   Friend of... (give name)

Line 4   Who loves... (list three objects, people or places)

Line 5   Who feels... (list three items)

Line 6   Who needs... (list three items)

Line 7   Who fears... (list three items)

Line 8   Who gives... (list three items)

Line 9   Who would like to see... (list three items)

Line 10   Choose a description of yourself What parts of your self-portrait do you see reflected in the media? Are these images presented as positive or negative?

Critiquing Advertising

The $130 billion advertising industry in the United States is a powerful educational force. The average person is exposed to over 1500 ads every day and will spend a year and a half of her life watching television commercials.[13] Girls wield substantial clout as consumers due to the fact that parents give them an estimated $6 billion in allowances. At a very young age they are already being trained in the sport of shopping. Even if we press the mute button or discount the advertising, it has a cumulative effective on girls.

• Identify a product that you have seen advertised on television.
• Visit a store that has the product.
  ▪ Ask girls how the product is different than imagined.
  ▪ Which is more exciting, the product in the store or the one on television?

• Monitor the types of commercials that appear on children's programming or on the programs watched by adolescent girls. Keep a record of how many of each type of advertising (food, toys, clothing, beer, CDs, cars) are shown in a given period of time.

• Chose two products that feature women in their commercials. Identify the spokeswoman:
  ▪ Encourage girls to speculate about why an advertiser may have chosen that particular person.
  ▪ How is the product made more attractive or interesting by virtue of its association with that person?

• Design an advertising campaign for a product which girls find useless. Their job is to present this product to the class, group or family in a way that makes it appealing and then to sell it. Younger girls can put the product in a box and dress it up as if it were going to appear on television. They can use crayons or markers to decorate the box and shine a flashlight on the product to make it stand out. Older girls can be more sophisticated in packaging and marketing. They can create a 'real' advertising campaign by designing a slogan, creating a song, targeting their audience, checking their demographics, deciding on profit potential, creating a need for the product and finally selling it.

Media Activism

Media activism refers to efforts to change the messages that are portrayed by the media. You can encourage girls to become media activists in the following ways:

Educate the Media

• Educate the media about responsible reporting and advertising practices with respect to body shape and size, gender roles and diversity.

• Provide members of the media with information on how media can affect self-esteem, disordered eating and prejudice against fat.

• Provide members of the media with accurate information about the dangers of dieting and the myths around fat.

• Encourage members of the media to avoid focusing on a narrow range of ideal body types and to present a wider and more realistic range of body types as acceptable.

Organize Letter Writing Campaigns

The media's main goal is to deliver audiences to advertisers. When we as consumers express our disapproval of a program or advertisement, media producers take notice because their profits depend upon us. For example, teen magazine *YM* has decided not to included diet tips or articles about diets. They have also featured a size fourteen model in one issue and included several others in their prom issue. What kind of statement does it make, however, when someone who is a size fourteen is described as 'plump' and when ads featuring thin girls permeate the magazine?

In 1998, Hershey Foods Corporation decided to advertise a chocolate bar with the slogan 'You can never be too rich or too thin.' ANAD (Anorexia Nervosa And Related Disorders) protested with a petition and letter-writing campaign. The advertisement was withdrawn.

Our comments do count. As a result of a media advocacy campaign conducted by NEDA (National Eating Disorders Association) Avia Sportswear stopped featuring a promotion with the caption 'Although fitness trainers gave advice, the mirror was her dedicated coach.' Nicole Shoes apologized for claiming, 'The pair to wear to your cooking class will also look fabulous at your weight loss seminar.'[14]

• Encourage girls to write letters to newspapers and television and radio stations to protest media products that have been identified and analyzed as conveying undesirable/unhealthy messages about women and girls or about treating them unfairly (or to praise those contradicting such views). This chapter begins with excerpts from one such letter.

• Encourage girls to write letters praising media outlets and companies for their efforts in empowering girls and women and promoting a healthy sense of their bodies. One such company, for example, is the Body Shop who promoted Ruby–a full-figured Rubenesque Barbie-like doll reclining on a love seat and encouraging women to 'love your body.' Ruby emphasizes that there are 3 billion women who don't look like supermodels and only 8 who do.

• Encourage girls to write letters to the editors of newspapers and magazines about how they feel about the pressure to be thin. By speaking out, girls validate themselves as well as other girls who feel the way that they do. In writing a letter always include your name, address, phone number and the date. Anonymous letters are not taken seriously.

• Encourage girls to organize petitions

Students in a middle-school asked Coca-Cola to remove what they saw as subliminal images of curvaceous women from onsite pop dispensers, saying it was wrong to use sexual messages to sell products in school. The students were offended by the images and felt the advertising on the school's machines was unethical, insulting and degrading.

The National Association of Eating Disorders developed a petition for professionals protesting advertising for Serafina pasta printed in the July 2000 issue of *Hamptons* magazine which read 'Supermodels love our pasta. It comes up as easily as it goes down.'

Your petition must present the facts accurately, clearly and concisely and present the reasons why you want a certain ad withdrawn. You can use the instructions on how to write an effective comment letter as a guide.

Research and Support Media Literacy

Support organizations that sponsor media literacy and media activism. One such organization is Adbusters Media Foundation—a network of artists, writers, students, educators and entrepreneurs whose goal is to galvanize resistance against those who would destroy the environment, pollute our minds and diminish our lives. Adbusters Media Foundation publishes *Adbusters* magazine, operates the web site <www.adbusters.org> and offers its creative services through its advocacy advertising agency, Powershift. See Resources for other such resources.

New Moon Magazine, an international bi-monthly magazine edited by and for girls ages 8 to 14 has been holding a "Turn

Beauty Inside Out" campaign for the last three years after girls voiced a need for a definition of beauty that fits them. They encourage girls to present a definition of beauty that is not defined by the size of their bust but rather the size of their character. The TBIO campaign celebrates girls who rejoice in their inner beauty, the beauty of good works, caring hearts and activism. In 2002 the TBIO campaign challenged the film industry's harmful depictions of girls and women. Girls finished the sentence "If I made the movies…" and rewrote the movies the way they wanted them to be.

Writing an Effective Comment Letter

Reprinted with adaptations by permission of MediaWatch Canada

Write as soon as possible. The information will be fresh in your mind and you will be taking advantage of the energy from your initial reaction. Encourage friends to write also.

Direct your letter to the appropriate contact.

Identify yourself. Include your name, address, city, province or state, postal or zip code and phone number. Anonymous letters are not taken seriously.

Identify the medium and format. If you are writing about a TV commercial, for example, indicate when you saw it and on which station. For a magazine article indicate which issue. Try to include a copy of the newspaper article that you are writing about.

Write persuasively. You want to sway the reader to be open to your point of view so that he or she will take action.

Criticize constructively. Focus criticism on the issue, not the organization or individual. Be specific about what you find offensive and why.

Give praise where it is due. If you can find something positive to say about the service or product or presentation that you are objecting to, add these details.

Be clear. Explain your position in a clear and concise manner. Try not to assume that the reader observes the same negative aspects that you do.

Suggest alternatives. If you can think of an alternative image or reference that you find acceptable, describe it. Some media producers are unaware of the issues that concern us and appreciate positive and specific suggestions.

Remind the recipient of what's at stake. You, your friends and family are part of the market the advertiser or broadcaster wants to reach. If you are considering a boycott of the product involved, mention that in your letter.

Ask for a response. Follow up with another letter or phone call if necessary.

Copy and circulate. In addition to copying to MediaWatch, ask yourself who else might be interested.

Pat yourself on the back. Most people complain but don't do anything. You have taken a proactive step in curtailing the negative images of women and girls in the media. In doing so you have fought the body thieves.

Write Letters to the Editor

Encourage girls to write letters to the editors of their newspapers. Make sure that they put their full name and address and daytime telephone number in the letter because often the newspaper will phone them to confirm that the letter is indeed theirs. Let girls know that not only are they expressing their views but they are also expressing the views of many other girls their age. This is important because often girls don't acknowledge the value in what they do.

Sample Comment Letter:
[Reprinted with permission of MediaWatch Canada]

Sarah Serious Complainant
1267 Angry Drive
Somewhere, BC V2A 1L9
March 8, 2000

Ms Laura Dallal
Advertising Standards Canada (ASC)
350 Bloor Street East, Suite 402
Toronto, ON   M4W 1H5

Dear Ms Dallal:

I am writing to express my concern over an advertisement for Fetish perfume that appeared on the outside of a Translink bus in Vancouver. In the ad a white, blond, very young and very thin woman is featured sporting a typical blank, passive look, pouting mouth and make-up bruised eyes. Her neck and face are strewn with sparkles (presumably where the perfume would be applied). The ad copy reads: "Fetish #16: Apply generously to your neck so that he can smell the scent as you shake your head 'no'."

I find the imagery in this ad very disturbing. *NO means NO* campaigns have been working hard to create an understanding of sexual consent and to make us aware of the reality of date rape. The imagery in the Fetish ad implies that women are constantly sexual, that they like being able to "turn a man on," and that NO is a part of the ritual of flirtation. This feeds the idea that rape victims are actually "asking for it" and minimizes and trivializes the very real problem of violence against women.

I hope that you will assist us in getting this ad pulled as soon as possible as it is in a very public place. I look forward to hearing from you.

Sincerely

Sarah Serious Complainant

cc. Houbigant (Fetish), Toronto Transit Commission, Translink, MediaWatch

[When notified of the consumer complaint, the advertiser voluntarily withdrew the advertisement even before the ASC Council heard the formal complaint and ruled that the Fetish ad violated their *Advertising Code of Ethics*.]

Sample Letter to the Editor:
[Printed with permission of Alexandra Webster and her parents]

The Vancouver Province
Wednesday, May 17, 2000

I am writing in complaint of the blatant sexism of the large breakfast cereal companies. I have recently realized that every single cereal box's symbolic character is MALE! Fruit Loops has Toucan Sam. Frosted Flakes has Tony the Tiger. Sugarcrisp has the Sugar Bear and Rice Crispies has three male characters known as Snap, Crackle and Pop.

As a female I am extremely offended by this. Women represent over 50% of the population and yet no female graces the front of a cereal box. It doesn't cut it to say that males are 'easier' to draw. How hard is it to draw a hair bow on top of a tiger's head and call her Tina instead of Tony?

Do they think females don't eat cereal? Perhaps cereal company executives don't think that women can see cereal, that we are not macho enough to fit the standards of the tiger or the honeybee. Or is it that females have never noticed this disparity in representation? Or do they think that women who do most of the shopping won't buy a cereal with a female character on the front?

Whatever it is, it is still discrimination against women. To me it is saying that women are not worthy of being respected and admired.

Women have been fighting for equality for years and now that we are finally getting closer to our goal of equal rights, we find more and more obstacles to overcome.

Alexandra Webster, Grade 9

FEATURE RESOURCE

GO GIRLS™

GO GIRLS ™ (Giving Our Girls Inspiration and Resources for Lasting Self-esteem!) is a program for high school students developed by NEDA: National Eating Disorders Association (formerly EDAP) that integrates media awareness and analysis, media activism and advocacy with relational group work.

The program consists of a 12-week curriculum that focuses on key issues affecting young women in today's society such as body image, media awareness and the power of speaking out. The program provides an organized but flexible set of media-related activities to give adolescent girls a chance to understand, through experience and action, that they have a voice as consumers and citizens, and that together they can use their voice to effect social, political, corporate and social change.

Through discussions and team meetings, participants explore their own body image issues, discuss general principles related to eating disorders and prevention, and learn about the strong connection between body image and the media. Projects include making presentations to executives at retail corporations, writing letters to national advisers, participating in TV and radio interviews, and creating peer awareness campaigns in local high schools. The projects are designed to educate and empower participants to change the way they feel about themselves, to change the way teens are portrayed in the media, and to learn that even one considered voice can make a difference.

Endnotes

1. *New York Times Magazine*, September 2, 2001/Section 6
2. Gerbner,G. (1998) Bell Atlantic Professor of Telecommunication, Temple University, Philadelphia
3. Graydon, S. and E. Verrall, *Gender Issues in the Media*, MediaWatch website <www.mediawatch.ca>
4. Kilbourne, J. (1994) "Still killing us softly: Advertising and the obsession with thinness," in Fallon et al *Feminist Perspectives on Eating Disorders*, New York: The Guilford Press, p. 397
5. Steiner-Adair, C. and A. P. Vorenberg (1999) "Resisting weightism: Media literacy for elementary-school children," in Piran, N., Levine, M.P. and C. Steiner-Adair (Eds.) *Preventing Eating Disorders: A Handbook of Interventions and Special Challenges.* Philadelphia: Brunner/Mazel, p. 112
6. Kimball, M.M. (1986) "Television and sex-role attitudes," in T.M. Williams (ED.) *The Impact of Television: A Natural Experiment in Three Communities.* Orlando, FL: Academic Press
7. Steiner-Adair and Vorenberg, Op Cit. p. 113
8. Shaw, J. and G. Waller (1995) "The media's impact on body image: Implications for prevention and treatment," *Eating Disorders: Journal of Treatment and Prevention*, 3(2):115-123
9. Maine, M. *Body Wars: Making Peace with Women's Bodies.* Carlsbad, CA: Gurze Books, 2000
10. Center for Medial Literacy, <www.medialit.org>
11. Berel, S. (1998) "Media and disturbed eating: Implications for prevention," *Journal of Primary Prevention*, 18(4): 415-430
12. Mizell, L. "Using the film with middle and high school students," in *Study Guide for Beyond Killing Us Softly: The Strength to Resist*, edited by Carlene Larsson <www.cambridgedocumentaryfilms.org>
13. Kilbourne, J. (1994) "Still killing us softly: Advertising and the obsession with thinness," in Fallon et al, p. 395
14. In *Healthy Eating Journal*, Vol. 12, No. 4- July/August 1998

15

∞

With Courage and Determination

After the game, Danièlle Sauvageau gathered her
victorious players together and reminded them:

"You have to go through tough times in your lives, so
remember what you have to come back with:
Responsibility
Determination
Courage
And never, ever give up!"

Danièlle Sauvageau, Coach of the Canadian Women's Hockey Team,
Gold Medal Winners, Salt Lake City Olympics, 2002

Girls come in all shapes and sizes. Their individual body
type and structure is determined by the genetic makeup of their
families, including people who lived many generations ago in
very different times. They should be able to feel some sense of
pride that they take after their father who has a great sense of
humor and a stocky build, or their Aunt Tessie who is a promi-
nent lawyer with wide hips, or their Grandma Vera who is a
social activist with big thighs, or even Uncle Al who has a big
nose but always comes to their soccer games to cheer them on.

Yet girls are not encouraged to celebrate their physical heritage, but berate themselves for not being someone else. Girls
try to change their natural bodies to look like people that they
see in magazines and on television. Instead of using their bodies and being connected to them, they turn them into objects
that they scrutinize and judge. In the process of trying to make
themselves into something they can never be, girls dissociate
from their bodies and their selves.

Girls gain weight as they go through puberty and make the transition through adolescence. This biological change is necessary to become women, but since our society has an extreme distaste and fear of fat, girls are encouraged to accept a cultural standard for thinness that is dangerously close to the very minimal weight necessary for them to get their periods, prevent osteoporosis and have children.[1]

At the same time that girls are dealing with the changes in their bodies they have to deal with changes to their lives. For example, starting high school means they move into an unknown environment and may have to make new friends—because some of their closest friends may not be in their classes or may even go to a different school. Increased academic expectations are placed upon them and they suddenly become interested in boys.

When girls reach adolescence the way they engage in relationships begins to change, which alters their sense of self. Girls develop their identities in the context of relationships with others. When relationships are open, honest and mutual both participants feel connected to one another and this provides a foundation out of which both personalities can develop and grow.

Before adolescence, girls' speak their minds, voice their opinions, get angry, fight and make up with great regularity. When girls reach adolescence, there is pressure to be kind and nice and hold back their feelings and opinions so that they won't hurt someone else. This makes it difficult for girls to be honest with one another. Girls become anxious and insecure about their friendships. They become afraid that they will place the friendship at risk if they tell someone they are angry with her, especially if they think her other friends will alienate them for hurting their friend.

When girls can't express themselves directly for fear of hurting someone else, they express their anger indirectly and their friendships take on a dark side. They gossip about each other behind their backs and exclude each other from their groups. Girls transform the relational skills that nurture them into weapons that they can use against one another. The same secrets that once brought them closer together become part of the arsenal that they draw upon for relational assaults. Not being able to speak their truths and to express and acknowledge their feelings (even to themselves) silences girls' voices and completes their disconnection from themselves.

Girls are socialized to internalize their distress. When they can't express their feelings and address their experiences directly they do so indirectly by learning to speak in code through a negative voice. They are 'hit by the *grungies*'—a term coined to describe the things girls tell themselves that make them feel badly about themselves. Whenever girls feel angry, lonely, disappointed, hurt or insecure (or experience other feelings they have difficulty acknowledging) they repress those feelings by telling themselves they are stupid or ugly. Because fat is considered bad in our society, girls learn to speak 'fat talk' and encode their feelings in the language of fat.

Think how exciting it would be if we could help girls relate to their natural bodies and live in them in a creative way—one that honors the cyclical nature of women.

Instead, girls are initiated into a cult of dieting so that they can change their bodies to fit a narrowly defined beauty ideal. Preparation for this ritual begins when girls are young. Little girls watch their mothers and copy what they do. In the same way they play dress-up, they emulate the rituals and language of deprivation. They make comments about their bodies, talk about foods they 'shouldn't eat' and tell themselves and each other they feel fat. Those who diet do so not simply because they believe it will make them thinner but because this is what they have seen grown women do.

Adolescent girls reinforce with each other the importance society places on thinness. They do this by replacing self-expression with fat talk, by constantly comparing themselves to each other and by watching and commenting on what each other eats. The rejection of fatness becomes a shared value in their group and reinforces society's obsession with weight and with prejudice towards people who are fat. In order to fit in with their friends, girls have to be preoccupied with losing weight and changing their natural bodies even when they feel good about them.

Girls diet because that's what we teach them. They diet because constant messages about the dangers of obesity tell them fat is bad and dieting is good. They diet because they believe it will relieve what they think is the discomfort of feeling fat but is really a discomfort with feelings that lie underneath their daily experiences.

Eating disorders and being fat+plus (or in medical jargon: obese) are two of the three major health risks for girls. The other is asthma and I'm just waiting for the day someone somewhere will link its 'cure' to being thin...

Diets don't produce happy endings no matter how much we hope and believe they might. At one end of the dieting spectrum there are girls who get caught up in the dynamics of anorexia and bulimia. At the other are girls who become trapped in a cycle of weight loss/regain that alters their body metabolism and progressively increases their body weight.

Dieting can and does make girls sick. Anorexia and bulimia can kill them. Yo-yo dieting puts them at higher risk for cardiovascular disease, high blood pressure and Type 2 diabetes that can disable them later in life.

Disordered eating, chronic dieting and the preoccupation with food and weight may not put the girls in the middle of the spectrum at immediate medical risk. However, being held hostage to the bathroom scale robs them of their self-esteem and negatively affects their relationships with others and their performance in school and at work and their quality of life. How can you feel good about yourself, try out new things or learn about yourself and the world around you if everything you do is overshadowed by worrying about how you look and how much you weigh?

What We Can Do

As parents and teachers and those who work with and care about girls, we can become *Size Acceptance Warriors* and fight the body thieves so that our girls can reclaim their natural bodies and take charge of their lives. We need to ensure that our girls can express their feelings constructively, have a good sense of their boundaries, build and maintain healthy connections with people, develop their self-esteem in ways other than looking good and are physically active and healthy and strong in their bodies.

Fighting the body thieves is not an easy task. It takes a lot of courage to be a Size Acceptance Warrior. It means that we have to examine and challenge our own beliefs about body size, and change our behavior when it has an adverse effect on our girls. It takes determination to be a Size Acceptance Warrior because the process of creating change in our schools, communities and in our society is often very slow and frustrating work.

Build Healthy Relationships

First and foremost we must develop, nurture and maintain our relationships with girls when they are going through adolescence despite however difficult this sometimes seems. We need to engage honestly with girls by letting them know what we think and feel and by sharing our own experiences of the world. We need to schmooze with them in order to maintain our connection with them. We must give them permission to raise certain topics, and let them know they have a right to their feelings, and assure them they are not alone in how they feel. We need to listen carefully to girls and provide them with a sounding board so that they can make sense of the world around them and learn to make good decisions.

We need to engage girls in dialogue instead of talking at them. What we tend to do is give them information in the hope that they will learn from someone else's experiences. What they need to do is learn from their own. This means we encourage girls to tell their truths in the context of their own experiences and we validate these as a genuine source of knowledge. It helps if we can interact with girls with sincere interest and curiosity about their feelings and opinions. Otherwise we run the risk of seeming to interrogate them in our desire to fix things and keep them from harm.

We need to be aware of the relationships that girls have with each other so we can help them deal with conflicts as they arise. If we don't do this we run the risk of failing to recognize things such as the effects of bullying, and our classes and teams become unsafe for everyone—not only for those involved.

We need to teach girls communication skills and support them as they try out new behavior. In my practice as a therapist and in my groups and in my community talks the key issue that comes up over and over again concerns the interpersonal dynamics between girls.

Understand and Teach Girls About Gender

We need to have a solid understanding of gender because it is the underpinning of how we parent, teach and work with girls in a way that honors who they are and how they learn.

We need to teach girls about gender and development so they have a context for their behavior and their own experiences. Knowing why they think and act the way they do and understanding the similarities between themselves and other girls and women makes many frustrating experiences less a personal failure and more of a collective trait. At the same time we need to help girls understand the continuum of behavior so they know not everyone is exactly the same and to understand why they are different from their friends.

Our lessons about gender need to include male development so girls can understand that the glitches in their relationships with their fathers and with boys have nothing to do with fault or blame and everything to do with difference. We also need to teach boys about gender. One seventeen year old girl emailed my website recently to ask me why girls cry so much and so easily compared to guys and how she could make her boyfriend understand.

Accept and Celebrate All Body Shapes and Sizes

We will not be able to prevent or end eating disorders nor rapid weight gain by children until it is acceptable by everyone and every institution in our society for girls (and boys) to be fat. By this I do not mean paying lip service to or grudgingly accepting different body sizes because it's politically correct, or accepting those who are just a teeny bit larger than what we consider to be average, but by accepting and valuing those who are truly fat and fat+plus.

This, the most important part of fighting the body thieves, requires the most courage because we must be honest about our own prejudice towards fat. It challenges our beliefs about health, and requires us to rethink the mythology that fat is necessarily bad. Changing our beliefs is extremely difficult when every day we are bombarded with messages paid for by our own government that obesity kills, and when every time we turn on the television or pick up a magazine the only people we see are thin.

Accepting and celebrating all body shapes and sizes means neutralizing fat so that it becomes just a descriptive word and not a character flaw. It means accepting our children as they are and not trying to pressure them to change their body size. It means helping them be fat with dignity and letting them know how beautiful they are. It means having pictures of fat people on the walls of our classrooms and addressing bullying so that our schools are safe for children of all body types. It means encouraging all children to be physically active and developing programs so that everyone can feel a measure of confidence and success.

Because we have such a genetically diverse population there will always be fat people in our society. It is not the fat that should be the center of our concern but the underlying causes that are making our children progressively fatter. It is not the fat that is the problem. It is the fact that our children are leading sedentary lives, consuming large amounts of high-fat food and using food to deal with their psychological distress.

Provide Opportunities for Girls to be Physically Active

Girls are pressured not only to be beautiful but also to be smart, accomplished and confident. Yet no matter how successful they are at other things, if they are not thin and good looking they are still considered something of a failure. When we socialize girls to treat their bodies like commodities to be looked at and worked on, it becomes difficult for them to make the connection between being strong in their bodies and feeling good about themselves.

Girls need to use their bodies. They need to run and jump and kick and throw. They need to wave their arms, raise their voices and take up space. They need to sweat. Not only will they be physically and emotionally healthier doing so but they will be able to move from seeing their bodies as 'decorative' to living in them and experiencing them as a vital part of who they are.

It is shameful that today three out of five children aged five to seventeen are not active enough for optimal growth and development.[2] Children are being sent contradictory messages. They are teased and ostracized when they are fat, yet natural play opportunities are being curtailed and they receive little physical education and have little chance to be physically active.

We need to make physical activity and sports accessible, enjoyable and safe at home, at school and in our communities and recreation centers. Physical education must become more relevant for girls. It must be fun—which means we need to provide girls with a balance between skills and challenges and with opportunities for interactions with their friends. Physical education must include more than traditional sport and must provide girls with activities they enjoy and at which they can have a measure of success. We need to ensure that physical education curriculums are treated as seriously in our schools as those of more academic subjects and we need to support teachers who are innovative and to ensure the changes that are happening in educational curriculums address the specific needs of girls.

We need to integrate physical activity into our girls' daily lives so that it is seen as a lifelong and enjoyable activity and not dependent upon organized sports. We can do this by teaching girls to 'snack on exercise' at home and incorporate these 'snacks' into our classroom routines. We can be physically active with them and walk or cycle instead of taking the car everywhere. We can join activities together and plan active family events. We can even get up from watching television and bend and stretch during the commercials. The two or three hours a week of soccer that our girls may play are great, but they are simply not enough.

We need to be careful that when we encourage girls to participate in sports we ensure they have the opportunity to learn skills. This means making sure that they have girl-only time and lots of practice. We need to place the emphasis on having fun instead of winning. When girls do participate in organized sports we need to be very clear about whose need is being satisfied. One little girl was enrolled in baseball not because she wanted to play but because the daughters of her mother's friends were on that team and it was a perfect opportunity for her mother to socialize as she was watching the game.

Put an End to Dieting

We need to stop girls from dieting and support them while they disengage. Dieting has serious consequences. It robs girls of their natural bodies, contributes to the silencing of their voices and damages their sense of self. Adolescent girls who diet or exercise obsessively just to lose weight or pursue other weight-control efforts are significantly more likely to gain weight and become very fat later on.[3] They are also at high risk of developing an eating disorder.

Adolescent girls who diet are four times more likely to smoke than those who do not diet. Smoking is one of the most popular weight-control strategies among adolescents. And dieting itself may create a craving for nicotine, leading to a cycle of weight loss and increased tobacco consumption.[4] Dieting affects girls' attention span and can lower their IQ and affect their performance in school.[5] It contributes to changes in girls' moods making them depressed, irritable, anxious and frequently angry, and affects girls' self-esteem and their relationships with others.

Because girls learn their dieting behavior from us, we need to get off diets ourselves. Says one young woman who struggled with anorexia "When I was nine years old I went on a diet so that I could be just like my mom. I finally asked my mother why she kept dieting because she never stuck with it and it never really worked. I became anorexic trying to show her that I could be better at it than her."

In workshop after workshop that I do there is at least one woman who expresses her concerns about her daughter's preoccupation with weight. When I ask if she is dieting herself, nine times out of ten the answer is yes—just to lose a few pounds or she's struggling to keep off the weight she lost before or doing it because she feels better at a certain weight and because it's good for her health. She never makes the connection that this reinforces in her daughter the very behavior that she would like to stop.

We often don't realize the powerful effect our behavior has on girls. Yet a careless remark that we quickly forget remains with girls. Many girls start to diet after their fathers or teachers made comments about their weight.

The most effective way to prevent girls from dieting is to encourage their healthy self-expression, help them find a passion so that their focus is not solely on how they look, teach them the skills to become media literate and encourage them to use their bodies.

The most effective way of getting girls off diets is through groups that validate their experiences and provide them with the opportunity to talk about their concerns. Groups are a powerful way of teaching girls new behaviors and providing them with a safe place to practice with their peers. Because friendships are so important to girls you can't just get one girl off her diet, you have to get her friends off their diets as well.

Become a Social Activist

Once we become Size Acceptance Warriors we start to realize that it's not enough to work with or parent girls. We also need to change the social environment in which we live. There are many ways we can be social activists. We can fight fat prejudice by writing letters to media advertisers and manufacturers. We can work with schools and communities to stop bullying and to provide girl-only programs.

While I've addressed what we can do individually to make physical activity a way of life, we also need changes in our society. We need to make our streets and parks safe for girls to play in and so they can walk to stores and community centers instead of being driven all the time. We can lobby for girl-friendly park space and for safe bicycle trails. For example, most girls won't use skate board pits because they are intimidated byboys.

We need to look at the way most people's time is structured. How can we expect parents to be physically active if they put in long work days and longer commutes? We need to make physical activity affordable. This may mean subsidizing rapid transit to make it easier for everyone to get out and about. It may mean subsidizing community center activities and sports organization fees and equipment.

We need to support organizations that advocate for gender equity such as Promotion Plus, CAAWS and the Women's Sports Foundation. We can start by becoming members as a way of showing that we believe in what they do.

As Size Acceptance Warriors it is important to realize that we are all in this together. No one person is responsible for everything, no one person will win the fight all alone and no one person has to do it all. We need to pick one thing to work on that interests us and then give it whatever time we have. Some of us will writing letters, some will lobbying for change, some will fight fat prejudice in our society and schools and organizations and some will educate people about the dangers of dieting and the even greater danger of focusing on obesity instead of addressing the inactivity that lies underneath.

Above all we have to make sure that we never ever give up until all girls can celebrate their physical heritage and be proud of the body they were born with and be proud of themselves.

Endnotes:

1. Steiner-Adair, C. (1990) "The body politic: Normal female adolescent development and the development of eating disorders," in Gilligan, C., Lyons, N.P. & T. J. Hanmer, (Eds.) *Making Connections: The Relational Worlds of Adolescent Girls at Emma Willard School.* Cambridge: Harvard University Press
2. *Canadian Fitness and Lifestyle Institute* in Vancouver Province, October 21, 2001
3. Stice, E., Cameron, R.P., Hayward, C.et al. (1999) "Naturalistic weight-reduction efforts prospectively predict growth in relative weight and onset of obesity among female adolescents," *J Consult Clin Psychol.*, 67: 967-974
4. *American Journal of Public Health* as reported in the Globe and Mail, September 8, 2001
5. *Healthy Weight Journal* (2000) 14: 6, 83/ Kenyon G., "Dieting may harm girls' I.Q." in Reuters Health London 8/1/00

Bibliography

Acosta, R.V. & Carpenter, L.J. (1985) "Women in athletics—A status report," *Journal of Physical Education, Recreation and Dance* 56: 42-43

Aldridge, S. (September 2001) "Obesity and heart failure," *Journal of the American College of Cardiology*

American Journal of Health Promotion, 1996, Vol. 10: 171-174

Anderson, C. (Summer 1997) "Are kids having enough fun?" *Melpomene*, Vol. 16, No. 2, pp. 4-8

Anderson, R. E. (2000) "The spread of the childhood obesity epidemic," *Canadian Medical Association Journal*, 163(11): 1461-1462

Araton, H. (2002) *Alive and Kicking: When Soccer Moms Take the Field and Change their Lives Forever*. New York: Simon and Schuster

The Associated Press in the *New York Times*, December 14, 2001, "U.S. Warning of Death Toll From Obesity"

Avery, J. & J. Stevens, (1998) *Too Many Men on the Ice: Women's Hockey in North America*. Vancouver: Polestar Books

Barrett-Conner, E. "Obesity, Atherosclerosis and Coronary Heart Disease," paper presented at the conference on Health Implications of Obesity in Bethesda, MD

Bennet, W. & J. Gurin. (1982) *The Dieter's Dilemma*. New York: Basic Books

Berel, S. (1998) "Media and disturbed eating: Implications for prevention," *Journal of Primary Prevention*, 18(4): 415-430

Berg, F.M. (July/August 1998) "Rethinking low-fat advice," *Healthy Weight Journal*, Vol. 12. No. 4

Berg, F.M. (May/June 1992) "Who is dieting in the United States?" *Obesity and Health*

Berg, F.M. (September/October 1999) "Integrated approach: Health at any size," *Healthy Weight Journal*

Berger-Sweeny, J. (February 9, 1996) "The Developing Brain: Genes, Environment and Behavior." AAS Symposium

Berry, B. J. "The implications of the 1999 Ontario secondary school reforms on physical education," OPHEA website <www.ophea.net>

Birch, L.L. (1992) "Children's preferences for high fat food," *Nutrition Review*, 50:249-255

Birch, L.L., McPhee, L., Shoba, B.C. et al. (1987) "Clean up your plate: effects of child feeding practices on the conditioning of meal size," *Learning and Motivation*: 18:301-317

Blum, D. (1997) *Sex on the Brain: The Biological Differences Between Men and Women*. New York: Viking

Blum, D. (July 1999) "What's the Difference Between Boys and Girls?" *Life Magazine*

Brody, J.E. (September 12, 2000) "Added Sugars are Taking a toll on Health," *New York Times*

Brown, C. (Fall 1994) "Danger: children at risk," *Canadian Woman Studies: Women and Girls in Sport and Physical Activity*, Vol. 15, No. 4

Brownell, K.D., Greenwood, M.R.C., Stellar, E., & E.E. Shrager. (1986) "The effects of repeated cycles of weight loss and regain in rats," *Physiology and Behavior*, 38:459-464

Cahn, S.K. (1993) "From the muscle moll to the butch ballplayer: Mannishness, lesbianism and homophobia," in *U.S. Women's Sport Feminist Studies*, p. 334

Canadian Association for Health, Physical Education, Recreation and Dance (CAHPERD). (1997) *Girls in Action Speaking Out*

Canadian Association for Health, Physical Education, Recreation and Dance. (1999) *Girls and Boys in Elementary Education: Issues and Action*

Canadian Fitness and Lifestyle Research Institute. (1996) "How active are Canadians?" *Progress in Prevention*, Bulletin No. 1

Cash, T. F. (May 17, 2001) "Beyond body image as a trait: The development and validation of the body image states scale," *Eating Disorders: The Journal of Treatment and Prevention*

Centers for Disease Control and Prevention. (1991) "Body weight perceptions and selected weight management goals and practices of high school students," *JAMA* :2811-2812

Center for Media Literacy   <www.medialit.org>

Center for Science in the Public Interest (2000) in *Healthy Weight Journal*, Vol. 14, No. 2, March/April

Chapman, G. & H. MacLean. (1993) "Junk food and healthy food: Means of food in adolescent women's culture," *Journal of Nutritional Education*, No. 25

Coaches' Game Plan developed by the Sport and Community Development Branch of British Columbia

Cohen, Joyce. (May 19, 2001) "He-Mails, She-Mails: Where Sender Meets Gender." *New York Times*

Communique. (September 1999) "Gender Equity," British Columbia Recreation and Parks Association (BCRPA) and Canadian Parks and Recreation Association (CPRA)

Cooper, P.J. & I. Goodyer. (1997) "Prevalence and significance of weight and shape concerns in girls aged 11-16 years old," *Br J Psychiatry*, Dec: 171:542-544

Council on Size and Weight Discrimination, Inc. (2000)

Crawford, P.B. & L.R. Shapiro (1991) "How obesity develops: A new look at nature and nuture," in *Obesity and Health*, F.M. Berg (ed.) Hettinger, N.D. Healthy Living Institute

Dahlgren, W. (1988) *A Report of the National Task Force on Young Females and Physical Activity*, Ottawa, ON: Department of Fitness and Amateur Sport

Did You Know? (1996, January 30) Parents, 71, 30

Edwards, P. *Evening the Odds: Adolescent Women: Tobacco and Physical Activity*, Gloucester, ON: Canadian Association for the Advancement of Women and Sport and Physical Activity

Erikson, E. (1968) *Identity, Youth and Crisis*. New York: W.W. Norton

Ernsberger, P. & R.J. Koletsk. (January/February 2000) "Rationale for a wellness approach to obesity," in *Healthy Weight Journal*, Vol. 14 No. 1, pp 8-15

Erkut, S. (Spring 1999) Research Report, Wellesley College Center for Research on Women

Esquire Magazine (February 1994)

Feldman, W.F., Feldman, E. & J. Goodman. (1986) "Health concerns and health related behaviors of adolescents," *CMAJ*, No. 134: 489-493

Fenton, J.M. (1996) "Linking girls' experiences in physical activity to school culture and social and political contexts: Elements of an exemplary model," University of British Columbia unpublished Master's degree thesis

Fisher, H. (1999) *The First Sex: The Natural Talents of Women and How They are Changing the World.* New York: Random House

Fisher, J.O. & L.L. Birch. "Parents' restrictive feeding practices are associated with young girls' negative self-evaluation of eating," *J Am Diet Assoc*, 100:1341-1346, taken from *Healthy Weight Updates*, (July 2000)

Fleming, A.T. (November 1994) "Daughters of Dieters," *Glamour Magazine*

Friedman, S. (1999) *Just for Girls Program Manual.* Vancouver: Salal Books

Friedman, S. (2000) *Nurturing girlpower: Integrating Eating Disorder Prevention/Intervention Skills into your Practice.* Vancouver: Salal Books

Friedman, S. (2000) *When Girls Feel Fat: Helping Girls Through Adolescence.* Toronto: HarperCollins (Firefly: U.S. edition)

Frisancho, A.R. (2000) "Prenatal compared with parental origins of adolescent fatness," *American Journal of Clinical Nutrition,* Novembers; 72(5): 1198-1190

Gaesser, Glenn A. (1996) *Big Fat Lies: The Truth About Your Weight and Your Body.* New York: Fawcett Columbine

Garner, D.M. & Wooley, D. (1991) "Confronting the failure of behavioral and dietary treatments for obesity," *Clin Psychol Rev*: 729-780

Garrow, J. (1974) *Energy Balance and Obesity in Man.* New York: American Elsevier

George, Elizabeth. (2001) *A Traitor to Memory.* New York: Bantam Books

Gerbner, G. (1998) Bell Atlantic Professor of Telecommunication, Temple University, Philadelphia

Gibbons, S., Higgins, J.W., Gaul, C. & G. Van Gyn. (1999) "Listening to female students in high school physical education," *Avante*, Vol. 5, No. 2: 1-20

Gilligan, C. & L. M. Brown. (1992) *Meeting at the Crossroads: Women's Psychology and Girl's Development*. Cambridge: Harvard University Press

Goodman, E. I. (1996) "Eating disorders on the rise in preteens, adolescents," *Psychiatry News,* 24(2): 10

Goodman, N., Richardson, S.A., Dornbush, S.M. & A.H. Hastorf. (1963) "Variant reactions to physical disabilities," *American Sociological Review,* 28: 429-435

Gordon-Larson, P. (2001) "Obesity-related knowledge, attitudes and behaviors in obese and non-obese urban Philadelphia female adolescents," *Obes Res*, Feb: 9(2):112-118

Gorski, R. (1991) "Sexual differentiation of the brain," in Krieger, D.T. & J.C. Hughes. (Eds.) *Neuroendocrinology*. Sunderland, MA: Sinauer Associates

Gortmaker, S.L., Dietz, W.H., Sobol, A.M., & C.A. Wehler. (1987) "Increasing pediatric obesity in the United States," *American Journal Dis Child,* 141:535-540

Graydon, S. & E. Verrall. *Gender Issues in the Media,* MediaWatch website <www.mediawatch.ca>

Greendorfer, S. (June 1987) "Hop, step and jump away: Socialization of females into sport," A presentation given at the New Agenda II Conference, Indianpolis, IN

Griffin, P.S. (1989) "Equity in the gym: What are the hurdles?" *Canadian Association for Health, Physical Education and Recreation Journal,* 55(2): 23-26

Guo, S.S., Roche, A.F., Chumlea, W.C., Gardner, J.C & R.M. Siervogel. (1994) "The predictive value of childhood body mass index values for overeweight at age 35," *American Journal of Clinical Nutrition,* 59:810-819

Gurian, M. (1996) *The Wonder of Boys: What Parents, Mentors and Educators Can Do To Make Boys Into Exceptional Men.* New York: Tarcher/Putnam

Habib, Marlene. "Study suggests exercise–not counting calories–the cornerstone of health." *The Vancouver Province*, (January 2, 2002)

Hall, J. (1984) *Nonverbal Sex Differences: Communication Accuracy and Expressive Style*. Baltimore: Johns Hopkins University Press

Hancock, E. (1989) *The Girl Within*. New York: Ballantine Books

Hardman, K. & J. Marshall. (1999) "The world-wide survey of the state and status of physical education in schools," University of Manchester, England. <http://www.icsspe.org/eng/forschung/hardman_eng.htm>

Hay J. & Donnelly, P. (1996) "Sorting out the boys from the girls: Teacher perception of student physical ability," *Avante*, Vo.2, No. 1:36-52

Healthy Eating Journal, (July/August 1998) Vol. 12, No. 4

Healthy Weight Journal (2000) 14: 6, 83/ Kenyon G., "Dieting may harm girls' I.Q." in *Reuters Health London* 8/1/00

Heart Health Coalition. (1997) *British Columbia–Setting the Pace: A Plan To Improve The Health Of British Columbians Through Physical Activity*, Vancouver, BC: Heart and Stroke Foundation of B.C. & Yukon

Heilbrun, C. (1988) *Writing A Woman's Life*. New York: Ballantine Books

Hill & Silver. (1995) in Michael I. Loewy, "Working with fat children in schools." *Radiance Magazine*, Fall Issue, 1998

Humbert, M.L. (1995) "On the sidelines: The Experiences of young women in physical education classes," *Avante*, Vol. 1, No. 2: 58-77

Huston, A. (1992) *Big World, Small Screen: The Role of Television in American Society*. Lincoln: University of Nebraska Press

Hutchinson, M. G. (1994) "Imagine ourselves whole: A feminist approach to treating body image disorders," in Fallon, Patricia, Katzman, Melanie A. & Susan C. Wooley (Eds.) *Feminist Perspectives on Eating Disorders*. New York Guilford Press

Irving, L. M. & D. Neumark-Sztainer. (2002) "Integrating the prevention of eating disorders and obesity: Feasible or futile?" *Preventive Medicine*

Jaffee, L & P. Wu. (Summer 1996) "After-school activities and self-esteem in adolescent girls," *Melpomene*, Vol 15, No. 2

Johnson, S.L. & L.L. Birch. (1994) "Parents' and children's adiposity and eating style," *Pediatrics*, 94:653-661

Jones, J.M., Bennett, S., Olmsted, M.P., Lawson, M. L. & G. Rodin. (2001) "Disordered eating attitudes and behaviours in teenaged girls. A school-based study," *CMAJ*, 165(5):547-52

Kater, K. J. (1998) *Healthy Body Image: Teaching Kids to Eat and Love their Bodies Too*. Seattle: EDAP (National Eating Disorders Association)

Kearney Cook, A. Eating Disorders Workshop. Washington State University, Vancouver Washington, February 23, 2001

Keays, J.J. & K.R. Allison (1995) "The effects of regular moderate to vigorous physical activity on student outcomes: A review," *Canadian Journal of Public Health*, Vol. 86, No. 11

Kilbourne, J. (1994) "Still killing us softly: Advertising and the obsession with thinness," in Fallon et al *Feminist Perspectives on Eating Disorders*, New York: The Guilford Press, p. 397

Killen, J.D., Taylor, C.B., Hammer, L.D., Litt, I., Wilson, D.M., Rich, T., Hayward, C., Simmons, B., Karemer, H. & A. Varady. (1993) "An attempt to modify unhealthful eating attitudes and weight regulation practices of young adolescent girls," *International Journal of Eating Disorders*, 13:369-78

Killen, J.D., Taylor, C.B., Telch, M.J., Saylor, K.E., Moaron, D.J. & T.N. Robinson. (1986) "Self-induced vomiting, laxative and diuretic use among teenagers: Precursors of the binge-purge syndrome," *Journal of the American Medical Association*, 255:1442-1449

Kimball, M. M. (1986) "Television and sex-role attitudes," in T.M. Williams (ed.) *The Impact of Television: A Natural Experiment in Three Communities*. Orlando, FL.: Academic Press

Landsberg, M. (1989) *'This is New York, Honey:' A Homage to Manhattan, with Love and Rage*. Toronto: McClelland & Stewart, Inc.

LeCrone, H. (1950) "How preoccupation with food leads to loss of control," in Ancel Keys et al *The Biology of Human Starvation*, Minneapolis: University of Minnesota Press

Lee, C.D., Jackson, A.S. & S.D. Blair. (August 22, 1998) "US weight guidelines: Is it also important to consider cardiorespiratory fitness?" *Int J Obes Relat Metabl Disord*, Suppl. 2:S2-7

Lenskyj, H.J. (1986) *Out of Bounds: Women, Sports and Sexuality.* Toronto: The Women's Press

Lenskyj, H.J. (Fall 1994) "What's sport got to do with it?" *Canadian Woman Studies: Women and Girls in Sport and Physical Activity*, Vol. 15, No. 4

Levine, M. P, Smolak, L., Moodey A. F., Shuman, M. D. & L.D. Hessen. (1994) "Normative developmental challenges and dieting and eating disturbance in middle school girls," *International Journal of Eating Disorders*, 15: 11-20

Ludwig, D.S., Peterson, K.E., & S.L. Gortmaker. (2001) "Relations between consumption of sugar-sweetened drinks and childhood obesity. A prescriptive observational analysis," *The Lancet*: 357 (9255): 505-508

Lyons, P.A. & D. Burgard. (1988/2000) *Great Shape: The First Fitness Guide for Large Women.* Lincoln, NB: iUnivers.com.Inc

Lyons, P. (1996) "Fat and fit: An idea whose time has come," *Melpomene*, Fall, Vol. 15, No. 3

Lyons, P. (Fall 2000) "Challenging the 'war on obesity," *Perspective: A Professional Journal of the Renfrew Center Foundation*, 6(1): 10

MacDonald, Gayle. (Saturday, January 13, 2001) "Girls Under the Knife," *The Globe and Mail*

Maine, M. (2000) *Body Wars: Making Peace with Women's Bodies: An Activist's Guide.* Carlsbad, CA: Gurze Books

Maloney, M.J., McGuire J., Daniels, S.R. & B. Specker. (1990) "Dieting behavior and eating attitudes in children," *Pediatrics*, May; 85(5): 714

Mandigo, J.L. & R.T. Couture. (1996) "An overview of the components of fun in physical education, organized sport and physical activity programs," *Avante*, Vol. 2, No. 3: 42-55

On the Move Newsletter, (Autumn, 1997) Melpomene

Miller, L. K. & V. Santini. (1986) "Sex differences in spatial abilities: Strategic and experiential correlates," *Acta Psychologica,* p. 62

Mizell, L. "Using the film with middle and high school students," in Study Guide for *Beyond Killing Us Softly: The Strength to Resist,* edited by Carlene Larsson, <www.cambridgedocumentaryfilms.org>

Moir, A. & D. Jessel. (1991) *Brain Sex: The Real Difference Between Men and Women.* New York: Bantam, Doubleday Dell

Mokdad, A.H., Sedrula, M.K., Dietz, W.H., Bowman, B.A., Marks, J.S. & J.P. Koplan (2000) "The continuing epidemic of obesity in the United States, " *JAMA* 284: 1650 - 1

Moore, T. (1993) *Lifespan: New Lives Longer and Why.* New York, Touchstone

National Association for Sport and Physical Education: *Shape of the Nation Survey,* 1997

National Women's Law Center <www.nwlc.org>

Nelson, M.B. (1994) *The Stronger Women Get, The More Men Like Football: Sexism and the American Culture of Sport.* New York: Avon Books

Neumark-Sztainer, D., Butler, R. & H. Palti. (1995) "Eating disturbances among adolescent girls: Evaluation of a school-based primary prevention program," *Journal of Nutrition Education,* 27:24-3

New York Times Magazine, September 2, 2001/Section 6

Nisbett, R.E. (1972) "Hunger, obesity and the ventromedical hypothalamus," *Psychological Review,* 79:433-533

Norgate, S. (1997) *Storm Clouds Over Party Shoes: Etiquette Problems for the Ill-Bred Woman."* Vancouver: Press Gang,

North American Association for the Study of Obesity, Annual Scientific Meeting. News release 11/1/00 taken from Healthy Weight Updates, July, 2000

Nutrition Recommendations Update: Dietary Fat and Children, Report of the joint working group of the Canadian Pediatric Society and Health Canada

O'Dea, J. & S. Abraham. (2000) "Improving the body image, eating attitudes and behaviors of young male and female adolescents: A new educational approach that focuses on self-esteem," *International Journal of Eating Disorders,* 28: 43-57

O'Dea, J. (2000) "School-based interventions to prevent eating problems: First do no harm," *Eating Disorders: Journal of Treatment and Prevention,* 8: 123-130

Offord, D., M.H. Boyle, P. Szatmari et al. (1987) "Ontario child and health study II: Six month prevalence of disorder and rates of service utilization," *Archives of General Psychiatry.* Vol. 44

Oliveria, S.A., Ellison, R.C., Moore, L.L., Gillman, M.E., Garrahie, E.J., & M.R. Singer. (1992) "Parent-child relationships in nutrient intake. The Framingham children's study," *American Journal of Clinical Nutrition,* 63: 593-598

Omichinski, L. (May/June 1993) "A paradigm shift from weight loss to healthy living," *Healthy Weight Journal*

Omichinski, L. (1995) *Hugs for Teens and Diet: No weigh; Building the road to Healthier Living,* VI Parents' Guide, Hugs International Inc.

Orbach, S. (1978/1998) *Fat is a Feminist Issue.* New York: Galahad Books

Patton, G.C., Selzer, R., Coffey, C., Carlin, J.B., & R. Wolfe (1999) "Onset of adolescent eating disorders. Population based cohort study," *BMJ,* March 20: 318(7186):765-768

Paxton, S. J. (1993) "A prevention program for disturbed eating and body dissatisfaction in adolescent girls: A one year follow-up," *Health Education Research,* 8:43-51

Paxton, S. J. (1999) "Peer relations, body image, and disordered eating in adolescent girls: Implications for prevention," in Piran, N., Levine, M.P. & C. Steiner-Adair (Eds.) *Preventing Eating Disorders: A Handbook of Interventions and Special Challenges,* Philadelphia: Brunner/Mazel

Pipher, M. (1994) *Reviving Ophelia: Saving the Selves of Adolescent Girls.* New York: Ballantine Books

Piran, N., Irving, L. & S. Friedman. (2001) "Assumptions of a Relational Approach to Prevention," Academy of Eating Disorders International Conference, Vancouver, BC

Polivy, J. & C.P. Herman. (1983) *Breaking the Diet Habit.* New York: Basic Book

Pollack, W. (1998) *Real Boys: Rescuing Our Sons from the Myths of Boyhood.* New York: Random House

The Presidents Council on Physical Fitness and Sports (1997) *Physical Activity and Sport in the lives of Girls: Physical and Mental Health Dimensions from an Interdisciplinary Approach,* Washington, D.C.: Department of Health and Human Services

Reinish, J. M. (1974) "Fetal hormones, the brain and human sex differences: A heuristic integrative review of the recent literature," *Archives of Sexual Behavior,* No. 3

Robertson, S. (Fall 1995) "The life and times of CAAWS," *Canadian Woman Studies: Women and Girls in Sport and Physical Activity,* Vol. 15, No 4:16-21

Rothblum, E.D. (1994) "I'll die for the revolution but don't ask me to diet: Feminism and the continuing stigmatization of obesity," in Fallon, Patricia, Katzman, Melanie A. & Susan C. Wooley *Feminist Perspectives on Eating Disorders.* New York Guilford Press

Rothblum, E.D., Miller, C.T. & B. Barbutt. (1988) "Stereotypes of obese female job applicants," *International Journal of Eating Disorders,* 7: 277-283

Reuters Health 11/1/00: Weight cycling appears to lower levels of HDL-C in women. Westport, CT *J Am Coll Cardiol* 2000, 26: 1565-1571

Ryan, J. (1995) *Little Girls in Pretty Boxes: The Making and Breaking of Elite Gymnasts and Figure Skaters.* New York: Doubleday

Rubin, J.Z., Provenzano, E. & Z. Luria. (1974) "The eye of the beholder: Parents' views on the sex of their newborns," *American Journal of Orthopsychiatry.,* No. 44

Sadker, M. & D. Sadker. (1994) *Failing at Fairness: How Our Schools Cheat Girls.* New York: Simon and Schuster

Satter, E. (1999) *Secrets of Feeding a Healthy Family.* Kelcy Press, Madison, WI

Scott, C. (Spring 1997) "Billie Jean King: A force for change in women's sports," *Melpomene,* Vol. 16, No. 1, p. 11

Seid, R.P. (1994) "Too 'close to the bone:' The historical context for women's obsessions with slenderness," in Fallon, Patricia, Katzman, Melanie A. & Susan C. Wooley (1994) (Eds.) *Feminist Perspectives on Eating Disorders.* New York: The Guilford Press

Shakeshaft, C. (March 1986) "A gender at risk," *Phi Delta Kappan.* Vol. 67, No. 73

Shaw, J. & G. Waller. (1995) "The media's impact on body image: Implications for prevention and treatment," *Eating Disorders: Journal of Treatment and Prevention,* 3(2):115-123

Sheldon, A. (1993) "Pickle fights: Gendered talk in preschool disputes," in Tannen, D. (Ed.). *Gender and Conversational Interaction.* New York: Oxford University Press

Shisslak, C. M., Crago, M.E., Estes, L.E. & L. Smolak. (1996) "Content and method of developmentally appropriate prevention programs," in Smolak, L. Levine, Michael P. & Ruth Streigel-Moore (Eds.) The *Developmental Psychopathology of Eating Disorders.* NJ: Lawrence Erlbaum Associates

Siegler, A. (1993) "Grieving the lost dreams of thinness" in Brown, C. & K. Jasper, (Eds.) *Consuming Passions: Feminist Approaches to Weight Preoccupation and Eating Disorders.* Toronto: Second Storey Press, pp. 152-154

Silverman, E. & M. Eals. (1992) "Sex differences in spatial abilities: Evolutional theory and data," in. J.Barkow, L. Cosmides & J.Tooby. (Eds.) *The Adapted Mind: Evolutionary Psychology and the Generation of Culture.* New York: Oxford University Press

Smolak, L, Levine, M.P., & F. Schermer. (1998) "A controlled evaluation of an elementary school primary prevention program for eating problems," *Journal of Psychosomatic Research,* 44:339-354

Snow, K. (Fall 1994) "Where are the role models: Exploring the invisibility of female athletes in the media," *Canadian Woman Studies: Women and Girls in Sport and Physical Activity,* Vol. 14, No. 4

Spraul, M. et al. (1997) "Mortality in obesity," *International Journal of Obesity,* 21 (Suppl 2):S24

Steinberg, L. & J. Belsky. (1991) *Infancy, Childhood and Adolescence: Development in Context.* New York: McGraw Hill

Steiner-Adair. C. (1990) "The body politic: Normal female adolescent development and the development of eating disorders," in Gilligan, C., Lyons, N.P. & T.J. Hanmer, (Eds.) *Making Connections: The Relational Worlds of Adolescent Girls at Emma Willard School.* Cambridge: Harvard University Press

Steiner-Adair, C. & A.P. Vorenberg. (1999) "Resisting weightism: Media literacy for elementary-school children," in Piran, N., Levine, M.P. & C. Steiner-Adair (Eds.) *Preventing Eating Disorders: A Handbook of Interventions and Special Challenge*s. Philadelphia: Brunner/Mazel

Stice, E., Agras, W.A. & L.D. Hammer. (1990) "Risk factors for the emergence of childhood eating disturbances. A five year prospective study," *International Journal of Eating Disorders,* 26:375-387

Stice, E., Cameron, R.P., Hayward, C. et al (1997) "Naturalistic weight-reduction efforts prospectively predict growth in relative weight and onset of obesity among female adolescents," *J Consult Clin Psychol,* 67: 967-974

Stunkard, A.J., Harris, J.R., Pederson, N.L. et al. (1990) "The body mass index of twins who have been reared apart," *New England Journal of Medicine,* 1483-1487

Stinson, K. M. (2001) *Women And Dieting Culture: Inside A Commercial Weight Loss Group.* New Brunswick, New Jersey: Rutgers University Press

Surrey, J. L. (1991) "The self-in-relation: A theory of women's development." in J. Jordan, A.G. Kaplan, J. B. Miller, I. P. Stiver & J. L. Surrey. (Eds.) *Women's Growth in Connection: Writings From the Stone Center.* New York: Guilford Press

Tannen, D. (1990) *You Just Don't Understand: Women and Men in Conversatio*n. New York Ballantine Books

Thelen, M.H., Powell, A.L., Lawrence, C. & M.E. Kuhnert. (1992) "Eating and body image concerns among children," *Journal of Clinical Child Psychology,* 21: 41-46

Tremblay, M.S. & D. Willms. (2000) "Secular trends in the body mass index of Canadian children," *Canadian Medical Association Journal*, 163(11): 1429-1433

University of Ca., Berkeley. (April 2001) *Wellness Letter*, Vol. 17, No. 7

US Continuing Survey of Food Intake by Individuals, (1994-1996)

US Department of Health, Education and Welfare, (1979)

Vertinsky, P. (1992) "Reclaiming space, revisioning the body: The quest for gender-sensitive physical education," *Quest*, 44:373:396

Waaler, H.T. (1984) "Height, weight and mortality: The Norwegian experience," *Acta Med Scan Suppl*: 1-56

Waterhouse, D. (1997) *Like Mother, Like Daughter: How Women are Influenced by Their Mothers' Relationship with Food—and How to Break the Pattern*. New York: Hyperion Books

Weight cycling appears to lower levels of HDL-C in women. Westport, CT, Reuters Health 11/1/00: *J Am Coll Cardiol* 2000, 26: 1565-1571

Werthner, P. (May 2001) "Understanding the differences between how women and men communicate," *Canadian Journal for Women in Coaching*, Vol. 1, No.5

Wolf, N. (1991) *The Beauty Myth: How Images of Beauty are Used Against Women*. New York: Morrow

Women's Sports Foundation (2001) *Why Sports Participation for Girls and Women*: *The Foundation Position*, Women's Sports Foundation <www.womensportsfoundation.org>

Women's Sports Foundation, *Health Risks and the Teenage Athlete*

Women's Sports Foundation (Fall 2001) "Arrows Can't Strike Down the Waves," *The Women's Sports Experience: A Newsletter for the Supporters of the Women's Sports Foundation*, Vol. 10, No. 3, pp. 9-10

Women's Sport Foundation Website, *Parents' Guide to Girls' Sports*

WTN program, "You, Me and the Kids," episode on body image. (1998)

Resources

Anti-Diet and Weight Acceptance

When Women Stop Hating Their Bodies: Freeing Yourself from Food and Weight Obsession. Jane R. Hirschmann & Carol H. Munter. New York, NY: Fawcett Columbine/Ballantine Books, 1995

Am I Fat? Helping Young Children Accept Differences in Body Size. J. Ikeda & P. Naworski. Santa Cruz, CA: ETR Associates, 1992

Making Peace with Food: Freeing Yourself from the Diet/Weight Obsession. Susan Kano. New York, NY: HarperCollins, 1989

Healthy Weight Journal, Frances Berg, editor
B.C. Decker, Inc.
P.O. Box 785, Lewiston, NY   14092-0785
☎ 1-800-568-7281   FAX 1-905-522-7839
<www.bcdecker.com>   info@bcdecker.com

No Weigh–a non-dieting program for use with teenagers
HUGS International
Box 102A, RR3, Portage La Prairie, MB   R1N 3A3
☎ 1-800-565-4847   <www.hugs.com>

Bodies

Real Gorgeous: The truth about body and beauty.
Kaz Cooke. New York, NY: Norton, 1995
[Good information presented with lots of humor.]

Body Talk: The Straight Facts about Fitness, Nutrition, and Feeling Great about Yourself!
Ann & Julie Douglas. Maple Tree Press, 2002
[Written by mother & daughter. Great book for girls!]

200 Ways to Love the Body You Have.
M. G. Hutchinson. Trumansburg, NY: Crossing Press, 1999
[Has the best information about body awareness]

Body Wars: Making Peace with Women's Bodies, An Activist's Guide. Margo Maine, PhD, Carlsbad, CA: Gurze Books, 2000 [Excellent information and resources including lists of media addresses.]

That Body Image Thing: Young Women Speak Out. Edited by Sara Torres. [Collection of the best 600 essays written by young women under the age of 20 for a competition sponsored by Chatelaine Magazine and CRIAW]. Cost is $11.95. (CRIAW)
Canadian Research Institute for the Advancement of Women
151 Slater Street, Suite 408, Ottawa, ON   K1P 5H4
☎ 613-563-0681   FAX 613-563-0682
<www.criaw-icref.ca>   info@criaw-icref.ca

About-Face
[A San Francisco based organization committed to promoting positive body image and self-esteem in girls and women.] <www.about-face>

Boys

The Wonder of Boys: What Parents, Mentors and Educators Can Do to Shape Boys into Exceptional Men. Michael Gurian. New York, NY: Jeremy P. Tarcher/Putnam, 1996

Boys Will Be Boys: Breaking the Link Between Masculinity and Violence. Miriam Miedzian. New York, NY: Anchor Books, 1991

Real Boys: Rescuing Our Sons from the Myths of Boyhood. William Pollack, New York, NY: Random House, 1998

The Brain

Sex on the Brain: The Biological Differences Between Men and Women. Deborah Blum. New York, NY: Viking, 1997

The First Sex: The Natural Talents of Women and How They are Changing the World. Helen Fisher, New York: Random House, 1999

Brain Sex: The Real Differences Between Men and Women. Anne Moir & David Jessel. New York, NY: Dell Publishing, 1989

Communication/Conflict Resolution

Viewpoints: A Guide to Conflict Resolution and Decision Making for Adolescents and *Teachers' Guide to Viewpoints.* Nancy G. Guerra, Ann Moore & Ronald Slaby. Research Press, 1995

Peer Mediation: Conflict Resolution in Schools. (Program Guide and Student Manual). Fred Schrumpf, Donna Crawford & Richard Bodine. Research Press, 1996

Eating Disorders

Anorexia's Fallen Angel. Barbara McClintock, Toronto: HarperCollins, 2002

Consuming Passions: Feminist Approaches to Weight Preoccupation and Eating Disorders. Catrina Brown & Karin Jasper, editors. Toronto, ON: Second Story Press, 1993

The Eating Disorder Sourcebook: A Comprehensive Guide to the Causes, Treatment and Prevention of Eating Disorders. Carolyn Costin, M.A., M.Ed, M.F.C.C., Los Angeles: Lowell House, 1997

Feminist Perspectives on Eating Disorders. Patricia Fallon, Melanie Katzman & Susan Wooley, editors. New York, NY: Guilford Press, 1994

When Your Child Has An Eating Disorder: A Step-by-Step Workbook. Abigail H. Natenshon. San Francisco: Jossey-Bass Publishers, 1999

Coping with Eating Disorders. (a book for adolescents). Barbara Moe. New York, NY: Rosen Publishing Group, 1991

Surviving an Eating Disorder: Strategies for Families and Friends. Michelle Siegel, Judith Brisman & Margot Weinshel. New York, NY: Harper Perennial, 1988

Eating Disorder Prevention/Intervention

Every Body is a Somebody: Facilitator's Guide.
[Designed for elementary and high school. Provides information and strategies on ways to promote positive body image among teen girls.] Cost: $30 includes shipping.
Body Image Coalition of Peel (c/o Peel Health Unit)
180B Sandalwood Pkwy East, Suite 200
Brampton ON   L6Z 4N1
☎ 905-791-7800 ext: 7665

Just for Girls.
Sandra Susan Friedman. Vancouver, BC: Salal Books, 1999
[Open discussion group helps girls become aware of when they are feeling fat and teaches skills to express the feelings and ideas that lie underneath. Contains session plans and handouts.]
Cost: $35 plus shipping
Salal Books
#309, 101-1184 Denman Street, Vancouver, BC   V6G 2M9
☎ + FAX 604-689-8399   <www.salal.com>   salal@salal.com

Nurturing girlpower: Integrating Eating Disorder Prevention/Intervention Skills into your Practice. [Prevention framework, user-friendly skills and practical strategies.]
Sandra Susan Friedman. Vancouver, BC: Salal Books, 2000
Cost: $35 plus shipping from Salal Books (as above)

When Girls Feel Fat: Helping Girls Through Adolescence. Sandra Susan Friedman. Toronto, ON: HarperCollins, 2000
(US edition: Firefly Books, 2000)

Liking the Me I See in the Mirror. Suzanne Hare and Dianne Drummond. [Designed for teachers in grades 4 and higher for use with girls and boys.]
Cost: $35–Manual $25–CD $8–Parent Workbook + shipping
Food and Nutrition Services
Grey Nuns Community Hospital
1100 Youville Drive West, Edmonton, AB   T6L 5X8
☎ 780-450-7342   FAX 780-450-7226

Preventing Eating Disorders: A Handbook of Interventions and Special Challenges. Niva Piran, Michael P. Levine & Catherine Steiner-Adair, editors. Philadelphia, PA: Taylor and Francis, 1999

Everybody's Different Program
Contact: Dr. Jennifer O'Dea at jodea@nature.berkeley.edu

Eating Disorder Organizations

Anorexia Nervosa and Related Eating Disorders, Inc. (ANRED) P.O. Box 5102, Eugene, OR   97405
☎ 503-344-1144   <www.anred.com>

National Eating Disorders Association (NEDA–formerly EDAP) 603 Stewart Street, Suite 803, Seattle, WA   98101
☎ 206-382-3587   FAX 206-292-9892   <www.neda.org>

National Association of Anorexia Nervosa and Associated Disorders (ANAD)
Highland Hospital, Highland Park, IL   60035
☎ 708-432-8000   <www.ANAD.org>

National Center of Overcoming Overeating
P.O. Box 1257, Old Chelsea Station, NY, NY   10113-0920
☎ 212-875-0442   <www.overcomingovereating.com>

The National Eating Disorder Information Centre (NEDIC)
CW 1, 304-200 Elizabeth Street, Toronto, ON   M5G 2C4
☎ 416-340-4146   FAX 416-340-5888   1-866-633-4220
<www.nedic.on.ca>

Food

Healthy Body Image: Teaching Kids to Eat and Love their Bodies Too! Kathy J.
Kater. [A comprehensive resource manual with introductory scripted
lessons for grades 4, 5 & 6.]
National Eating Disorders Association (NEDA)
603 Stewart Street, Suite 803, Seattle, WA   98101
☎ 206-382-3587   FAX 206-292-9892   <www.neda.org>

*Eating in the Light of the Moon: How Women Can Transform their Relationship
with Food Through Myths, Metaphors and Storytelling.* Anita Johnson,
Wiltshire Press, 2000

Secrets of Feeding a Healthy Family. Ellyn Satter
Kelcy Press, Madison, WI, 1999
1-877-844-0857   <www.ellynsatter.com>

Vitality Program
Health and Welfare Canada: Health Services and Promotion
Jeanne Mance Bldg., 4th floor, Ottawa, ON   K1A 1B4
☎ 613-957-8331

*Nourishing Your Daughter: Help Your Child Develop a Healthy relationship with
Food and Her Body.* Carol Beck, Perigee Books, 2001

Gender and Female Development

Meeting at the Crossroads: Women's Psychology and Girls' Development. Carol
Gilligan & Lyn Mikel Brown. Cambridge, MA: Harvard University
Press, 1992

*Making Connections: The Relational Worlds of Adolescent Girls at Emma
Willard School.* Carol Gilligan, Nona P. Lyons & Trudy J. Hanmer, editors. Cambridge, MA: Harvard University Press, 1989

Reviving Ophelia. Mary Pipher. New York, NY: Putnam, 1994

Women's Growth in Connection: Writings from the Stone Center. Judith Jordan,
Alexandra G. Kaplan, Jean Baker Miller, Irene P. Stiver & Janet L.
Surrey, editors. New York, NY: The Guilford Press, 1991

You Just Don't Understand: Men and Women in Conversation. Deborah Tannen. New York, NY: Ballantine Books, 1990

Media

GO GIRLS™ Program (Giving Our Girls Inspiration and Resources for Lasting Self-Esteem)
National Eating Disorders Association (NEDA)
603 Stewart Street, Suite 803, Seattle, WA   98101
☎ 206-382-3587   FAX 206-292-9892   <www.neda.org>

Where the Girls Are: Growing Up Female with the Mass Media. Susan J. Douglas. New York, NY: Random House, 1994

Deadly Persuasion: Why Women and Girls Must Fight the Addictive Powers of Advertising. Jean Kilbourne. New York, NY: The Free Press, 1999

No Fat Chicks: How Women are Brainwashed to Hate their Bodies and Spend their Money. Terry Poulton. Toronto, ON: Key Porter Books Ltd., 1996

Media Watch (U.S.) PO Box 618, Santa Cruz, CA   95061-0618
☎ 408-423-6355   <www.mediawatch.org>
[Organization dedicated to attacking sexism in advertising.]

MediaWatch (Canada)
517 Wellington St. West, Suite 204, Toronto, ON   M5V 1G1
☎ 416-408-2065   FAX 416-408-2069   <www.mediawatch.ca>
[Excellent resource. Has contact addresses for writing letters.]

Adbusters Media Foundation
1243 West 74th Avenue, Vancouver BC   V6H 1B7
☎ 604-736-9401   1-800-663-1243   <www.adbusters.org>
[Active media critic producing educational materials and the innovative *Adbusters* magazine.]

The Center for Media Literacy
4727 Wiltshire Blvd. Suite 403, Los Angeles, CA   90010
☎ 213-931-4177   <www.medialit.org>
[Resources concerning the impact of advertising, violence and other media influences.]

Media-Awareness Network   <www.media-awareness.ca>
[Developed by Health Canada: excellent resources and lesson plans that can be downloaded.]

Just Think Foundation
P.O. Box 475638, San Francisco, CA   94147
☎ 415-292-2900   FAX 415-292-1030
<www.justthink.org>   think@justthink.org

Physical Activity and Sports

Alive and Kicking: When Soccer Moms Take the Field and Change their Lives Forever. Araton, H. New York: Simon and Schuster, 2002

Black Tights: Women, Sport and Sexuality. Laura Robinson. Toronto: HarperCollins, 2002

The Bodywise Woman: Reliable Information about Physical Activity and Health (1990) The Melpomene Institute
1010 University Avenue, St. Paul MN   55104
☎ 612-642-1951   FAX 612-642-1871

Girls in Action....Speaking Out [Video and Leader's Guide]
Girls in Action [Peer Facilitator's Guide]
Girls & Boys in Elementary Physical Education, Issues and Action
(CAHPERD) Canadian Association for Health, Physical Activity, Recreation & Dance
2197 Riverside Drive, Suite 403, Ottawa, ON   K1H 7X3
☎ 613-523-1348   1-800-663-8708
<www.cahperd.ca>   info@cahperd.ca

GoGirlGo Project [Dedicated to the development and funding of girls' sports programs that combine athletic skill instruction and programming with the delivery of educational information aimed at reducing risk behaviors that threaten the health and social advancement of girls aged 10 to 14 years. A kit is provided to each group participating in the project.] Women's Sports Foundation
Eisenhower Park, East Meadow, New York   11554
☎ 516-542-4700   FAX 516-542-4716
<www.Womenssportsfoundation.org>   wosport@aol.com

Girls@Play Network [Provides girls with an opportunity to win prizes, meet new people, chat with Canadian sports heroes and gather information about physical activity programs, nutrition and "what's hot and what's not."]   (CAAWS) Canadian Association for the Advancement of Women and Sports and Physical Activity
N202-801 King Edward Avenue, Ottawa, ON K1N 6N5
☎ 613-748-5793   FAX 613-748 –57754
<www.caaws.ca>   caaws@caaws.ca

Girls on the Run [A 12 week program that combines training for a 3.1 mile running event with self-esteem enhancing workouts.] P.O. Box 268, Huntsville, NC   28070-0268
☎ 704-948-7016   1-800-901-9965   FAX 704-948-4063
<www.girlsontherun.com>   Gr8runrz@aol.com

Great Shape: The First Fitness Guide for Large Women. Pat Lyons & Deb Burgard. Lincoln, NB: iUnivers.com.Inc, 1998/2002

National Association for Girls and Women in Sport (GWS) and American Alliance for Health, Physical Education, Recreation and Dance (AAHPERD)
1900 Association Drive, Reston, VA   22091-1599
☎ 703-476-3450   FAX 703-476-9527

New Moves Program
Contact: Dr. Dianne Neumark-Sztainer
University of Minnesota
Ste 300, 1300 South Second St., Minneapolis, MN 55454-1015
☎ 612-624-1818   FAX 612-624-0315

On the Move: Increasing Participation of Girls and Women in Physical Activity & Sport   Cost $10 plus shipping.
Promotion Plus: Girls and Women in Physical Activity & Sport
#305-1367 West Broadway, Vancouver, BC   V6H 4A9
☎ 604-738-7175   FAX 604-737-3075
<www.promotionplus.org>   promotion.plus@telus.net

Ontario Physical and Health Education Association (OPHEA)
1185 Eglinton Avenue E., Suite 501, Toronto, ON   M3C 3C6
☎ 416-426-7120   FAX 416-426-7373
<www.ophea.net>   infor@ophea.net

Parents' Guide to Girls' Sports
[Excellent booklet that can be downloaded from the Women's Sports Foundation website (see above)]

Play Like a Girl: A Celebration of Women in Sports. Sue Macy & Jane Gottesman. New York: Henry Holt and Company, Inc, 1999

Premier's Sport Awards Program resources. c/o JW Sporta
#228 – 1367 West Broadway, Vancouver, BC   V6H 4A9
☎ 604-738-2468   FAX 604-737-6043
<www.psap.jwsporta.ca>   psap@jwsporta.ca

Proceedings: World Summit on Physical Education. Gudrum Doll-Tepper and Deena Scoretz, eds. Berlin, November 1999. Published by ICSSPE/CIEPSS (International Council for Sport Science and Physical Education) Germany 2001
[Contains best practices and rationale for physical education.]
Available from <www.icsspe.org>

Promoting Fitness and Self-Esteem in Your Overweight Child. Teresa Pitman & Miriam Kaufman, MD. Toronto, ON: HarperPerennial, 1994 (Firefly Books, 2000)

Raising Our Athletic Daughters: How Sports can Build Self-Esteem and Save Girls' Lives. J. Zimmerman & G. Reavill, New York: Doubleday, 1998

Straight Talk about Children and Sport. Janet LeBlanc and Louise Dickson. Coaching Association of Canada
141 Laurier Avenue West, Suite 300, Ottawa, ON K1P 5J3
☎ 613-235-5000   FAX 613-235-9500

Relationships

Where to Draw the Line: How to Set Healthy Boundaries Every Day. Anne Katherine, M.S. New York: Fireside Books, 2000

Dating Violence: Young Women and Danger.
 Barrie Levy, ed. Seattle, WA: Seal Press, 1991

Relationships and Communication Activities. Patricia Rizzo Toner. The Centre for Applied Research in Education, 1996

Dads and Daughters: How to Inspire, Support and Understand Your Daughter When She is Growing Up So Fast. Joe Kelley. Broadway Books, 2002

Stress

Stress Management and Self-Esteem Activities. Patricia Rizzo Toner. Center for Applied Research in Education, 1993

You and Stress: A Guide for Adolescence and Leaders' Guide to You and Your Family and School and Stress. Gail C. Roberts & Lorraine Guttormson. Minneapolis, MN: Free Spirit Publishing. 1990

Talk with Teens about Self and Stress. Jean Sunde Peterson. Minneapolis, MN: Free Spirit Publishing Inc., 1993

Magazines

GIRL – Beauty for Every Face; Fashion for Every Body
22 East 49th Street, New York, NY
☎ 1-888-419-0427   girlpub@aol.com

In 2 Print   [Publishes original works by young male and female
adults 12 to 20 including poetry, short stories, one-act plays, painting,
photography, computer art and cartoons.]
P.O. Box 102, Port Colborne, ON   L3K 5V7
☎ 905-834-1539   FAX 905-834-1540

New Moon: The Magazine for Girls and Their Dreams (girls 8-12)
New Moon Publishing
P.O. Box 3587, Duluth, MN   55803-3587
☎ 218-728-5507   1-800-381-4743   <www.newmoon.com>

Reluctant Hero Magazine (girls 13-16)
189 Lonsmount Drive, Toronto, ON   M5P-2Y6
☎ 416-656-8047   <www.reluctanthero.com>

Teen Voices (13-20)
515 Washington Street, Floor 6, Boston, MA   02111
☎ 617-426-5577   1-888-882-TEEN   <www.teenvoices.com>

Film/Video

BODY IMAGE
Half hour program designed to separate media hype from reality, to
help young people learn to make right choices and develop an effective, healthy lifestyle. (Grades 6-10)
Heartland Releasing
1102- 8th Avenue, 3rd Floor, Regina, SK   S4R 1C9
☎ 306-777-0888   FAX 306-586-3537

MODEL PERFECT from *Ready or Not* series. "Amanda" and "Bizzy"
have great appeal in story format for Grades 5-7
Distributor: McNabb and Connolly
60 Briarwood Avenue, Port Credit, ON   L5G-3N6
☎ 905-278-2801   FAX 905-278-0566

TAKE ANOTHER LOOK [1994] 24 min
This film is a dramatic fantasy on self-esteem for viewers aged 11-13.
Encourages discussion on self-esteem, body image, beauty and diet
industries, self-respect and the need for peer support.
Produced by: Lisa O'Brien and Bernice Vanderlaan

Distributor: McNabb and Connolly (see above)

SCANNING TELEVISION: Videos For Media Literacy In Class
Four one-hour videos plus Teacher's Guide. Copyright-cleared video excerpts that allow teachers to use real media while teaching media literacy.
Harcourt and Brace Canada
55 Horner Avenue, Toronto, ON   M8Z 4X6
☎ 1-800-387-7278

KILLING US SOFTLY: Advertising's Image Of Women [1979]
28 min   American feminist Jean Kilbourne casts a critical eye on the power and influence of advertising.
Produced by: Cambridge Documentary Films
Distributor: National Film Board of Canada (cat # 0179 389)

STILL KILLING US SOFTLY [1987]   30 min
This sequel to *Killing Us Softly* offers tools for developing a critical approach to mass media.
Produced by: Cambridge Documentary Films
Distributor: National Film Board of Canada (cat # 0187 145)

SLIM HOPES: Media's Obession With Thinness [1995]   29 min
Jean Kilbourne film. Excellent for high school.
Kinetic Video Inc.   409 Dundas East, Toronto, ON   M5A 2A5
☎ 416-963-5979   1-800-263-6910   FAX 416-925-0653

BEYOND KILLING US SOFTLY: The Strength To Resist   33 min
Jean Kilbourne film that presents leading authors in the fields of the psychology of girls and women, eating disorders, gender studies, violence against women and media literacy and focuses their ideas on practical solutions and the best tactics for reclaiming our female culture.
Cambridge Documentary Films
PO Box 390385, Cambridge, MA   02139
☎ 617-484-3393   FAX 617-484-0754   cdf@shore.net

BEYOND THE LOOKING GLASS   28 min
Grade 8-10 teacher resource (can be used for younger girls). Focuses on self-esteem, thoughts, feelings, identification of attitudes, stereotypes, body image and provides direction to garner support for problem solving.Produced in the US.
Canadian distributor:
McIntyre Media   30 Kelfield Street, Rexdale, ON   M9W 5A1
☎ 1-800-565-3036   FAX 416-245-8660

THE FAMINE WITHIN [1990]   60 or 120 min
Ages 8-15. Explores the obsession with thinness and prejudice against fat. Reviews what dieting does to individuals.
Produced by: Katherine Kilday
Available from: McNabb and Connolly (see above)

BREAKING SIZE PREJUDICE   23 min   An education video to promote body-size acceptance for youth aged 11 to 17 years.
Developed by Mary Kay Wardlaw, M.S., Family & Consumer Science Educator, University of Wyoming.
UW FCS Department   attn: WIN Wyoming
P.O. Box 3353, Laramie, WY   82071
☎ 307-766-5375   FAX 307-766-5686   studer@uwyo.edu

Index

JUST FOR GIRLS
Program Facilitator's Manual

ISBN# 0-9698883-1-7   160 pages
Vancouver: Salal Books (1999) $35.00

Sandra Friedman's *JUST FOR GIRLS* is an open discussion group program that addresses what happens to girls in the process of growing up female that silences them and encourages them to redefine themselves by the numbers on the bathroom scale. The program looks at what 'feeling fat' means to girls, teaches them skills to decode the language of fat and encourages them to tell the stories and express the feelings that lie underneath.

JUST FOR GIRLS helps girls understand the societal pressures that they face during adolescence and the physical and emotional changes they are experiencing. It provides them with an awareness of their own bodies that goes beyond how they look. It teaches girls how to strengthen their friendships and support one another. The manual contains the complete blueprint for the program, 18 structured session plans and 25 reproducible handouts.

NURTURING GIRLPOWER
Integrating Eating Disorder Prevention/Intervention into Your Practice

ISBN# 0-9698883-2-5   176 pages
Vancouver: Salal Books (2000) $35.00

Sandra Friedman's *NURTURING GIRLPOWER* manual provides a comprehensive framework for prevention that addresses the changes in girls' bodies and the changes in girls' lives during adolescence. It helps you enhance your individual practice and assess and develop prevention strategies and teamwork in your schools and communities. The manual includes information, skills and strategies on issues such as body image and awareness, the myths around fat and dieting, communication, stress, media literacy and bullying. The section on application helps you integrate these skills into your practice, develop classroom lessons, prepare presentations, and facilitate a girls' day program.

NURTURING GIRLPOWER provides background information on eating disorders and demystifies them-so that you can relate to and support the girl instead of the disorder. It provides counseling skills so that you can intervene with girls who are just experimenting with eating disorder behaviors. The manual contains 16 tools, 20 exercises and a section on contemporary resources.

WHEN GIRLS FEEL FAT
Helping Girls through Adolescence

ISBN# 0-00-638609-1   272 pages
Toronto: HarperCollins (2000) $19.95 Canada

ISBN# 1-55209-459-6   272 pages
Firefly Books (2000) $14.95 USA

Sandra Friedman's friendly guide *WHEN GIRLS FEEL FAT* helps adults (and girls themselves) to understand and cope with the difficult process of adolescence. It demystifies the relationships girls have with body image, sexuality, eating disorders, friends, parents, school and the media. Using case notes from her private practice and feedback from her successful *JUST FOR GIRLS* discussion groups, Sandra draws upon a wealth of useful experiences and coping techniques to explain how feeling fat provides a key to opening discussion about what happens to girls growing up female in a male world – a process that puts tremendous pressure on girls.

WHEN GIRLS FEEL FAT gives parents, teachers and professionals who work with girls clear and proven strategies to deal with conflict, to recognize that 'worries about weight' can lead to serious eating disorders, to maintain a connection in the face of 'tuning out' and to cope with the *grungies* – the voice of girls' self-deprecating negative feelings.

SALAL BOOKS

#309, 101 - 1184 Denman Street
Vancouver, BC, Canada V6G 2M9
☎ + fax 604-689-8399

www.salal.com   salal@salal.com

GST 120074331   SAN 1173189

ORDER FORM

___ BODY THIEVES   ISBN 0-9698883-3-3 $19.95..._____

___ BODY THIEVES (US edition)   ISBN 0-9698883-3-3   US$14.95..._____

___ JUST FOR GIRLS program   ISBN 0-9698883-1-7 $35.00..._____

___ NURTURING GIRLPOWER   ISBN 0-9698883-2-5 $35.00..._____

___ WHEN GIRLS FEEL FAT   ISBN 0-00-638609-1 $19.95..._____

___ WHEN GIRLS FEEL FAT (US edition)   ISBN 1-55209-459-6   US$14.95..._____

Shipping (within North America) $3/book x ____..............._____

Canada: add 15% HST for postal codes beginning A, B or E only..._____

or add 7% GST for all other postal code..........................._____

Total: $_____

Ship to: Date: _____

Name:_____

Position:_____

Agency:_____

Street Address:_____

_____

City:_____ State/Prov:_____ PostCode:_____

Phone:_____wk / home FAX (option):_____

eMAIL (option):_____

VISA # _____ expiry:_____/_____

(Please keep a photocopy as a record of your order. Books are shipped regular
mail. Allow approximately three weeks for delivery. Customers outside North
America please inquire about shipping fees.)